THE XXL UK SLOW COOKER RECIPE BOOK

333 Dishes for Everyday Enjoyment incl. Breakfast, Lunch, Dinner and Sides

Sara R. Adams

ISBN - 9798774487226

TABLE OF CONTENTS

Dinner 44

Sides

Snacks

Desserts 132

Drinks 146

Disclaimer 153

INTRODUCTION

Slow cookers are cheap to buy, economical to use and a great way to make the most of the cheapest ingredients or leftovers. Whether you have just bought yourself a slow cooker, been handed one down from a relative or given one as a gift, there are a huge range of ways that you can make use of this handy device if you just know where to start.

Read on to find out more about how to use a slow cooker, and then get started enjoying our wide selection of recipes for each meal of the day!

What is a slow cooker?

A slow cooker (sometimes known as a crockpot) is a counter-top appliance that relies on simmering to cook food. Slow cookers cook at a much lower temperature than your oven, hob, or microwave, which leads to a longer cook time.

Slow cookers are an affordable appliance that come in a range of styles and price points, with some having more features than others. All slow cookers, however, should have a choice of low, medium, and high cooking modes.

What is slow cooked food like?

Slow cooking is a great choice if you want tender meat and vegetables. The long cook time means that food can end up buttery soft, which is ideal for most meats, potatoes, and vegetables. You can even make great pasta or rice in a slow cooker!

Using a slow cooker is not too dissimilar to using a casserole pot with a lid. Most things that you cook in a slow cooker will turn out in a very similar way.

Slow cookers trap in a lot of moisture, and so they make light work of stews, casseroles, and curries that are cooked with quite a lot of moisture.

All slow cooker recipes do require liquid, so slow cooking might not be ideal if you require a finished meal that is dry without any additional steps.

How do you use a slow cooker?

Slow cookers are very easy to use.

Just plug in the slow cooker, add your ingredients, set the temperature and put the lid on.

You might need to pre-cook certain ingredients from your recipe before putting them in the slow cooker, however for the most part, you can put your ingredients in and walk away!

Benefits of using a slow cooker

Slow cookers are an easy appliance that generally allow you to put your ingredients in, then walk away and just leave it to do its thing. This is ideal for cooking meals overnight or if you want to start a dish in the morning to have ready when you finish work.

The long cook time means that slow cookers will bring out the flavour in the ingredients in a recipe, combining them into a fresh explosion of smells and tastes.

Slow cookers do a great job of tenderising meat, meaning you can achieve something delicious even if you use cheap cuts of steak, pork, or chicken.

You are much less likely to burn food in a slow cooker because the temperatures are so low. In the same way, the low temperature of a slow cooker means that your finished dish will have greater nutritional value than it may have done if you had oven baked it.

Slow cookers are also much cheaper to run than standard ovens, which can help you save money in the long term.

You can even make food in bulk and freeze some for later on.

How long does food take in a slow cooker?

Most dishes in a slow cooker will take several hours to cook. As a rule, dishes that take:
- 15 to 30 minutes will need 1 to 2 hours on high or 4 to 6 hours on low
- 30 to 60 minutes will need 2 to 3 hours on high or 5 to 7 hours on low
- 1 to 2 hours will need 3 to 4 hours on high or 6 to 8 hours on low
- 2 to 4 hours will need 4 to 6 hours on high or 8 to 12 hours on low

Some ingredients will need longer to cook, such as potatoes or dense meats. By placing these in the slow cooker first, you will get the best results.

How can I make the most of a slow cooker?

There are a range of methods that can be used to help you make the most of a slow cooker. From optimising preparation time to using cheap cuts, here's how to get the most out of your slow cooker.

Prep time

Ease of use is something that attracts households to using the humble slow cooker. Many slow cooker recipes require little preparation, however, if your chosen recipe does, try to do this the night before cooking to save you time.

If you think you will be short on time in the morning, prepare everything for the meal the night before and put it in the slow cooker bowl and keep it in the fridge overnight. Get the bowl out of the fridge about 20 minutes before putting it on to let it warm up to room temperature.

Cheap cuts

We might all usually avoid cheap cuts of meat; however, a slow cooker will make the most of them. Whether it is brisket, pork shoulder, lamb shoulder or chicken thighs, the low cook temperature of the slow cooker will extract great flavour from the meat, and you will end up with melt-in-the-mouth tender food at the end of the cook time.

Trim your meat

Slow cookers rarely need oil as the cooking temperatures are too low for food to catch on the bottom. In the same way, you don't need to keep a lot of fat on your meat.

Normally when you fry or bake meat, the fat drains away, however this cannot happen with a slow cooker. To avoid pools of fat ending up sitting in your food, just trim the meat before you start to cook. This will be healthier, and it will still be delicious.

Flour

The lid of a slow cooker means water will not evaporate during the cook time. As a result, the liquid will not reduce, and it will not thicken unless the recipe contains a thickening agent. To tackle this, roll meat in seasoned flour, or just add cornflour towards the end to thicken the sauce.

Common slow cooker mistakes to avoid

A slow cooker might be a simple appliance; however, many people do find themselves making some common mistakes. To ensure you get the best possible results, you want to limit these mistakes where possible.

Removing the lid too often

It can be tempting to lift the lid to see how your food is getting on, however you should avoid this unless you need to add an ingredient in during the cook time. By lifting the lid, all the heat will escape, meaning it can take longer to cook the food.

Adding too much liquid

Adding too much liquid can leave you with a watery dish. Ideally, the liquid in most dishes should only just cover the meat and vegetables. If you think you have too much, ladle some out before cooking.

Not reducing alcohol

The lid and lower temperature of a slow cooker means liquid will not evaporate or reduce during the cooking time. A slow cooker simply does not get hot enough to boil off alcohol, so if your recipe includes wine, boil it in a saucepan first and let it reduce slightly. If you skip this step, your finished meal will end up tasting very boozy.

Soggy vegetables

Soft vegetables, such as courgettes and peas, should be added close to the end of recipes with long cook times. If they are added too early, they can end up mushy and overcooked.

Lacking flavour

If you are adapting a recipe that isn't designed to be used in a slow cooker, you might find that the flavour of any dried herbs you have added disappears. As a rule, if the recipe in question calls for a tablespoon of dried oregano, add an extra half tablespoon.

Uneven cooking

New users can often struggle with unevenly cooked food; however, this can be easily rectified. Dense foods, such as root vegetables, should be added to the slow cooker first so that they are closer to the heat source. Foods that are softer and easier to cook should then be closer to the top of the dish.

Rubbery chicken skin

If you are cooking with skin-on chicken, cook the pieces in a frying pan first until the skins are crisp. When the chicken comes out of the slow cooker, it will have lost some of this crispness, but this can be easily recovered by just cooking the chicken under the grill for a few minutes.

SARA R. ADAMS

BREAKFAST

BIO YOGHURT

MAKES 2 LITRES | PER SERVING - CALORIES: 120, FAT: 5G, CARBOHYDRATES: 11G, PROTEIN: 8G

INGREDIENTS

- 2 litres of whole milk
- 100ml live yoghurt, either from a store or one you made earlier

INSTRUCTIONS

1. First, tip the milk into the slow cooker. Cook the milk on high for 2 to 3 hours until the milk reaches 82C. Turn the slow cooker off and let the milk cool until it reaches 43C.
2. Mix a cup of the milk into the yoghurt, then stir back into the slow cooker. Cover the slow cooker with a tea towel and leave it to sit undisturbed for between 9 and 12 hours until the yoghurt has set.
3. Serve with cereal, porridge, or fresh fruit, or make into marinades and smoothies.
4. If you prefer a thicker yoghurt, leave it to set for longer. The finished yoghurt can be kept in the fridge for up to 14 days.

TURKISH BREAKFAST EGGS

SERVES 4 | PER SERVING - CALORIES: 165, FAT:8G, CARBOHYDRATES: 13G, PROTEIN: 9G

INGREDIENTS

- 1 slice sourdough bread, cubed
- 2 onions, sliced
- 1 red pepper, chopped
- 1 small red chilli, finely sliced
- 1 tbsp olive oil
- 4 eggs
- 8 cherry tomatoes
- 2 ½ tbsp skimmed milk
- Small bunch parsley, finely chopped
- 4 tbsp natural yoghurt, to serve

INSTRUCTIONS

1. Grease the inside of the slow cooker. Warm the rest of the oil in a pan, and cook the chilli, pepper, and onions until they start to soften.
2. Put the contents of the frying pan in the slow cooker, and stir in the bread and tomatoes. Season to taste.
3. Whisk the eggs with the milk and parsley and pour this over the top, making sure all the other ingredients are covered by the milk and eggs. Cook for 5-6 hours. Serve with a spoonful of natural yoghurt.

BREAKFAST BEANS

SERVES 4 | PER SERVING - CALORIES: 149, FAT:3G, CARBOHYDRATES: 21G, PROTEIN: 6G

INGREDIENTS

- 400g canned pinto beans, rinsed and drained
- 1 ½ tbsp soft brown sugar
- 1 tbsp wine vinegar, red or white
- 2 garlic cloves, cut into thin slices
- 1 onion, finely sliced
- 225ml tomato passata
- 1 tbsp olive oil
- Small bunch coriander, chopped

INSTRUCTIONS

1. Set the slow cooker on low. Fry the onion in a frying pan with the oil until it starts to colour, then stir in the garlic and cook for a minute longer. Add the vinegar and sugar and bubble for a minute. Stir in the beans and passata and season with black pepper. Put everything in the slow cooker.
2. Cook for 5 hours. If the sauce is thin, turn the temperature up to high and cook until it thickens to your taste. Stir through the coriander.

CINNAMON ROLL

MAKES 12 SLICES | PER SERVING - CALORIES: 240, FAT:7G, CARBOHYDRATES: 41G, PROTEIN: 4G

INGREDIENTS

DOUGH

- 7g active dried yeast
- 180ml lukewarm water
- 70g rolled oats
- 55g brown sugar
- 2 tbsp butter, melted
- 1 egg
- 1 tsp salt
- 240g plain flour

FILLING

- 3 tbsp butter, softened
- 70g caster sugar
- 2 tsp ground cinnamon

ICING

- 125g icing sugar
- 2 tbsp single cream
- 4 tsp butter, softened

INSTRUCTIONS

1. Put the yeast in warm water and leave to dissolve.
2. Add the oats, brown sugar, butter, egg, salt, and half of the plain flour and beat on a medium speed until smooth. Gradually stir in the rest of the flour until you have a soft dough.
3. Sprinkle a clean work area with flour, and knead the dough until it is smooth. Roll into an 18 x 12-inch rectangle.
4. For filling, spread dough with butter, then combine sugar and cinnamon; sprinkle over dough, leaving a ½ inch gap around the edges.
5. Roll up the dough, starting with the long side. Pinch the seam to seal.
6. Cut crosswise in half to form 2 rolls. Place rolls side by side; pinch top ends together to seal. Cut the rolls in half lengthwise using a sharp knife, and loosely twist the strips around each other. Pinch the bottom ends together to seal. Shape into a coil; place on baking paper.
7. Put the dough in the slow cooker. Let rise until doubled, or about 1 hour.
8. Cook, covered, on low until bread is lightly browned, 3-1/2 to 4 hours. Let the cinnamon buns cool until they can be handled. Beat icing ingredients until smooth. Spread over warm roll.

BREAKFAST HASH

SERVES 4 | PER SERVING - CALORIES: 446, FAT:25G, CARBOHYDRATES: 42G, PROTEIN: 14G

INGREDIENTS

- 8 to 10 sausages, frozen
- 680g diced potatoes
- 4 medium carrots, sliced
- 2 spring onions
- 4 eggs
- 2 tbsp extra virgin olive oil
- 1 tbsp red wine vinegar
- 1 tsp salt
- ½ tsp ground pepper
- ¼ tsp chilli flakes
- 1 tbsp plus 2 tsp fresh dill
- 1 tbsp butter
- 2 tbsp crumbled feta
- 2 tbsp maple syrup

INSTRUCTIONS

1. Brown the sausages in a frying pan, turning regularly until they start to cook in the middle. This should take about 8 to 9 minutes.
2. Combine next 5 ingredients in a slow cooker. Stir in a tablespoon of dill, a sprinkle of salt, ¼ tsp pepper, and chilli flakes.
3. Arrange sausages on top of vegetable mixture.
4. Cook for 5 to 6 hours on low. Serve the vegetables on a serving platter sprinkled with feta cheese and topped with the sausages.

STICKY PECAN BUNS

MAKES 12 BUNS | PER BUN - CALORIES: 173, FAT: 4.9G, CARBOHYDRATES: 29.5G, PROTEIN: 2.9G

INGREDIENTS

FOR THE DOUGH:

- 240g whole wheat flour
- ½ tbsp unsalted butter, melted
- 7g dry yeast
- 6 tbsp semi-skimmed milk
- 1 tsp vanilla extract
- ¼ tsp salt
- 4 tbsp maple syrup

FOR THE CARAMEL SAUCE:

- 4 tbsp maple syrup
- 2 tbsp unsalted butter
- 2 tbsp semi-skimmed milk
- 28g chopped pecans

FOR THE FILLING:

- ½ tbsp unsalted butter, melted
- 1½ tsp ground cinnamon
- 3 tbsp maple syrup

INSTRUCTIONS

1. Grease the slow cooker. Wipe the rim of the pot with a clean paper towel.
2. To make the dough, mix the milk, butter, vanilla, and maple syrup in a microwave-safe bowl. Cook in the microwave on high in 20 second intervals. Stir the mixture for a minute after each interval, until the butter melts. The mix should be warm, but not hot. Tip in the yeast, and leave the bowl to sit until frothy. This should take between 10 and 15 minutes.
3. Fold the flour into the bowl gradually to form a dough that no longer sticks to the bowl. Sprinkle the flour over the work surface, then tip the dough out onto the work surface. Knead the dough for a couple of minutes until it springs most of the way back if you touch it. Leave the dough to rest whilst you prepare the sauce and filling.
4. To make the caramel sauce, mix the syrup, milk, and butter in a pan. Cook over a high heat until everything melts, stirring constantly. Carry on stirring the pan until the sauce starts to darken and thicken. Pour the caramel sauce into the slow cooker and sprinkle the nuts over the top. Leave a 1cm border around the edge of sauce.

5. Whisk together the cinnamon and maple syrup in a bowl to make the filling.
6. Clean the work surface, and sprinkle with fresh flour. Roll the dough into a rectangle around 10 x 14" in size. Brush the dough with the melted butter, and then the syrup mixture. Leave a 1cm border on the two long sides. Roll the dough up to make a log, rolling from a long edge.
7. Slice the dough into 12 rolls, and place each roll straight into the sauce in the slow cooker. If any of the syrup filling falls out, spoon it into the caramel sauce after putting all rolls in the slow cooker.
8. Put the lid on the slow cooker, and use the "Keep Warm" setting until the cinnamon rolls rise and double in size. This should take about 45 minutes.
9. Set the slow cooker on low, and bake for between 1 ¼ and 1 ½ hours. Take off the lid, and leave the rolls to cool for about 10 minutes before carefully turning out onto a rack.

MINI CHOCOLATE CHIP MUFFINS

MAKES 14 MUFFINS | PER MUFFIN - CALORIES: 114, FAT: 4G, CARBOHYDRATES: 18.2G, PROTEIN: 2.2G

INGREDIENTS

- 125g flour
- 30g cocoa powder
- 100g caster sugar
- 2 tsp baking powder
- 75g milk chocolate chips
- 120ml semi-skimmed milk
- 1 tsp vanilla extract
- 1 egg
- 40ml vegetable oil

INSTRUCTIONS

1. Stir the baking powder, caster sugar, cocoa powder, and chocolate chips into the flour in a large bowl.
2. Mix the milk, egg, vanilla extract, and vegetable oil together in a separate bowl.
3. Add the wet ingredients to the dry in the bowl gradually, mixing roughly until combined.
4. Using a pastry brush and a little extra vegetable oil, carefully oil mini silicone muffin moulds.
5. Fill each mould halfway with the mixture.
6. Put the muffin moulds in the slow cooker. Put a tea towel or couple pieces of kitchen paper across the top, and put the lid on top. Cook on high for around 1 hour 45 minutes.
7. Check the muffins periodically. Test the muffins with a cake tester, metal skewer or toothpick. If the tester comes out clean, the muffins are ready.

BREAKFAST QUINOA

SERVES 4 | PER SERVING - CALORIES: 326, FAT: 17G, CARBOHYDRATES: 39G, PROTEIN: 7G

INGREDIENTS

- 170g quinoa
- 475ml water
- 240g canned coconut milk
- 2 tbsp maple syrup
- ¼ tsp salt
- Splash of milk
- Toppings of your choice, such as berries, honey, or cinnamon

INSTRUCTIONS

1. Rinse the quinoa well under cold running water.
2. Add the rinsed quinoa, maple syrup, salt, water and coconut milk to the slow cooker and put the lid on. Cook for 8 hours on the low setting. Serve hot with a splash of milk and toppings of choice.

SARA R. ADAMS

BREAKFAST FRITTATA CASSEROLE

SERVES 8 | PER SERVING - CALORIES: 166, FAT: 12G, CARBOHYDRATES: 5G, PROTEIN: 10G

INGREDIENTS

- 2 tsp olive oil
- 140g baby kale
- Non-stick spray or oil to grease the slow cooker if needed
- 170g roasted red peppers, diced
- 1 sliced spring onion
- 140g crumbled feta
- 8 eggs, beaten
- ½ tsp multi-purpose seasoning
- Ground black pepper to taste

INSTRUCTIONS

1. Wash the kale if needed, and dry with paper towels.
2. Over a medium to high heat, warm up the oil in a pan.
3. Once the oil is hot, sauté the kale until it has softened and flattened out. This should only take a couple of minutes.
4. If you are using a regular slow cooker, spray it well with non-stick spray or oil and transfer the cooked kale to the slow cooker. If using, turn the slow cooker down to low.
5. Drain the peppers and chop.
6. Slice the green onions and crumble the Feta.
7. Tip the red pepper, spring onion, and kale into the slow cooker.
8. Beat the eggs and stir into the slow cooker.
9. Season with the multi-purpose seasoning and black pepper, then sprinkle on the feta.
10. Cook on low for 2 to 3 hours and the cheese has melted and the egg has set.
11. Serve hot, with a dollop of low-fat sour cream if desired.

BREAKFAST PIE

SERVES 4 | PER SERVING - CALORIES: 367, FAT: 27.2G, CARBOHYDRATES: 7.1G, PROTEIN: 22.8G

INGREDIENTS

- 8 eggs
- 1 sweet potato, grated
- 450g pork sausage, broken up
- 1 onion, diced
- 1 tbsp garlic powder
- 2 tsp dried basil
- Salt and pepper to taste

INSTRUCTIONS

1. Grease the slow cooker with coconut or vegetable oil.
2. Put everything in the slow cooker and mix together.
3. Cook the pie on low for 6 to 8 hours.

GRANOLA APPLE CRUMBLE

SERVES 3 | PER SERVING - CALORIES: 369, FAT: 15G, CARBOHYDRATES: 56G, PROTEIN: 5G

INGREDIENTS

- 2 Granny Smith apples
- 150g granola
- 30ml maple syrup
- 60ml apple juice
- 2 tbsp butter
- 1 tsp ground cinnamon
- ½ tsp ground nutmeg

INSTRUCTIONS

1. Peel, core and cut the apples into slices and then chunks.
2. Put everything in the slow cooker and stir together.
3. Cook on low for 4 hours.

BACON, CHEDDAR AND EGG CASSEROLE

SERVES 8 | PER SERVING - CALORIES: 530, FAT: 33G, CARBOHYDRATES: 30G, PROTEIN: 28G

INGREDIENTS

- 340g cubed French bread or ciabatta
- 2 tbsp butter
- 226g sliced mushrooms
- 9 eggs
- 475ml semi-skimmed milk
- ½ tsp chilli flakes
- 225g grated cheese
- 450g cooked, sliced bacon
- 1 green pepper, chopped
- Small bunch of fresh parsley, chopped

INSTRUCTIONS

1. Preheat the oven on 150C. Bake the bread cubes on a large baking sheet until dry, this should take about 20 to 30 minutes.
2. Line the slow cooker's sides with foil, and grease with oil or a non-stick cooking spray.
3. Melt the butter in a pan, and cook the mushrooms until starting to soften, about 5 minutes.
4. Beat the eggs with the milk and chilli flakes. Mix in a quarter of the pepper, bacon, and cheese, along with 2 tablespoons of the chopped parsley. Fold in the bread cubes, then spoon the contents of the bowl into the slow cooker.
5. Cook on low for 4 to 5 hours, or 2 to 3 hours on high.
6. Sprinkle the reserved cheese and remaining parsley over the top. Cook for 10 minutes longer until the cheese is melted.

MEXICAN BREAKFAST CASSEROLE

SERVES 8 | PER SERVING - CALORIES: 540, FAT: 38G, CARBOHYDRATES: 20G, PROTEIN: 29G

INGREDIENTS

- c9 corn tortillas
- 8 eggs
- 350ml milk
- 450g cooked chorizo, chopped
- 250g grated cheddar
- 1 jalapeno chilli, chopped
- 3 spring onions, sliced
- 1 red pepper, chopped
- 3 spring onions, sliced
- 2 tbsp coriander, chopped
- 230ml salsa

INSTRUCTIONS

1. Grease the slow cooker pot with oil or cooking spray. Put 3 of the tortillas in the slow cooker, tearing to fit if needed.
2. Beat the eggs with the milk and chilli. Set aside 2 tablespoons of the chopped pepper, 2 tablespoons of the spring onions, and half of the cheese.

SARA R. ADAMS

3. Top the tortillas with half of the sausage mixture, and half of the remaining peppers, spring onions, and cheese. Repeat layers. Top with the remaining 3 tortillas, and pour the egg mix into the slow cooker.
4. Cook the casserole for 2 to 3 hours on high, or 4 to 5 hours on low until the centre has set.
5. Sprinkle with the reserved cheese, pepper, spring onions and coriander. Serve with the salsa.

BREAKFAST LASAGNE

SERVES 8 | PER SERVING - CALORIES: 429, FAT: 31G, CARBOHYDRATES: 18G, PROTEIN: 21G

INGREDIENTS

- Non-stick cooking spray
- 450g sausage
- 1 green pepper, chopped
- 1 jalapeno chilli, chopped
- 5 eggs
- 2 tsp vegetable oil
- 2 spring onions, sliced
- Small bunch of chopped fresh parsley
- ½ tsp salt
- ½ tsp ground cumin
- 9 corn tortillas
- 225g grated cheddar cheese
- 400g Italian salsa Verde
- Sour cream to serve, if desired

INSTRUCTIONS

1. Grease the slow cooker. Brown the sausages in a frying pan. Break the sausage into chunks as it cooks.
2. Drain the fat from the pan, then tip in the chilli and pepper. Cook for a minute, then transfer the contents of the pan to a large bowl.
3. In the same pan, cook the eggs until just set, stirring the eggs to break them up. Transfer the eggs to the bowl with the sausage mixture.
4. Stir in the spring onions, parsley, salt, and cumin.
5. Put 3 tortillas in the slow cooker and add half the sausage mix and a quarter of the cheese. Top the cheese with a third of the salsa. Repeat the process for a second layer.
6. Finish with a layer of 3 tortillas, cheese, and salsa.
7. Cook for 2 to 3 hours on low, and leave to stand for 15 t0 30 minutes before serving.

HAM AND BRIE BREAD PUDDING

SERVES 6 | PER SERVING - CALORIES: 370, FAT: 16G, CARBOHYDRATES: 34G, PROTEIN: 23G

INGREDIENTS

- Non-stick cooking spray
- 4 eggs
- 700ml milk
- 2 cloves of garlic, minced
- 1 tsp dried thyme
- ¼ tsp ground black pepper
- Herbed focaccia, cubed
- 250g cooked ham, chopped
- 130g Brie, cut into small cubes
- 70g dried tomatoes

INSTRUCTIONS

1. Grease the inside of the slow cooker.
2. Beat the eggs with the milk, garlic, pepper, and thyme. Gently stir in bread cubes, ham, Brie, and dried tomatoes. Spoon into prepared cooker.
3. Cook on low for 3 ½ to 4 hours. Turn off cooker, and leave it to stand for 30 minutes. Note that the pudding will fall slightly as it cools.

LEMON AND POPPY SEED BREAD

SERVES 12 | PER SERVING - CALORIES: 264, FAT: 12G, CARBOHYDRATES: 35G, PROTEIN: 5G

INGREDIENTS

- Non-stick cooking spray
- 260g plain flour
- 40g poppy seeds
- 1 tbsp baking powder
- ½ tsp salt
- 200g caster sugar
- 3 eggs
- 120ml vegetable oil
- 120ml Greek-style yoghurt
- 60ml semi-skimmed milk
- 1tsp grated lemon peel
- 60ml fresh lemon juice
- 1 tsp vanilla

INSTRUCTIONS

1. Coat the slow cooker in cooking spray. Stir the baking powder, salt, and poppy seeds into the flour in a bowl. Set aside.
2. In another bowl, whisk the eggs with the sugar, oil, yoghurt, milk, vanilla, lemon peel and lemon juice until the sugar has dissolved. Add the sugar mixture all at once to flour mixture. Stir just until combined (mixture should still be slightly lumpy). Spoon batter into prepared slow cooker.
3. Cook for 1.5 to 2 hours on high until the top appears set, then switch off the slow cooker. Carefully remove lid so condensation from lid does not drip onto bread. Cover opening of slow cooker completely with paper towels; place lid on top.
4. Let the bread stand for 15 to 30 minutes. To remove the bread from the slow cooker, first run a knife around the edge to free it, before tipping it out to cool on a wire rack. If desired, drizzle with Lemon Icing.

FRY UP

SERVES 2 | PER SERVING - CALORIES: 926, FAT: 60.7G, CARBOHYDRATES: 52G, PROTEIN: 42G

INGREDIENTS

- 6 sausages
- 6 rashers of bacon
- 400g tin chopped tomatoes
- 400g baked beans
- 100g button mushrooms, sliced
- 4 eggs
- 30g butter

INSTRUCTIONS

1. Place the tomatoes, beans, mushrooms, and eggs into separate mugs.
2. Add 15g butter to the eggs and the same to the mushrooms.
3. Put the mugs in the middle of the slow cooker.
4. Stand the sausages and bacon around the edges of the slow cooker.
5. Turn the slow cooker onto a low heat and set the timer for 9 hours.

SARA R. ADAMS

BANANA BREAD

SERVES 12 | PER SERVING - CALORIES: 330, FAT: 16G, CARBOHYDRATES: 43G, PROTEIN: 7G

INGREDIENTS

- 3 bananas
- 2 eggs
- 90g butter
- 225g caster sugar
- 400g plain flour
- ½ tsp bicarbonate of soda
- 1 tsp baking powder
- ½ tsp salt
- ¼ tsp nutmeg
- ¼ tsp cinnamon
- 225g sliced almonds, optional

INSTRUCTIONS

1. Prepare your slow cooker by buttering or using non-stick cooking spray to coat the bottom half of the slow cooker.
2. Beat the sugar and eggs into the butter until combined.
3. Stir the baking soda, baking powder, salt, nutmeg, and cinnamon into the butter.
4. Fold the flour into the bowl. The mixture will be a little dry at this point.
5. Combine the dough with the mashed bananas and almonds. Mix well.
6. Tip the dough into the pot of the slow cooker. Lay 2 or 3 paper towels over the slow cooker, then place the lid on top. This will keep the bread moist while cooking.
7. Cook the bread for 4 hours on low. The top will be slightly browned when done and toothpick inserted in the middle will come out warm.

BACON CASSEROLE

SERVES 12 | PER SERVING - CALORIES: 306, FAT: 19G, CARBOHYDRATES: 13G, PROTEIN: 18G

INGREDIENTS

- 450g bacon, chopped
- 800g potatoes
- 12 eggs
- 250g grated cheese
- 235ml semi-skimmed milk
- ½ tsp salt
- ½ tsp pepper

INSTRUCTIONS

1. Cook the bacon in batches in a frying pan until crisp. Place on paper towels to drain.
2. Grease the slow cooker, and layer a third of the cheese, bacon, and potatoes. Repeat the layers twice.
3. In a bowl, whisk the eggs with the salt, pepper, and milk. Pour the egg into the slow cooker. Cook for 4 to 5 hours on low until the egg has set.
4. Take the lid off and leave to stand for 30 minutes before serving.

CHILAQUILES

SERVES 6 | PER SERVING - CALORIES: 325, FAT: 11G, CARBOHYDRATES: 51G, PROTEIN: 9G

INGREDIENTS

- 340g minced beef
- 340g minced pork
- ½ onion, chopped
- 2 cloves of garlic, minced
- 400g enchilada sauce
- 400g can of chilli beans in chilli gravy
- 300g pitted olives, drained
- 120ml beef broth
- 100g tortilla chips, crushed
- 225g grated cheese
- Cherry tomatoes and sour cream to serve (optional)

INSTRUCTIONS

1. Over a medium heat, cook the meats, garlic, and onion until the meat has coloured and the onion is soft. Drain off fat.
2. Line a slow cooker with a disposable slow cooker liner. Combine the next four ingredients (through broth) in cooker. Add meat mixture, broken tortillas, and the cheese. Stir to combine.
3. Cook for 4 hours on low, then take the lid off, and let the dish stand for 30 minutes.
4. If desired, serve with cherry tomatoes and sour cream.

CINNAMON AND BLUEBERRY FRENCH TOAST

SERVES 8 | PER SERVING - CALORIES: 265, FAT: 6G, CARBOHYDRATES: 42G, PROTEIN: 11G

INGREDIENTS

- 250g French bread, cubed
- 475ml semi-skimmed milk
- 110g blueberries, thawed if frozen
- 3 large eggs
- 50g sugar
- 1 tsp ground cinnamon
- 1 tsp vanilla extract
- ¼ tsp salt
- Maple syrup to serve

INSTRUCTIONS

1. Whisk together the eggs, milk, sugar, cinnamon, vanilla, and salt.
2. Place half of the bread in the bottom of the slow cooker.
3. Top with half of the blueberries, and half of the milk mixture. Repeat layers. Refrigerate ideally overnight, but for a minimum of four hours.
4. Cook for 4 hours on low. Serve warm with maple syrup.

OMELETTE FRITTATA

SERVES 6 | PER SERVING - CALORIES: 314, FAT: 19G, CARBOHYDRATES: 10G, PROTEIN: 25G

INGREDIENTS

- 12 eggs
- 230g cooked ham, chopped
- ½ green pepper, chopped
- 1 potato
- 1 onion, sliced
- 120g grated cheese
- 235ml water
- 1 tbsp olive oil
- 1 to 2 tsp hot sauce
- ½ tsp salt
- ¼ tsp pepper

INSTRUCTIONS

1. Put a rack in the slow cooker, if you have one. Alternatively, layer two 24-inch pieces of aluminium foil, and starting with the long side, fold to create a 1-inch-wide strip. Roll the strip to make a coil, and place it in the slow cooker. Pour over the 235ml of water.
2. Heat the oil in a frying pan over a medium to high heat. Cook the potato and onion for between 4 and 6 minutes until the potato is starting to brown. Transfer to a greased baking dish that fits in the slow cooker.
3. In a bowl, whisk the eggs, hot sauce, salt, and pepper. Fold in the green pepper, ham, and half of the cheese. Pour the egg into the slow cooker, and sprinkle over the rest of the cheese. Carefully put the dish in the slow cooker.
4. Cook on low until set, around 3 to 4 hours.

HAM AND CHEESE BREAKFAST CASSEROLE

SERVES 12 | PER SERVING - CALORIES: 324, FAT: 19G, CARBOHYDRATES: 17G, PROTEIN: 22G

INGREDIENTS

- 12 eggs
- 235ml milk
- 1 tsp salt
- ½ tsp pepper
- 850g grated potato
- 250g cooked ham, chopped into small cubes
- 1 onion, chopped
- 450g grated cheese

INSTRUCTIONS

1. Beat the eggs with the milk and seasoning. Put a third of the potatoes in the slow cooker, and add a third of the cheese, ham, and onion. Repeat the layers twice. Pour the egg over the top, and refrigerate, covered, overnight.
2. Cook for 4 to 5 hours on low until the middle has set. Let it stand for 30 minutes before serving.

RASPBERRY AND COCONUT FRENCH TOAST

SERVES 12 | PER SERVING - CALORIES: 280, FAT: 12G, CARBOHYDRATES: 35G, PROTEIN: 9G

INGREDIENTS

- 6 eggs
- 350ml coconut milk
- 1 tsp vanilla extract
- 450g French bread, cubed
- 225g cream cheese
- 300g seedless raspberry jam
- 50g desiccated coconut
- Whipped cream and raspberries to serve (optional)

INSTRUCTIONS

1. Whisk the eggs with the vanilla and coconut milk. Place half of the bread in a greased slow cooker. Layer half of the cream cheese, jam, coconut, and egg mixture. Repeat the layers. Refrigerate, covered, overnight.
2. Cook for 2 ½ to 3 ¼ hours on low. Serve with a dollop of whipped cream and a handful of fresh raspberries.

BREAKFAST BURRITOS

SERVES 12 | PER SERVING - CALORIES: 359, FAT: 15G, CARBOHYDRATES: 39G, PROTEIN: 16G

INGREDIENTS

- 450g pork sausage
- 800g potatoes
- 230g grated cheddar cheese
- 12 eggs
- 150ml semi-skimmed milk
- ¼ tsp salt
- 1/8 tsp pepper
- 12 tortillas
- Salsa, sliced jalapenos, and tomatoes to serve (optional)

INSTRUCTIONS

1. Fry the sausages until they are no longer pink. This should take about 8 to 10 minutes. Break into chunks and drain.
2. In a greased slow cooker, layer the potatoes, sausage, and cheese. Whisk the eggs in a bowl with the seasoned salt, pepper, and milk until blended. Tip the mixture into the slow cooker.
3. Cook for 3 ½ to 4 hours on low until the eggs are set. Let the dish stand without the lid for 10 to 15 minutes before serving. Serve in tortillas with toppings of your choice.

CHILLI BREAKFAST CASSEROLE

SERVES 12 | PER SERVING - CALORIES: 272, FAT: 16G, CARBOHYDRATES: 16G, PROTEIN: 15G

INGREDIENTS

- 850g grated potato
- 450g pork sausage, cooked and drained
- 1 onion, chopped
- 115g canned green chillies, drained
- 170g grated cheddar cheese
- 12 eggs
- 240ml semi-skimmed milk
- ½ tsp salt
- ½ tsp pepper

INSTRUCTIONS

1. In a greased slow cooker, layer half of the potatoes, sausage, onion, chillies, and cheese. Repeat the layers.
2. Whisk the eggs in a bowl with the salt, pepper, and milk and pour into the slow cooker. Cook on low for 7 to 9 hours.

DOUGHNUT BREAKFAST BAKE

SERVES 12 | PER SERVING - CALORIES: 609, FAT: 36G, CARBOHYDRATES: 64G, PROTEIN: 8G

INGREDIENTS

- 4 eggs
- 240ml double cream
- 2 apples, peeled and cut into chunks
- 24 mini doughnuts, cut into pieces
- 1 tbsp vanilla extract
- 100g brown sugar
- 1 tsp ground cinnamon
- Whipped cream and berries to serve (optional)

INSTRUCTIONS

1. Line the inside of the slow cooker with two pieces of aluminium foil, and grease. Put half of the doughnut pieces in the bottom of the slow cooker, followed by half of the apples. Repeat the process until you have used all of the ingredients.
2. Whisk the cream, vanilla, and eggs together in a bowl. Tip the mixture over the doughnut mixture.
3. Cook on low for 4 to 5 hours, then leave it to stand without the lid on for at least 20 minutes. Enjoy with berries and cream.

FRITTATA PROVENCAL

SERVES 6 | PER SERVING - CALORIES: 245, FAT: 14G, CARBOHYDRATES: 12G, PROTEIN: 15G

INGREDIENTS

- 120ml water
- 1 tbsp olive oil
- 1 medium potato, peeled and sliced
- 1 onion, sliced
- ½ tsp smoked paprika
- 12 large eggs
- ½ tsp dried thyme
- 1 tsp hot sauce
- ½ tsp salt
- ¼ tsp pepper
- 140g fresh goats' cheese, crumbled
- 30g chopped sun-dried tomatoes

INSTRUCTIONS

1. Put a rack in the slow cooker. Alternatively, layer two 24-inch pieces of aluminium foil, and starting with the long side, fold to create a 1-inch-wide strip. Roll the strip to make a rack to go in the bottom of the slow cooker. Place the coil in the bottom of the slow cooker. Pour in the water.
2. Heat the oil in a frying pan, then add the potato and onion; cook and stir until potato is lightly browned, 5-7 minutes. Stir in the paprika. Transfer to a greased baking dish (dish must fit in slow cooker).

3. Beat the eggs with the chilli sauce, thyme, and salt and pepper. Stir in half of the cheese. Pour over the potato mixture. Top with tomatoes and the remaining goat cheese. Place the dish on foil rack.

4. Cook on low until set and a knife inserted in the centre comes out clean, around 3 to 4 hours.

HAM AND EGGS

SERVES 6 | PER SERVING - CALORIES: 315, FAT: 18G, CARBOHYDRATES: 17G, PROTEIN: 21G

INGREDIENTS

- 6 eggs
- 135g flour
- 150ml semi-skimmed milk
- 75ml sour cream
- 2 tbsp fresh parsley, chopped
- 2 garlic cloves, minced
- ½ tsp salt
- ½ tsp pepper
- 135g cooked ham, cubed
- 120g grated cheese
- 1 onion, chopped
- 40g grated Parmesan

INSTRUCTIONS

1. In a large bowl, whisk the eggs, flour, milk, sour cream, parsley, garlic, salt, and pepper. Stir in the remaining ingredients and pour into the slow cooker.

2. Cook on low for 3 to 4 hours. Cut into wedges.

SAUSAGE AND WAFFLE BAKE

SERVES 6 | PER SERVING - CALORIES: 442, FAT: 31G, CARBOHYDRATES: 20G, PROTEIN: 19G

INGREDIENTS

- 900g pork sausage
- 1 tbsp sage
- ½ tsp fennel seeds
- 350g waffles, cut into small pieces
- 8 eggs
- 300ml single cream
- 50ml maple syrup
- ¼ tsp salt
- ¼ tsp pepper
- 260g grated cheese
- More maple syrup to serve

INSTRUCTIONS

1. Fold two 18-inch pieces of foil into two strips, 4 inches wide. Line the slow cooker with the foil and grease with cooking spray.

2. Fry the sausage over a medium heat until starting to colour, then drain and break into pieces. Stir through the safe and fennel.

3. Put the waffle in the bottom of the slow cooker and tip over the contents of the pan. In a bowl, mix eggs, cream, syrup, and seasonings. Pour over the sausage and waffles. Top with cheese. Cook on low for 5 to 6 hours. Let stand, uncovered, 15 minutes. Serve with added maple syrup.

FRITTATA WITH COURGETTES, TOMATOES, AND FETA

SERVES 3 TO 4 | PER SERVING - CALORIES: 264, FAT: 15.3G, CARBOHYDRATES: 17.3G, PROTEIN: 17.5G

INGREDIENTS

- 2 courgettes, grated with ½ tsp salt
- 6 eggs
- ¼ tsp paprika
- ¼ tsp thyme
- ¼ tsp salt
- ¼ tsp black pepper, ground
- 3 tbsp parsley, chopped
- 150g feta, crumbled
- 10 cherry tomatoes, halved
- Oil to grease the slow cooker

INSTRUCTIONS

1. Put the grated courgette in a sieve or colander and sprinkle over the salt. Leave the courgette to drain naturally, but then squeeze by hand to get most of the moisture out.
2. Grease the inside of the slow cooker.
3. Beat the eggs with the seasoning, then stir in the tomatoes, courgette, and feta. Tip into the slow cooker.
4. Cook for 2 ½ to 3 hours on low until the middle appears dry. Insert a knife into the centre, if it comes out dry, it is ready.

BAKED BEANS WITH BACON

SERVES 6 | PER SERVING - CALORIES: 241, FAT: 6G, CARBOHYDRATES: 40G, PROTEIN: 11G

INGREDIENTS

- 6 to 8 rashers of bacon, chopped into pieces
- 30g brown sugar
- ½ tsp mustard powder
- 120ml ketchup or chilli sauce
- 3 cans of baked beans

INSTRUCTIONS

1. Cook the bacon in batches in a frying pan until crisp.
2. Place the bacon on paper towels to drain.
3. Mix the brown sugar, mustard powder, and sauce. Pour the bacon and beans into the slow cooker and stir. Add the sauce mixture to the beans and mix well to combine.
4. Cook on low for 4 to 5 hours, or high for 2 hours.

SAUSAGE AND AVOCADO BREAKFAST BURRITOS

MAKES 10 BURRITOS | PER BURRITO - CALORIES: 905, FAT: 53G, CARBOHYDRATES: 70G, PROTEIN: 39G

INGREDIENTS

- 900g pork sausage
- 850g grated potato
- 14 eggs
- 1 tsp pepper
- 1 tbsp salt
- 2 tbsp hot sauce
- 1 onion, diced
- 1 green pepper, diced
- 130g grated cheese, plus extra to serve
- 2 avocados, sliced
- Salsa, sour cream, and tortillas to serve

INSTRUCTIONS

1. Brown the sausage, then drain and set aside.
2. Fry the grated potato until starting to cook, dry out and brown. Set aside.
3. Grease the slow cooker and place the potatoes in the bottom.
4. Sprinkle the onions and green pepper over the top of the potatoes.
5. Beat the eggs together with the cheese, hot sauce, pepper, and season salt. Pour the eggs over the onions and potatoes. Then top with the cooked breakfast sausage.
6. Cook on low, overnight. The low setting cooks for eight hours; be careful not to let it cook much longer than eight hours.
7. Stir the ingredients together again to combine.
8. Serve with warmed tortillas, avocado, cheese, salsa, and sour cream.

DECADENT BABY BREAKFAST POTATOES

SERVES 8 | PER SERVING - CALORIES: 192, FAT: 6G, CARBOHYDRATES: 32G, PROTEIN: 4G

INGREDIENTS

- 2 tbsp extra-virgin olive oil
- 1.2kg baby potatoes, quartered
- ½ onion, diced
- 1 red pepper, diced
- 1 green pepper, diced
- 4 garlic cloves, minced
- 2 tbsp unsalted butter
- 2 tsp smoked paprika
- 2 tsp salt

INSTRUCTIONS

1. Grease the inside of the slow cooker. Add the potatoes, green pepper, red pepper, onion, garlic, seasoned salt, paprika, and butter. Drizzle the olive oil over the top, then stir.
2. Cook for 2 ½ to 3 hours on high or for 4 to 5 hours on low until the potatoes are tender. Check on the potatoes in the last hour of cooking time to make sure they don't overcook.
3. Stir well and season.

CHEESY BREAKFAST POTATOES

SERVES 8 | PER SERVING - CALORIES: 377, FAT: 24G, CARBOHYDRATES: 20G, PROTEIN: 19.5G

INGREDIENTS

- 3 potatoes, peeled and diced
- 1 red pepper, diced
- 1 green pepper, diced
- 1 onion, diced
- 370g chorizo, sliced
- 175g cheddar cheese
- 120ml sour cream
- ¼ tsp dried oregano
- ¼ tsp dried basil
- Can of cream of chicken soup
- 2 tbsp chopped fresh parsley

INSTRUCTIONS

1. Place potatoes, peppers, onion, chicken sausage, cheese, sour cream, oregano, and basil into a slow cooker. Stir in chicken soup; season to taste.
2. Cook for 2 to 3 hours on high, or 4 to 5 hours on low.
3. Serve with a sprinkling of parsley.

BREAKFAST QUINOA

SERVES 8 | PER SERVING - CALORIES: 326, FAT: 17G, CARBOHYDRATES: 39G, PROTEIN: 7G

INGREDIENTS

- 170g quinoa, uncooked
- 475g water
- 240g coconut milk
- 2 tbsp maple syrup or honey
- ¼ tsp salt
- Toppings of your choice, such as fruit and nuts

INSTRUCTIONS

1. Place quinoa in a fine mesh colander and rinse very well under cold running water, for about a minute.
2. Add rinsed quinoa, water, coconut milk, maple syrup and salt to a small slow cooker and cover with a lid. Cook for 8 hours on low. Serve hot with a splash of milk and toppings of choice.

CARROT CAKE PORRIDGE

SERVES 6 | PER SERVING - CALORIES: 184, FAT: 4G, CARBOHYDRATES: 32G, PROTEIN: 5G

INGREDIENTS
- 90g porridge oats
- 450ml almond milk
- 450ml coconut milk
- 75g grated carrots
- 40g raisins
- 1 tsp ground cinnamon
- ½ tsp ground nutmeg
- Brown sugar, coconut flakes and chopped pecans to serve

INSTRUCTIONS
1. Grease the slow cooker.
2. Add the porridge to the slow cooker.
3. Stir the almond milk, coconut milk, raisins, carrot, and spices together, then pour into the slow cooker.
4. Cook on low for 6 to 8 hours.
5. Serve topped with brown sugar, coconut flakes, and chopped pecans.

PUMPKIN PIE PORRIDGE

SERVES 4 | PER SERVING - CALORIES: 242, FAT: 4G, CARBOHYDRATES: 45G, PROTEIN: 8G

INGREDIENTS
- Cooking spray to grease the slow cooker
- 90g porridge oats
- 600ml water
- 360ml almond milk
- 240ml pumpkin puree
- 3 tbsp maple syrup
- 1 tsp vanilla
- ½ tsp cinnamon
- ¼ tsp salt
- Chopped pecans, maple syrup, and almond milk to serve

INSTRUCTIONS
1. Grease the slow cooker with coconut oil, butter, or cooking spray. Put everything in the slow cooker and mix.
2. Cook for 6 to 8 hours on low.
3. In the morning, give the porridge a good stir as the oats will settle to the bottom. Serve in bowls topped with pecans, maple syrup and almond milk.

GIANT BLUEBERRY PANCAKE

SERVES 8 | PER SERVING - CALORIES: 174, FAT: 2G, CARBOHYDRATES: 30G, PROTEIN: 6G

INGREDIENTS
- 2 eggs
- 170g plain flour
- 375ml milk
- 1 tsp vanilla
- 2 tbsp sugar
- 2 ½ tsp baking powder
- 60g fresh blueberries

INSTRUCTIONS
1. Beat the eggs with the vanilla and milk.
2. Stir the sugar and baking powder into the flour in a second bowl.
3. Add the wet ingredients to the dry and stir just until mixed. Do not over mix!
4. Tip the batter into the slow cooker, then top with the blueberries.
5. Cook on low for around 4 hours or until cooked through. Insert a knife in the centre, if it comes out clean, it is ready.
6. Serve with toppings of your choice.

FARMER'S BREAKFAST CASSEROLE

SERVES 8 | PER SERVING - CALORIES: 386, FAT: 29G, CARBOHYDRATES: 4G, PROTEIN: 26G

INGREDIENTS

- 9 eggs
- 185g ricotta
- ¾ tsp salt
- ¼ tsp pepper
- ½ tsp dried thyme
- ½ tsp dried dill
- 5 bacon rashers, cooked and sliced
- 115g diced cooked ham
- 450g cheddar cheese
- 2 tomatoes, sliced

INSTRUCTIONS

1. Cube two thirds of the cheese and grate the rest. Save the grated cheese for later.
2. Whisk the eggs, ricotta, seasoning, and spices in a bowl. Whisk until you can get it smooth, though chunks of ricotta are fine.
3. Grease the slow cooker with cooking spray or oil. Add the cubed cheese, bacon, and ham. Whisk the egg mixture one more time to get it combined again, then pour over the ham, bacon, and cheese.
4. Cook on high for 2 ½ hours. If there is any liquid on top of the casserole, blot it with a paper towel. Add remaining cheese and cover for 5-10 minutes more.

LUNCH

AFRICAN-INSPIRED PEANUT AND SWEET POTATO STEW

SERVES 8 | PER SERVING - CALORIES: 349, FAT: 9G, CARBOHYDRATES: 60G, PROTEIN: 10G

INGREDIENTS

- 550g chopped fresh kale
- 100g peanut butter, ideally chunky
- 2 cans of chopped tomatoes
- 3 tbsp chopped coriander leaves
- 6 medium sweet potatoes, cubed
- 3 garlic cloves, chopped
- 2 tsp ground cumin
- 1 tsp salt
- ½ tsp ground cinnamon
- ½ tsp smoked paprika
- 400g chickpeas, rinsed and drained
- 240ml water

INSTRUCTIONS

1. Place the tomatoes, coriander, peanut butter, garlic, cumin, salt, cinnamon and paprika in a food processor and puree. Transfer to the slow cooker, then stir in the potatoes, chickpeas, and water.
2. Cook the dish for between 6 and 8 hours on low, adding the kale for the last 30 minutes.

ASIAN STYLE PORK

SERVES 12 | PER SERVING - CALORIES: 203, FAT: 7G, CARBOHYDRATES: 11G, PROTEIN: 23G

INGREDIENTS

- 2 large onions, thinly sliced
- 3 garlic cloves, minced
- ½ tsp salt
- ½ tsp pepper
- 1.3kg pork loin
- 1 tbsp oil
- 3 bay leaves
- 60ml hot water
- 60ml honey
- 60ml reduced sodium soy sauce
- 2 tbsp rice vinegar
- 1 tsp ground ginger
- 3 tbsp cornflour
- 60ml cold water
- Cooked rice to serve

INSTRUCTIONS

1. Place the onions in the slow cooker. Cut the pork joint in half, and rub in the garlic, salt, and pepper. In a large non-stick frying pan, brown the pork in oil on all sides. Add the pork and bay leaves.
2. In a bowl, stir together the hot water and honey. Mix in the vinegar, soy sauce, and spices, then tip over the pork. Cook for 4 to 5 hours on low until the pork is tender.
3. Remove the pork, and wrap in foil to keep warm.
4. Discard bay leaves. Mix cornstarch and cold water until smooth; gradually stir into the slow cooker. Cook on high for 30 minutes to thicken, stirring twice.
5. Coarsely shred pork into bite-sized pieces; serve with sauce over rice. Sprinkle with sesame seeds and, if desired, green onions.

ASIAN STYLE STEAK

SERVES 8 | PER SERVING - CALORIES: 237, FAT: 8G, CARBOHYDRATES: 14G, PROTEIN: 29G

INGREDIENTS

- 900g steak, cut into strips
- 2 tbsp oil
- 3 stalks of celery, chopped
- 1 onion, chopped
- 60ml reduced sodium soy sauce
- 1 tsp sugar
- ½ tsp minced garlic
- ¼ tsp ground ginger
- ¼ tsp pepper
- 2 green peppers, chopped
- 400g tomato passata
- Can of beansprouts, rinsed and drained
- 225g canned sliced water chestnuts, drained
- 125g canned sliced mushrooms, drained
- 1 tbsp cornflour
- 120ml cold water
- Rice to serve

INSTRUCTIONS

1. In a large frying pan, brown meat in oil on all sides. Transfer the meat and drippings to the slow cooker. Combine the celery, onion, soy sauce, sugar, garlic, ginger, and pepper, and pour over the meat. Cook on low until the meat is tender, around 5 ½ to 6 hours.
2. Add the tomato sauce, water chestnuts, mushrooms, green peppers, and bean sprouts, and cook for a further hour.
3. Combine cornflour and water until smooth and stir into the beef mixture. Cook on high to thicken the sauce for 30 minutes. Serve with rice.

BEEF AND RICE CABBAGE ROLLS

SERVES 6 | PER SERVING - CALORIES: 204, FAT: 7G, CARBOHYDRATES: 16G, PROTEIN: 18G

INGREDIENTS

- 60ml semi-skimmed milk
- 12 cabbage leaves
- 225g cooked brown rice
- 1 onion, chopped
- 1 egg
- ¼ tsp pepper
- ½ tsp salt
- 425g minced beef

FOR THE SAUCE:

- 1 tbsp lemon juice
- 1 tbsp light brown sugar
- 200g tomato passata
- 1 tsp Worcestershire sauce

INSTRUCTIONS

1. In batches, cook the cabbage in boiling water 3-5 minutes or until crisp-tender. Drain and cool slightly. Trim the thick vein from the bottom of each cabbage leaf, making a V-shaped cut.
2. Stir together the rice with the egg, onion, milk, salt, and pepper. Add the beef and fold together. Place about 3 tbsp of the beef mixture on each cabbage leaf. Pull together cut edges of the leaves to overlap and fold over the filling. Fold in the sides and roll up.
3. Place 6 rolls in the slow cooker, seam side down. Mix the sauce ingredients together and pour half of the sauce over cabbage rolls. Top with remaining rolls and sauce. Cook for 6 to 8 hours on low.

BUTTERNUT SQUASH AND CINNAMON SOUP

SERVES 14 | PER SERVING - CALORIES: 135, FAT: 7G, CARBOHYDRATES: 17G, PROTEIN: 2G

INGREDIENTS

- 2 tbsp butter
- 1 onion, chopped
- 1 medium butternut squash, peeled and cubed
- 1.2L vegetable stock
- 1 tbsp brown sugar
- 1 tbsp minced ginger
- 1 garlic clove, minced
- 1 cinnamon stick
- 225g cream cheese

INSTRUCTIONS

1. Melt the butter in a pan, and cook the onion until softened, about 3 to 5 minutes. Combine the broth, brown sugar, ginger, garlic, and cinnamon, then pour over the squash. Cook on low until the squash softens, about 6 to 8 hours.
2. Leave the soup to cool slightly and discard the cinnamon stick. Process the soup in batches in a blender until smooth, then return to the slow cooker.
3. Stir in the cream cheese, and cook until the cheese melts.

BUTTERNUT SQUASH WITH WHOLE GRAINS

SERVES 12 | PER SERVING - CALORIES: 97, FAT: 1G, CARBOHYDRATES: 22G, PROTEIN: 3G

INGREDIENTS

- 1 medium butternut squash, cut into cubes
- 210g uncooked wholegrain rice blend
- 1 onion, chopped
- 120ml water
- 3 garlic cloves, minced
- 2 tsp fresh thyme
- ½ tsp salt
- ¼ tsp pepper
- 450ml vegetable stock
- 175g fresh baby spinach

INSTRUCTIONS

1. Put everything except the spinach in the slow cooker and stir.
2. Cook for 4 to 5 hours on low. Stir in the spinach before serving.

CAROLINA-STYLE VINEGAR BBQ PULLED CHICKEN

SERVES 6 | PER SERVING - CALORIES: 134, FAT: 3G, CARBOHYDRATES: 3G, PROTEIN: 23G

INGREDIENTS

- 480ml water
- 240ml white vinegar
- 60g sugar
- Reduced salt chicken stock cube
- 1 tsp chilli flakes
- ¾ tsp salt
- 675g chicken breasts, chopped

INSTRUCTIONS

1. Mix the sugar, chilli flakes and salt with the water, vinegar, and stock. Add the chicken and pour over the vinegar mix.
2. Cook on low for 4 to 5 hours.
3. Take out the chicken, and let it cool slightly. Reserve about 240ml of the cooking juices and discard the rest. Using 2 forks, shred the meat.
4. Put the meat back in the slow cooker with the reserved juice. Heat back through for a few minutes before serving.

CARROT AND LENTIL CHILLI

SERVES 8 | PER SERVING - CALORIES: 310, FAT: 10G, CARBOHYDRATES: 47G, PROTEIN: 13G

INGREDIENTS

- 1L vegetable stock
- 12 medium carrots, chopped
- Can chopped tomatoes
- 180g dried green lentils, rinsed
- 180g dried red lentils, rinsed
- 2 medium avocados, cubed
- 6 garlic cloves, minced
- 1 onion, chopped
- 2 tbsp olive oil
- 2 tsp paprika
- 1 tsp salt
- 1 tbsp ground cumin
- 1 tsp chilli powder

INSTRUCTIONS

1. Heat the oil in a pan and cook the onions until soft. Tip in the lentils and garlic and cook for another minute. Tip into the slow cooker.
2. Add the carrots, broth, and seasoning. Cook on low for 4 to 6 hours.
3. Fold through the tomatoes and cook for 30 minutes longer.
4. Serve with the avocado.

CHICKEN TOMATILLO SOUP

SERVES 8 | PER SERVING - CALORIES: 290, FAT: 8G, CARBOHYDRATES: 36G, PROTEIN: 21G

INGREDIENTS

- 400g can of black beans
- 400g can of chickpeas, rinsed
- 400g sweetcorn, fresh or frozen
- 950g tomatillos or green tomatoes, chopped
- 1 red pepper, chopped
- 3 medium tomatoes, chopped
- 1 onion, chopped
- 3 garlic cloves, minced
- 2 tbsp olive oil
- 900g chicken breast
- 1L reduced salt chicken stock
- 2 tbsp taco seasoning

INSTRUCTIONS

1. Heat the oil in a pan and cook the onion until tender. Add the garlic and cook for another minute.
2. Stir in the stock, tomatillos, tomatoes, and red pepper. Bring to a boil, and simmer, covered for 15 minutes. Leave the pan to cool slightly, then puree.
3. Put the chicken and taco seasoning in the slow cooker. Pour the pureed soup over the chicken and add the beans. Cook on low for 3 ½ to 4 ½ hours.
4. Shred the chicken with two forks, then put back in the slow cooker. Add the sweetcorn and cook for a further 30 minutes.

CHICKPEA AND POTATO CURRY

SERVES 6 | PER SERVING - CALORIES: 240, FAT: 6G, CARBOHYDRATES: 42G, PROTEIN: 8G

INGREDIENTS

- 600ml vegetable stock
- 400g can of chopped tomatoes
- 2x 400g cans of chickpeas, rinsed
- 1 large potato, peeled and cubed
- 1 onion, chopped
- 2 garlic cloves, minced
- 2 tsp minced fresh ginger
- 1 tsp garam masala
- 1 tbsp oil
- 2 tsp ground coriander
- 1 tsp chilli powder
- ½ tsp ground cumin
- ¼ tsp ground turmeric
- 1 tsp salt
- 1 tbsp lime juice
- Small handful of fresh coriander, chopped

INSTRUCTIONS

1. Heat the oil in a pan and cook the onion over a medium to high heat until soft. Stir in the garlic, ginger, and seasoning, and cook for another minute. Fold in the tomatoes, and tip everything into the slow cooker.
2. Stir in the chickpeas, potato, and stock. Cook for between 6 and 8 hours on low until the potato is softening.
3. Stir in the lime juice and sprinkle with the coriander.

GREEK STYLE SAUSAGE AND PEPPERS

SERVES 12 | PER SERVING - CALORIES: 504, FAT: 41G, CARBOHYDRATES: 10G, PROTEIN: 23G

INGREDIENTS

- 1.7kg smoked sausage, sliced
- 1 onion, chopped
- 3 peppers, chopped
- 1 whole garlic bulb, minced
- 480ml beef stock
- 1 tsp sea salt
- 1 tsp ground black pepper
- 1 tbsp fresh oregano
- 500g cherry or plum tomatoes

INSTRUCTIONS

Put everything excluding the tomatoes in the slow cooker. Cook for 5 to 6 hours on low until the vegetables are softening. Tip in the tomatoes, then cook for 30 minutes longer.

PORK BEAN SOUP

SERVES 12 | PER SERVING - CALORIES: 207, FAT: 2G, CARBOHYDRATES: 30G, PROTEIN: 18G

INGREDIENTS

- 450g dried cannellini beans
- 1 large onion, chopped
- 3 medium carrots, chopped
- 3 stalks of celery, chopped
- 450g pork tenderloin
- 1 tsp garlic powder
- 1 tbsp fresh minced chives
- 1 tsp dried oregano
- ½ tsp dried thyme
- 1 tsp pepper
- 1.3L reduced salt chicken stock
- 330ml pale ale
- 400g can chopped tomatoes
- 140g fresh spinach
- 2 tsp salt

INSTRUCTIONS

1. Tip the beans in a bowl and add cool water to cover. Soak 5 hours or overnight. Drain beans, discard the water, and rinse with clean water.
2. In the slow cooker, layer the beans, onions, carrots, celery, and pork. Add the seasonings, stock, and ale. Cook for 6 to 8 hours on low until the pork and beans are cooked through and softening.
3. Take the pork out of the slow cooker, and shred with forks. Stir in the tomatoes, spinach, and salt. Return the pork to slow cooker. Cook for a further 15 to 20 minutes until heated through.

ITALIAN BEEF AND VEGETABLE SOUP

SERVES 6 | PER SERVING - CALORIES: 127, FAT: 3G, CARBOHYDRATES: 14G, PROTEIN: 11G

INGREDIENTS

- 225g minced beef
- Half an onion, chopped
- 680g cabbage, chopped
- 2 medium carrots, chopped
- 150g Brussel sprouts, quartered
- 100g chopped kale
- 1 stalk of celery, chopped
- 1 tbsp fresh parsley
- ½ tsp pepper
- ½ tsp dried basil
- ¼ tsp salt
- 720ml beef stock
- 400g can chopped tomatoes

SARA R. ADAMS

INSTRUCTIONS

1. Brown the beef and onion in a pan. Crumble the meat up as you go. Stir in the rest of the ingredients.
2. Cook on low for 5 to 6 hours until the carrots are tender.

MOROCCAN LAMB LETTUCE WRAPS

SERVES 8 | PER SERVING - CALORIES: 221, FAT: 8G, CARBOHYDRATES: 13G, PROTEIN: 24G

INGREDIENTS

- 900g lamb chunks
- 200g chunky salsa
- 100g apricot preserves
- 6 tbsp dry red wine
- 2 tbsp ras el hanout
- 2 tsp chilli powder
- ½ tsp garlic powder
- 1 cucumber, thinly sliced
- Lettuce leaves to serve

INSTRUCTIONS

1. In a bowl, mix the lamb, salsa, preserves, ras el hanout, chilli powder, garlic powder, and 4 tablespoons of the red wine. Transfer to the slow cooker.
2. Cook for 5 to 6 hours on low. Remove lamb from the slow cooker and shred. Skim the fat from the slow cooker, and strain the remaining juices.
3. Put the lamb and cooking juices back in the slow cooker. Stir in remaining wine, and heat until warm.
4. Serve the lamb in lettuce leaves topped with the cucumber.

BUFFALO CHICKEN SALAD

SERVES 6 | PER SERVING - CALORIES: 385, FAT: 26G, CARBOHYDRATES: 12G, PROTEIN: 28G

INGREDIENTS

- 675g chicken breast, chopped
- 160ml buffalo or chilli sauce
- 3 tbsp butter
- 1 carrot, grated
- 1 medium avocado, peeled, and cubed
- 50g crumbled blue cheese
- 50ml blue cheese salad dressing
- Salad leaves of your choice

INSTRUCTIONS

1. Put the chicken in the slow cooker, and cover with the sauce and butter. Cook on low for 2 ½ to 3 hours.
2. Remove the chicken and shred with two forks. Reserve about 100ml of the cooking juices and discard any that remain. Return the chicken and reserved juices to the slow cooker and head through.
3. Serve the chicken and vegetables on top of your salad leaves of choice with a drizzle of blue cheese dressing.

SWEET POTATO CHOCOLATE SOUP

SERVES 8 | PER SERVING - CALORIES: 203, FAT: 6G, CARBOHYDRATES: 31G, PROTEIN: 4G

INGREDIENTS

- 500ml reduced salt chicken stock
- 1L reduced salt vegetable stock
- 1 large onion, finely chopped
- 4 sweet potatoes, peeled and cubed
- 3 garlic cloves, minced
- 75g bittersweet chocolate, finely chopped
- 1 tsp dried oregano
- 2 tbsp chilli powder
- 1 tsp dried tarragon
- ½ tsp ground cinnamon
- 1 tsp ground cumin
- ½ tsp pepper
- ¾ tsp salt
- 2 tbsp olive oil
- 2 tbsp tequila (optional)

INSTRUCTIONS

1. Heat the oil over a medium to high heat and cook the onion with the seasonings for 5 to 7 minutes. Stir in the garlic, and cook for another minute. If desired, add in tequila, stirring constantly.
2. Transfer to the slow cooker. Add the stock and sweet potatoes. Cook the soup on low for between 6 and 8 hours until tender. At the end of the cook time, stir through the chocolate until melted. Let the soup cool slightly, then process in batches in a blender until smooth.

CHICKEN CAESAR WRAPS

SERVES 8 | PER SERVING - CALORIES: 472, FAT: 25G, CARBOHYDRATES: 29G, PROTEIN: 31G

INGREDIENTS

- 675g chicken breast
- 480ml chicken stock
- 180ml Caesar salad dressing
- 100g grated Parmesan
- 3 tbsp minced fresh parsley
- ½ tsp pepper
- Tortillas and lettuce to serve

INSTRUCTIONS

1. Place the chicken in the slow cooker and pour over the stock. Cook for 3 to 4 hours on low. Remove the chicken and discard the cooking juices. Shred the chicken, then put it back.
2. Stir through the dressing, Parmesan, parsley, and pepper, then heat through. Serve immediately in tortilla wraps with lettuce.

TOMATO BALSAMIC CHICKEN

SERVES 6 | PER SERVING - CALORIES: 235, FAT: 11G, CARBOHYDRATES: 12G, PROTEIN: 23G

INGREDIENTS

- 950g chicken thighs, bone-in
- 75ml balsamic vinegar
- 1 shallot, sliced
- 2 carrots, chopped
- 120ml chicken stock
- 400g can chopped tomatoes
- 1 tbsp olive oil
- 2 garlic cloves, minced
- ½ tsp Italian herb mix
- ½ tsp salt
- ¼ tsp pepper
- 1 bay leaf
- 1 tbsp plain flour
- Hot cooked orzo

INSTRUCTIONS

1. Place the carrots and shallots in slow cooker and top with chicken. In a bowl, whisk the flour and broth until smooth; stir in tomatoes, vinegar, oil, garlic, and seasonings. Pour into the slow cooker. Cook on low for 6 to 8 hours.
2. Remove the chicken; cool slightly. Discard bay leaf and, if desired, skim fat from carrot mixture.
3. Remove chicken from bones; shred slightly with two forks. Serve with orzo.

ENCHILADA ORZO

SERVES 6 | PER SERVING - CALORIES: 331, FAT: 7.8G, CARBOHYDRATES: 54.6G, PROTEIN: 12.1G

INGREDIENTS

- 400g sun-dried chopped tomatoes
- 280g enchilada sauce
- 125g canned chopped green chillies, drained
- 120ml vegetable stock
- 100g sweetcorn
- 100g canned black beans, drained and rinsed
- Salt and pepper to taste
- 200g cream cheese
- 420g orzo
- 2 tbsp fresh coriander

INSTRUCTIONS

1. Put the chopped tomatoes, enchilada sauce, green chillies, vegetable stock, sweetcorn, and beans into a slow cooker. Season to taste and stir. Put the cream cheese on top.
2. Cook on high for 3 to 4 hours, or on low for 7 to 8 hours.
3. Uncover and stir until cream cheese is well combined. Stir in orzo. Cook for a further 15 to 30 minutes on high. Add extra stock if needed.

CHEESY TORTELLINI

SERVES 6 | PER SERVING - CALORIES: 437, FAT: 19.9G, CARBOHYDRATES: 34G, PROTEIN: 32G

INGREDIENTS

- 2x 400g cans of chopped tomatoes
- 900g beef mince
- 250g grated mozzarella
- 275g fresh cheese tortellini
- 2 garlic cloves, minced
- 1 onion, diced
- 130g grated cheddar
- 280g canned tomatoes in chilli sauce
- 1 tbsp olive oil
- ¼ tsp chilli flakes
- ½ tsp dried oregano
- ½ tsp dried basil
- 2 tbsp fresh parsley, chopped
- Salt and pepper to taste

INSTRUCTIONS

1. Heat the oil in a frying pan. Add the beef, garlic, and onion to the pan. Cook, stirring regularly, until the beef has browned, about 3-5 minutes. Crumble the mince as it cooks. Once cooked, drain away the excess fat.
2. Put the tomatoes, beef, basil, oregano, and chilli in the pot, and season to taste. Stir well.
3. Cook for 7 to 8 hours on low, or 3 to 4 hours on high.
4. Stir through the tortellini and top the pasta with the cheese. Cook on low heat for 15-30 minutes more, or until the tortellini is tender.
5. Serve immediately with a sprinkling of parsley.

HAWAIIAN CHICKEN WITH PINEAPPLE

SERVES 6 | PER SERVING - CALORIES: 505, FAT: 10G, CARBOHYDRATES: 54G, PROTEIN: 50G

INGREDIENTS

- 900g chicken breasts, cut into pieces
- 600g canned pineapple chunks
- 1 tbsp olive oil
- 150g pineapple preserves or jam
- 120ml ketchup
- 80ml soy sauce
- 60g brown sugar
- 2 tbsp rice wine vinegar
- 1 tbsp sesame oil
- 1 tbsp lime juice
- 2 tsp ground ginger
- 2 to 3 tbsp Sriracha
- 2 cloves of garlic, minced
- ½ tsp salt
- ½ tsp pepper
- 50g cornflour
- 3 tbsp coriander
- 3 tbsp spring onions, finely sliced

INSTRUCTIONS

1. Whisk the pineapple juice and preserves, ketchup, soy sauce, vinegar, sesame oil, lime juice, chilli sauce, ginger, brown sugar, garlic, and salt and pepper in a bowl. Set the sauce aside.
2. Grease the slow cooker with oil.
3. Put the chicken and cornflour in a bag and toss to coat, then tip into the slow cooker.
4. Add the pineapple chunks, then pour the pineapple sauce mixture on top.
5. Cook for 4 hours on low, or 2 hours on high.
6. Add chicken and pineapple to a plate with as much extra cooking sauce spooned over the top as desired, garnish with coriander, green onions, and serve immediately.

CAULIFLOWER AND POTATO SOUP

SERVES 4 | PER SERVING - CALORIES: 542, FAT: 38G, CARBOHYDRATES: 46G, PROTEIN: 8.8G

INGREDIENTS

- 1 onion, chopped
- 3 garlic cloves, minced
- Pinch of cayenne pepper
- 1 tsp ground black pepper
- 1 ½ tsp salt
- 4 medium potatoes, peeled and cubed
- 500g cauliflower
- 1.2L chicken stock
- 240ml double cream
- 5 tbsp butter

INSTRUCTIONS

1. Mix the potatoes, garlic, onion, 400g of cauliflower, stock and seasonings in the slow cooker.
2. In the last 30 minutes, blend the soup in batches until smooth. Mix in the cream and continue cooking for 15 to 30 minutes.
3. Melt the butter in a pan, then fry the remaining cauliflower until brown. Set aside the cauliflower.
4. Serve the soup warm with fried cauliflower florets and a drizzle of the browned butter.

GNOCCHI WITH CREAMY PORK

SERVES 4 | PER SERVING - CALORIES: 513, FAT: 16G, CARBOHYDRATES: 57G, PROTEIN: 35G

INGREDIENTS

- 1 onion, chopped
- 6 garlic cloves, minced
- 1.8 to 2.3kg pork shoulder
- 1.5kg canned chopped tomatoes
- 1 tbsp Italian seasoning
- Salt and pepper to taste
- 120ml double cream
- 900g dried gnocchi

INSTRUCTIONS

1. Grease the inside of the slow cooker.
2. Place the garlic and onion in the slow cooker with the pork on top. Pour half of the tomatoes over the pork.
3. Sprinkle the Italian seasoning all over and season to taste. Tip over the remaining tomatoes, then cook for 11 hours on low.
4. Trim the pork and remove the bone. Stir through the cream and gnocchi, then cook for an hour longer. Serve with grated Parmesan.

KOREAN TACOS

SERVES 6 | PER SERVING - CALORIES: 305, FAT: 12G, CARBOHYDRATES: 25G, PROTEIN: 29G

INGREDIENTS

- 900g boneless pork loin, cut into 4 pieces
- 240ml hoisin sauce
- 3 garlic cloves, minced
- 3 spring onions, sliced thinly
- 3 tsp ground ginger
- 450g coleslaw
- 3 tbsp rice wine vinegar
- 2 tbsp brown sugar

INSTRUCTIONS

1. Add the pieces of pork in the insert/bowl of your slow cooker. Add hoisin sauce, garlic, green onions, and ground ginger.
2. Toss each piece of pork a few times to fully coat with the sauce and spices.
3. Cook for 8 to 9 hours on low.
4. Prior to serving, in a bowl, toss coleslaw or broccoli slaw mix with rice wine vinegar and brown sugar.

5. Take the pork out of the slow cooker and shred. Place pork back into the sauce and toss to coat.
6. Serve in warmed tortillas with slaw on top or spoon pork onto a bed of rice and a sprinkling of spring onions.

PASTA FAGIOLI

SERVES 8 | PER SERVING - CALORIES: 329, FAT: 6G, CARBOHYDRATES: 27G, PROTEIN: 22G

INGREDIENTS

- 1 litre beef stock
- 450g beef mince
- 2x 400g cans of chopped tomatoes
- 425g can cannellini beans, rinsed
- 425g can red kidney beans, rinsed
- 225g dried pasta
- 150g diced carrots
- 1 stick of celery, diced
- 1 onion, diced
- ½ tsp dried thyme
- 1 ½ tsp Italian seasoning
- 2 bay leaves
- Salt and pepper to taste

INSTRUCTIONS

1. Brown ground beef in a frying pan and break into tiny pieces. Add to the slow cooker with the rest of the ingredients, excluding the pasta and beans.
2. Cook for 3 to 4 hours on high, or 7 to 8 hours on low.
3. Prior to serving, add the beans and pasta to the slow cooker. Cook for a further 30 minutes.
4. Season to taste, and remove bay leaves prior to serving.

EASY BEEF AND BROCCOLI FAKEAWAY

SERVES 4 | PER SERVING - CALORIES: 370, FAT: 10G, CARBOHYDRATES: 24G, PROTEIN: 28G

INGREDIENTS

- 450g beef, sliced into thin strips
- 240ml beef stock
- 120ml low sodium soy sauce
- 60g dark brown sugar
- 1 tbsp sesame oil
- 3 cloves of garlic, minced
- 300g frozen broccoli
- 2 tbsp cornflour

INSTRUCTIONS

1. Whisk together the stock, soy sauce, sesame oil, brown sugar, and garlic in the slow cooker.
2. Gently place your slices of beef in the liquid and toss to coat.
3. Cook on low for 4 to 6 hours.
4. Mix the cornflour with a couple tablespoons of water, then stir into the slow cooker. Toss in your broccoli florets. Cook on low for an additional 30 minutes to thicken up the sauce.
5. Serve hot over white rice.

ITALIAN INSPIRED TURKEY MEATBALLS

SERVES 12 | PER SERVING - CALORIES: 239, FAT: 8G, CARBOHYDRATES: 23G, PROTEIN: 22G

INGREDIENTS

FOR THE MEATBALLS:

- 3 slices white bread, torn into small pieces
- 120ml semi-skimmed milk
- 900g turkey mince
- 50g grated Parmesan
- 3 tbsp fresh parsley
- 2 eggs
- 3 garlic cloves, minced
- 2 tsp Italian seasoning
- ½ tsp salt
- ½ tsp pepper

FOR THE SAUCE:

- 2 onions, chopped
- 1 green pepper, chopped
- 1.5kg canned chopped tomatoes
- 340g tomato passata
- 1 tbsp sugar
- 2 tsp Italian seasoning
- ½ tsp salt
- ½ tsp pepper
- 2 bay leaves

INSTRUCTIONS

1. Preheat the grill. Combine the bread and milk in a bowl, and let it stand until the liquid is absorbed. Add the remainder of the meatball ingredients and mix thoroughly. Shape into meatballs, and place on the greased rack of a grill tray. Cook for 5 to 6 minutes until browned.
2. Mix the sauce ingredients in the slow cooker. Gently stir the meatballs and bay leaves into the sauce.
3. Cook for 4 to 5 hours on low until the meatballs are cooked.
4. Serve with pasta.

MAPLE AND MUSTARD CHICKEN

SERVES 6 | PER SERVING - CALORIES: 289, FAT: 4G, CARBOHYDRATES: 24G, PROTEIN: 35G

INGREDIENTS

- 6 chicken breasts
- 120ml maple syrup
- 80ml mustard
- 2 tbsp tapioca starch

INSTRUCTIONS

Place the chicken in the slow cooker. Mix the syrup, mustard, and tapioca together and pour over the chicken. Cook for 3 to 4 hours on low. Serve with rice.

MUSHROOM MARSALA WITH BARLEY

SERVES 6 | PER SERVING - CALORIES: 235, FAT: 9G, CARBOHYDRATES: 31G, PROTEIN: 7G

INGREDIENTS

- 50g crumbled goat's cheese
- 180ml Marsala wine
- 440g cooked barley
- 675g small mushrooms, cut into chunks
- 2 shallots, thinly sliced
- 3 tbsp olive oil
- 3 tbsp reduced fat sour cream
- ½ tsp minced thyme
- 1 ½ tsp grated lemon zest
- 2 tbsp plain flour
- ¼ tsp salt
- 3 tbsp fresh parsley

INSTRUCTIONS

1. In a slow cooker, combine mushrooms, shallots, olive oil and thyme, with a third of the Marsala. Cook on low for 4 hours.
2. Stir in sour cream, flour, lemon zest, salt, and remaining Marsala. Cook for 15 minutes. Sprinkle with goat cheese and parsley. Serve with hot cooked barley.

RAINBOW MINESTRONE PASTA

SERVES 10 | PER SERVING - CALORIES: 231, FAT: 7G, CARBOHYDRATES: 34G, PROTEIN: 9G

INGREDIENTS

- 250g uncooked pasta
- 400g can of kidney beans, rinsed
- 400g can of chickpeas, rinsed
- 2x 400g cans chopped tomatoes
- 50g pesto
- 1.4L vegetable stock
- 250g baby spinach
- 1 medium carrot, chopped
- 1 red onion, chopped
- 1 courgette, sliced
- 1 red pepper, chopped
- 2 tbsp olive oil
- 2 garlic cloves, minced

INSTRUCTIONS

1. Chop the spinach, keeping stems and leaves separate. Cook the onion and spinach stems in a frying pan for 5 minutes. Transfer to the slow cooker.
2. Stir in the stock, tomatoes, beans, chickpeas, courgette, pepper, carrot, and garlic. Cook for 6 to 8 hours on low.
3. Fold in the pasta and spinach leaves, then cook for 20 to 25 minutes or until the pasta is cooked. Stir through to pesto to serve.

PULLED TURKEY

SERVES 5 | PER SERVING - CALORIES: 339, FAT: 4G, CARBOHYDRATES: 40G, PROTEIN: 36G

INGREDIENTS

- 560g turkey breast
- 480ml water
- 120ml sweet pickle juice
- Powdered onion soup or sauce mix
- 2 tbsp canned diced jalapenos
- 120ml fat-free Greek yoghurt
- 1 tbsp yellow mustard
- ¼ tsp pepper

INSTRUCTIONS

1. Add the turkey to the slow cooker. In a bowl, mix the pickle juice with the soup mix and jalapenos, then tip over the turkey. Cook for 6 to 8 hours on low. Remove the turkey and shred. Set aside.
2. Strain the cooking juices, reserving about 120ml. Stir together the cooking juices, yoghurt, mustard, and pepper. Pour over turkey and toss to coat.

ORANGE CHIPOTLE CHICKEN

SERVES 6 | PER SERVING - CALORIES: 246, FAT: 4G, CARBOHYDRATES: 15G, PROTEIN: 35G

INGREDIENTS

- 120ml orange juice
- 60ml BBQ sauce
- 1 red chilli, chopped
- ¼ tsp salt
- ¼ tsp garlic powder
- 6 chicken breasts
- Half a red onion, chopped
- 4 tsp cornflour
- 3 tbsp cold water
- Grated orange zest

INSTRUCTIONS

1. Put the BBQ, orange juice, garlic powder, chilli, and salt in a blender until smooth.
2. Put the chicken and onion in the slow cooker, and cover with the juice. Cook on low for 4 to 5 hours.
3. Remove the chicken, and wrap in foil to keep warm. Bring the juices to a boil in the saucepan.
4. Mix the cornflour and water together until smooth, and gradually stir this into the saucepan. Return to the boil, stirring constantly until thickened.

BEAN STUFFED PEPPERS

SERVES 4 | PER SERVING - CALORIES: 317, FAT: 10G, CARBOHYDRATES: 43G, PROTEIN: 15G

INGREDIENTS

- 4 red peppers
- 400g can of black beans, rinsed and drained
- 150g grated cheese
- 150g salsa
- 1 onion, chopped
- 120g frozen sweetcorn
- 90g uncooked long grain rice
- 1 ¼ tsp chilli powder
- ½ tsp ground cumin

INSTRUCTIONS

1. Cut the tops off the peppers and remove the seeds. Stir the rest of the ingredients together, then stuff into the peppers. Put in the bottom of the slow cooker.
2. Cook for 3 to 4 hours on low.

COSY VEGETABLE CURRY

SERVES 6 | PER SERVING - CALORIES: 304, FAT: 8G, CARBOHYDRATES: 49G, PROTEIN: 9G

INGREDIENTS

- 2x 400g cans of chickpeas, rinsed
- 2 tomatoes, seeded and chopped
- 250ml coconut milk
- 500ml chicken stock
- 225g fresh cauliflower florets
- 475g sweet potatoes, peeled and cubed
- 2 tbsp tomato paste
- 4 carrots, chopped
- 4 garlic cloves, minced
- 1 onion, chopped
- 1 tbsp oil
- 1 tsp ground ginger
- 2 tsp ground coriander
- 1 ½ tsp ground cinnamon
- ¼ tsp salt
- 1 tsp ground turmeric
- ½ tsp pepper
- ½ tsp cayenne pepper
- Chopped fresh coriander

INSTRUCTIONS

1. Fry the onion until it starts to colour, then add the spices and garlic and fry for another minute. Transfer to the slow cooker.
2. Mash one can of the beans until smooth, then add to the slow cooker. Stir in the remaining beans, vegetables, stock, coconut milk, pepper, and salt.
3. Cook on low for 5 to 6 hours.

CHICKEN TACO SALAD

SERVES 6 | PER SERVING - CALORIES: 143, FAT: 3G, CARBOHYDRATES: 4G, PROTEIN: 24G

INGREDIENTS

- 700g chicken breast
- 240ml chicken stock
- 1 tsp ground cumin
- 1 tsp salt
- 2 ½ tsp chilli powder
- ¼ tsp chilli flakes
- ½ tsp white pepper
- 1 tsp black pepper
- ¼ tsp dried oregano
- ½ tsp paprika

INSTRUCTIONS

1. Mix the seasonings together and rub into the chicken. Add the chicken to the slow cooker, and cover with the stock. Cook on low for between 3 and 4 hours.
2. Let the chicken cool slightly, then shred. Serve over salad of your choice.

CHICKPEA TAGINE

SERVES 12 | PER SERVING - CALORIES: 127, FAT: 3G, CARBOHYDRATES: 23G, PROTEIN: 4G

INGREDIENTS

- 10 dried apricots, chopped
- 400g can of chopped tomatoes
- 400g can of chickpeas, rinsed
- 1 butternut squash, peeled and cubed
- 2 courgettes, sliced
- 1 onion, chopped
- 1 red pepper, chopped
- 2 to 3 tsp harissa paste
- 2 tsp honey
- 2 garlic cloves
- 2 tsp paprika
- 1 tsp ground ginger
- ¼ tsp ground cinnamon
- 1 tsp ground cumin
- ½ tsp salt
- ¼ tsp pepper
- 2 tbsp olive oil
- Small bunch of fresh mint, chopped

INSTRUCTIONS

1. Place the butternut squash, courgettes, pepper, onion, chickpeas, and apricots in the slow cooker.
2. Cook the paprika, garlic, ginger, cumin, cinnamon, and salt and pepper in a frying pan until fragrant, about 2 minutes. Stir in the tomatoes, harissa and honey, and bubble for a few minutes. Pour over the vegetables and stir.
3. Cook for 4 to 5 hours on low. Stir through the mint just before serving.

THAI PEANUT NOODLES

SERVES 6 | PER SERVING - CALORIES: 378, FAT: 11G, CARBOHYDRATES: 37G, PROTEIN: 32G

INGREDIENTS

- 675g chicken, cut into cubes
- 1 onion, chopped
- 180g salsa
- 60g peanut butter
- 2 tbsp black bean sauce
- 1 tbsp reduced sodium soy sauce
- 225g uncooked linguine
- 1 tbsp oil
- 225g sliced baby mushrooms

INSTRUCTIONS

1. Place the chicken and onion in a slow cooker. Combine the salsa, peanut butter, bean sauce, and soy sauce, then add to the slow cooker. Cook on low for between 2 ½ and 3 ½ hours.
2. Cook the pasta.
3. Heat the oil in a frying pan, and cook the mushrooms for 6 to 8 minutes. Drain the pasta and stir it and the mushrooms into the slow cooker before serving.

CHICKEN WITH RAISINS, CAPERS AND BASIL

SERVES 8 | PER SERVING - CALORIES: 250, FAT: 12G, CARBOHYDRATES: 13G, PROTEIN: 23G

INGREDIENTS

- 2 tbsp olive oil
- 8 chicken thighs, boneless
- 1 tsp salt
- 1 tsp pepper
- 120ml Marsala wine
- 225g sliced fresh mushrooms
- 1 red pepper, sliced
- 1 onion, sliced
- 400g can chopped tomatoes
- 75g golden raisins
- 2 tbsp capers, drained
- Small bunch chopped fresh basil

INSTRUCTIONS

1. Heat 1 tablespoon of oil in a frying pan. Season the chicken with salt and pepper, then brown in the pan, adding extra oil if needed. When browned, place the chicken in the slow cooker.
2. Tip in the wine and stir to loosen any stuck bits. Add the rest of the ingredients and the wine into the slow cooker, excluding the basil.
3. Cook for 4 ½ to 5 hours on low. Sprinkle with the basil before serving.

TURKEY STEW

SERVES 6 | PER SERVING - CALORIES: 238, FAT: 4G, CARBOHYDRATES: 17G, PROTEIN: 33G

INGREDIENTS

- 675g turkey breast, cubed
- 200g salsa
- 400g can beans with chilli
- 400g can chopped tomatoes
- 3 garlic cloves
- 1 onion, chopped
- 1 red pepper, chopped
- 1 green pepper, chopped
- ¼ tsp salt
- ½ tsp ground cumin
- 1 ½ tsp chilli powder
- 2 tsp oil

INSTRUCTIONS

1. In a frying pan, brown the turkey. Add to the slow cooker, and stir in all of the ingredients.
2. Cook on low for 5 to 6 hours until the turkey is cooked through, and the vegetables are tender.

TANGY ORANGE CHICKEN THIGHS

SERVES 8 | PER SERVING - CALORIES: 248, FAT: 10G, CARBOHYDRATES: 15G, PROTEIN: 25G

INGREDIENTS

- 8 chicken thighs, boneless
- 4 bacon rashers, cooked and chopped
- 2 carrots, chopped
- 400g can chopped tomatoes
- 1 onion, sliced
- 125ml orange juice
- 175g tomato paste
- 2 garlic cloves, minced
- ½ tsp pepper
- 1 ½ tsp sugar
- 2 tsp grated orange zest
- 2 tsp dried basil
- ½ tsp dried thyme
- ½ tsp dried oregano
- ½ tsp dried rosemary
- 2 tbsp lemon juice

INSTRUCTIONS

1. Put everything, except the lemon juice and bacon in the slow cooker. Cook for 5 to 6 hours on low.
2. Stir through the lemon juice and sprinkle the bacon on top to serve.

VEGAN CABBAGE SOUP

SERVES 10 | PER SERVING - CALORIES: 110, FAT: 0G, CARBOHYDRATES: 24G, PROTEIN: 4G

INGREDIENTS

- 1L vegetable stock
- 700g cabbage, chopped
- 2 medium carrots, chopped
- 400g can chopped tomatoes
- 4 celery stalks, chopped
- 1 onion, chopped
- 175g tomato paste
- 2 garlic cloves, minced
- 2 tsp Italian seasoning
- Salt and pepper to taste

INSTRUCTIONS

Put everything in the slow cooker and stir. Cook for 6 to 8 hours on low.

VIETNAMESE CHICKEN MEATBALL SOUP

SERVES 8 | PER SERVING - CALORIES: 110, FAT: 0G, CARBOHYDRATES: 24G, PROTEIN: 4G

INGREDIENTS

- 225g minced chicken or turkey
- Half an onion, chopped
- 2 chilli peppers, seeded and finely diced
- 50g panko breadcrumbs
- 1 egg
- 1 garlic clove, minced
- 2 tbsp peanut oil

FOR THE SOUP:

- 400g can chopped tomatoes
- 1 onion, cut into strips
- 2 garlic cloves, minced
- 5 bok choy leaves, cut into strips
- 3 mild chillies, cut into small pieces
- ½ tsp salt
- 1 egg, beaten
- 1.4L chicken or vegetable stock
- Handful of fresh baby carrots, cut into thin strips

INSTRUCTIONS

1. Mix the meatball ingredients, then shape into balls. In a large pan, brown the meatballs in the oil in batches. Transfer to the slow cooker.
2. Tip all of the soup ingredients except the egg into the slow cooker and stir together. Cook on low for 6 to 8 hours.
3. Drizzle the beaten egg over the soup without stirring. Let the soup stand until the egg sets.

DINNER

SAUSAGES WITH BEER

SERVES 4 | PER SERVING - CALORIES: 822, FAT: 64G, CARBOHYDRATES: 8G, PROTEIN: 45G

INGREDIENTS

- 850g sausages, chopped
- 500g sauerkraut, drained
- 330ml beer

INSTRUCTIONS

Stir all the ingredients together in the slow cooker. Cook on low for 5 to 6 hours, or until the sausage is cooked.

SWEET AND SOUR SMOKED SAUSAGE

SERVES 8 | PER SERVING - CALORIES: 361, FAT: 16G, CARBOHYDRATES: 42G, PROTEIN: 12G

INGREDIENTS

- 2 large onions, sliced
- 220g dark brown soft sugar
- 400g tomato ketchup
- 3 tbsp cider vinegar
- 1 ½ tsp spicy mustard
- 1 tbsp Worcestershire sauce
- 2 tsp hot pepper sauce
- 450g sausages, cut into 2.5cm pieces

INSTRUCTIONS

1. Melt the butter in a frying pan and cook the onions until they soften. Stir in everything else excluding the sausages. Bring to a simmer, and cook for 20 minutes.
2. Place sausage and contents of the pan in the slow cooker. Cook for between 4 and 5 hours on low.

MOROCCAN CHICKEN AND APRICOT TAGINE

SERVES 6 | PER SERVING - CALORIES: 334, FAT: 4.2G, CARBOHYDRATES: 39G, PROTEIN: 33G

INGREDIENTS

- 800g chicken breast, cut into chunks
- 200g couscous
- 65g dried apricots, coarsely chopped
- 2 large onions, thinly sliced
- 50g raisins
- 250ml boiling water
- 300ml low salt chicken stock
- 2 tbsp lemon juice
- 2 tbsp tomato puree
- 2 tbsp plain flour
- ¼ tsp curry powder
- ¼ tsp cayenne pepper
- ½ tsp black pepper
- 1 tsp ground cinnamon
- 1 ½ tsp ground cumin
- 1 ½ tsp ground ginger

INSTRUCTIONS

1. Place the chicken, onions, apricots, and raisins into a slow cooker. Mix the stock, puree, lemon juice, ginger, cumin, cinnamon, black pepper, curry powder, cayenne, and flour together, then tip over the chicken. Cook on high for 2 ½ hours, or low for 5 hours .
2. Place the couscous into a saucepan, stir in the boiling water, cover, and let stand until the water is absorbed and the couscous is tender, about 5 minutes. Scoop onto plates and serve with chicken tagine.

SPICY CHICKEN AND BEAN SOUP

SERVES 8 | PER SERVING - CALORIES: 404, FAT: 5.8G, CARBOHYDRATES: 64G, PROTEIN: 23G

INGREDIENTS

- 1 onion, chopped
- 450g tinned chilli beans
- 410g tinned black beans
- 340g tinned sweetcorn, drained
- 225g passata
- 350ml beer
- 400g tinned chopped tomatoes with chilli
- Packet of taco seasoning
- 3 whole chicken breasts

INSTRUCTIONS

1. Place the onion, chilli beans, black beans, sweetcorn, passata, beer and chopped tomatoes in a slow cooker. Add taco seasoning and stir to blend. Lay chicken breasts on top of the mixture, pressing down slightly until just covered by the other ingredients. Set slow cooker for low heat, cover, and cook for 5 hours.
2. Remove chicken breasts from the soup and allow to cool long enough to be handled. Shred the chicken with two forks. Stir the shredded chicken back into the soup and continue cooking for 2 hours. Serve topped with grated Cheddar cheese, a dollop of soured cream and crushed tortilla chips, if desired.

LEEK AND POTATO SOUP

SERVES 8 | PER SERVING - CALORIES: 278, FAT: 8G, CARBOHYDRATES: 44.8G, PROTEIN: 7.5G

INGREDIENTS

- 8 potatoes, chopped
- 3 leeks, cut into rounds
- 1 onion, diced
- 3 tbsp margarine
- 2 cubes chicken stock
- 1 tbsp salt
- ½ tsp ground black pepper
- 350ml evaporated milk

INSTRUCTIONS

1. Put everything in the slow cooker and cover with water. Cook on high for about 4 hours.
2. Stir in the evaporated milk. Ladle soup into a liquidiser and blend until smooth. Serve hot.

PORK IN PEANUT SAUCE

SERVES 4 | PER SERVING - CALORIES: 372, FAT: 15G, CARBOHYDRATES: 24.3G, PROTEIN: 37G

INGREDIENTS

- 250ml chicken stock
- 75ml soy sauce
- 85g smooth peanut butter
- 3 tbsp honey
- 6 cloves garlic, finely chopped
- 2 tbsp finely chopped fresh ginger
- 1 tsp crushed chillies
- 2 red peppers, thinly sliced and cut into bite-size lengths
- 450g boneless pork chops

INSTRUCTIONS

1. Tip everything in the slow cooker and stir.
2. Cook for between 5 and 6 hours on low. Take the pork out, and shred. Put the pork back, and cook until warmed through.

WHISKEY BEEF AND MUSHROOM STEW

SERVES 2 | PER SERVING - CALORIES: 781, FAT: 13G, CARBOHYDRATES: 45G, PROTEIN: 97G

INGREDIENTS

- 500g diced stewing steak
- 60ml whiskey
- 300ml beef stock
- 3 onions, thickly sliced
- 2 potatoes, peeled and chopped
- 1 tsp dried mixed herbs
- 2 flat field mushrooms, thickly sliced
- 1 clove garlic, roughly chopped
- 1 heaped tsp smoked paprika
- Olive oil for frying
- Salt and pepper to taste
- Cornflour mixed with water (if needed)
- 1 tbsp chopped flat leaf parsley (optional)

INSTRUCTIONS

1. Turn slow cooker onto low. Boil the kettle and melt one beef stock in a mug with hot water. Stir well until melted down and set aside.
2. Fry the onion for 5 minutes, then add the garlic and cook for another minute. Transfer the onion with a slotted spoon to the slow cooker.
3. Turn up the heat to high in the frying pan, add more oil if needed and add the beef. Stir constantly. The idea is to sear the meat with a rich dark colour quickly. After a few minutes this should have sealed. Transfer to the slow cooker with a slotted spoon. There may be frothy juices left behind from the meat in the pan, but this is fine as it will only add to the flavour.
4. Put the whisky in the pan, and cook for a couple minutes, stirring. Turn down the heat and add half of the beef stock. Put the remaining stock in the slow cooker. Stir constantly, and when bubbling well, pour into the slow cooker. Stir through the potatoes, seasonings, paprika and herbs, then cook for 6 hours on low.
5. About 2 hours before serving, place the mushrooms in the pot. Stir well and replace the lid. After about an hour and a half check the consistency of the liquid. (Slow cookers to tend to produce a lot of liquid). The idea is to get a runny to thick gravy consistency. Add cornflour mixed with water if needed to thicken, stir, and cover.
6. Serve in a deep bowl. Garnish with chopped flat leaf parsley (optional).

KASHMIRI LAMB CURRY

SERVES 4 | PER SERVING - CALORIES: 830, FAT: 47G, CARBOHYDRATES: 19.8G, PROTEIN: 77G

INGREDIENTS

- 1kg lamb dried and cut into pieces
- 2 large onions, sliced thinly
- 3 tomatoes, chopped
- ½ pint plain yoghurt
- 4 dried red chillies
- 3 fresh green chillies
- 1 tsp cumin seeds
- 1 inch piece of root ginger, peeled and grated
- 5 cloves garlic, crushed
- 4 tbsp desiccated coconut
- 6 tbsp oil
- ½ tsp turmeric
- ½ tsp saffron
- 1 tsp Kashmiri garam masala
- 20 blanched almonds
- A handful chopped coriander
- Salt to taste

INSTRUCTIONS

1. Blend the grated coconut, cumin seeds, garam masala, ginger, red chillies, green chillies, garlic, and tomatoes together into a paste.
2. Cook the onions in a frying pan until starting to colour.
3. Add the paste to the pan and cook until it just starts to brown and the oil separates.
4. Add the lamb, and cook until nearly cooked, stirring regularly.

5. Add the yoghurt, turmeric, saffron and the blanched almonds and mix well.
6. Add everything to the slow cooker and cook for 4 to 5 hours on low.
7. Garnish with coriander and serve with rice.

SPICY TURKEY CHILLI

SERVES 10 | PER SERVING - CALORIES: 254, FAT: 5.6G, CARBOHYDRATES: 49G, PROTEIN: 28G

INGREDIENTS

- 700g turkey mince
- 120ml beer
- 120ml chicken stock
- 2x 400g tins diced tomatoes
- 400g tin kidney beans, drained
- 2 cloves garlic, minced
- 1 onion, chopped
- 1 tbsp chilli powder
- 1 tsp salt
- 1 tbsp olive oil
- 1 tsp black pepper
- 1 tbsp chopped green chillies
- ½ tsp dried oregano
- ½ tsp ground cumin
- 1 tsp cayenne pepper
- 1 tsp black pepper
- ½ tsp paprika

INSTRUCTIONS

1. Heat the oil in a pan, and cook the mince, breaking it up as you cook it. Mix in the garlic and onion, and cook for about 8 to 10 minutes. Add the salt, pepper, and chilli powder, and fry for 5 minutes. Add the beer, and simmer until reduced by half.
2. Put everything in the slow cooker, and cook on high for 2 to 3 hours.

PASTA BAKE

SERVES 6 | PER SERVING - CALORIES: 704, FAT: 32.9G, CARBOHYDRATES: 43.9G, PROTEIN: 56G

INGREDIENTS

- 650g beef mince
- 225g pasta
- 450g grated mozzarella
- 280ml cream of tomato soup
- 2 (400g) jars of pasta bake sauce of your choice
- 225g sliced pepperoni

INSTRUCTIONS

1. Cook the pasta until al dente, then drain. Brown the mince over a medium-high heat. Drain off any grease.
2. In slow cooker, alternate layers of minced beef, pasta, mozzarella cheese, soup, sauce, and pepperoni.
3. Cook for 4 hours on low.

BEEF AND TOMATO STEW

SERVES 8 | PER SERVING - CALORIES: 271, FAT: 9.1G, CARBOHYDRATES: 4.8G, PROTEIN: 40G

INGREDIENTS

- 1 tbsp vegetable or olive oil
- 1 kg beef stewing steak, cubed
- 1 large onion, diced
- 2 (400g) tins chopped tomatoes
- Salt and pepper, to taste

INSTRUCTIONS

1. Fry the beef until browned in the oil, transferring to the slow cooker once browned.
2. Fry the onion until starting to brown. Transfer to the slow cooker and add the tomatoes.
3. Stir, then cook for 6 hours on high. Season to taste with salt and pepper
4. Serve with baked potatoes or mash.

PORK CHOPS WITH CARAMELISED ONIONS AND PEAS

SERVES 2 | PER SERVING - CALORIES: 498, FAT: 26G, CARBOHYDRATES: 43G, PROTEIN: 23.5G

INGREDIENTS

- Oil for frying
- 2 pork chops
- 4 large onions, sliced into rings
- 1 clove garlic, crushed
- Good pinch sugar
- 200ml cider
- 4 tbsp frozen petit pois
- Knob butter

INSTRUCTIONS

1. Set the slow cooker on low.
2. Heat oil in a frying pan, then brown the pork on each side. Transfer to the slow cooker.
3. Fry the onions in the same pan until starting to caramelise, then add the sugar and garlic and cook for 2 to 3 minutes.
4. Pour in the cider, stir, and bring to the boil.
5. Pour the onion and cider mixture on top of the pork chops. Season well and cover.
6. Half an hour before the end, stir in the peas.
7. To serve, remove the pork chops and place onto a bed of mashed potato. Stir a knob of butter into the juices and pour over.

FRENCH ONION SOUP

SERVES 8 | PER SERVING - CALORIES: 290, FAT: 13.6G, CARBOHYDRATES: 27.5G, PROTEIN: 11.6G

INGREDIENTS

- 6 tbsp butter
- 4 large onions, sliced and separated into rings
- 1 tbsp sugar
- 2 cloves garlic, minced
- 120ml sherry
- 1.5L beef stock
- Salt, to taste
- ¼ tsp dried thyme
- 1 bay leaf
- 8 slices of French baguette
- 60g gruyere cheese, grated
- 40g Emmental cheese, grated
- 20g fresh Parmesan cheese, grated
- 2 tbsp mozzarella cheese, grated

INSTRUCTIONS

1. Melt the butter in a frying pan over a high heat and cook the onions for 10 minutes until soft. Add the sugar and turn the heat down to medium. Cook for 30 minutes, stirring constantly, until the onions are golden. Stir in the garlic and cook for a minute.
2. Tip in the sherry and scrape the pan to release any stuck bits on onion. Tip the onions into the slow cooker and pour in the stock. Season to taste with salt, then stir in the bay and thyme. Cook for 8 to 10 hours on low, or 4 to 6 hours on high.
3. About 10 minutes before serving, arrange bread slices on a baking tray and toast both sides under the grill.
4. Combine all the grated cheeses in a bowl, tossing lightly. Fill oven-safe soup bowls ¾ full of onion soup and set a bread slice in each bowl. Top with about 2 tbsp of cheese mixture per serving.
5. Place bowls on a baking tray and grill until cheese topping is lightly browned and bubbling, about 2 minutes.

LAMB BALTI

SERVES 4 | PER SERVING - CALORIES: 807, FAT: 54G, CARBOHYDRATES: 19G, PROTEIN: 56.7G

INGREDIENTS

- 900g lamb, cut into chunks
- 4cm piece root ginger, grated
- 400ml vegetable stock, warmed
- 200g chopped tomatoes
- 1 onion, finely chopped
- 1 to 2 red chilli peppers, seeded and minced
- 300g plain yoghurt
- 2 tbsp sunflower oil
- 2 cloves garlic, crushed and finely chopped
- 1 pinch saffron
- 1 ½ tbsp Balti medium curry paste
- 1 bunch fresh coriander, chopped
- Salt and pepper to taste

INSTRUCTIONS

1. Turn the slow cooker on low.
2. Fry the garlic and onion in oil for 3 to 4 minutes until starting to soften, but not colour. Add the ginger and red chilli, stirring constantly. Tip in the curry paste and stir well. Add the lamb and coat in the mixture, then cook for between 5 and 8 minutes until the lamb is brown, but still pink in the middle. Add half of the stock and tomatoes then simmer for 10 minutes. Tip the mixture into the slow cooker with the remaining stock, saffron, and half of the yoghurt. Season to taste.
3. Cook for 3 to 4 hours on high, or 7 to 8 hours on low.
4. Stir in the remainder of the yoghurt and some fresh coriander. Sprinkle over more fresh coriander to serve.

BUTTERNUT SQUASH, CHORIZO AND ROCKET RISOTTO

SERVES 4 | PER SERVING - CALORIES: 1097, FAT: 59G, CARBOHYDRATES: 92G, PROTEIN: 38G

INGREDIENTS

- 110g Parmesan, grated
- 1 butternut squash - peeled, seeded, and cubed
- 250ml white wine
- 650ml chicken stock
- 375g risotto arborio rice
- 350g chorizo, sliced
- 1 large onion, finely sliced
- 3 cloves garlic, minced
- 40g salted butter
- 3 tbsp olive oil
- Salt and pepper, to taste
- 2 large handfuls rocket leaves
- Chopped fresh flat leaf parsley, to taste

INSTRUCTIONS

1. Turn the slow cooker on the low setting. Fry the onion and garlic until soft, about 4 to 5 minutes. Transfer to the slow cooker.
2. Melt the butter in the frying pan, and tip in the chorizo and squash. Cook for 6 to 8 minutes, stirring regularly, until the butternut squash starts to colour. Tip into the slow cooker, leaving behind a little butter. Add the rice to the pan, and season. Add the butter and stir until covered. Increase the heat then add the white wine and chicken stock to the rice. Simmer for about 2 minutes.
3. Put everything in the slow cooker and cook for 1 ½ to 2 ½ hours on low, stirring every 30 to 45 minutes.
4. To serve, stir through the Parmesan cheese and parsley then add the rocket leaves. Serve immediately.

THAI GREEN FISH CURRY

SERVES 4 | PER SERVING - CALORIES: 432, FAT: 33G, CARBOHYDRATES: 14.9G, PROTEIN: 21.6G

INGREDIENTS

- 475g firm white fish, cubed
- 220ml vegetable stock
- 4 or 5 tsp Thai green curry paste
- ½ onion, chopped
- 3 carrots, peeled and chopped
- 400ml coconut milk
- 3 spring onions, chopped
- 2 tbsp sunflower oil
- 1 pinch ground nutmeg
- 1 green chilli, seeded and finely chopped
- 1 tbsp fish sauce
- 2cm piece root ginger, chopped
- Salt and pepper, to taste
- Juice of 1 lime
- 1 bunch chopped fresh coriander
- 1 sprig Thai basil, leaves chopped

INSTRUCTIONS

1. Set the slow cooker to low. In a large pan, heat the oil, and cook the onion, ginger, and chilli for 4 minutes, stirring constantly until the onions soften.
2. Add the curry paste, lime juice, nutmeg, and fish sauce, then stir for another 2 minutes. Add the stock and coconut milk, bring to a simmer, then add the carrots and fish.
3. Tip into the slow cooker, then season with salt and pepper to taste. Cook on high for 3 hours, or low for 4 to 5 hours. Just before serving, stir through the spring onions, basil, and coriander.

TURKEY AND APRICOT TAGINE

SERVES 4 | PER SERVING - CALORIES: 231, FAT: 9.5G, CARBOHYDRATES: 16.2G, PROTEIN: 20.9G

INGREDIENTS

- 450g boneless and skinless turkey breast, diced
- 600ml chicken stock
- 60ml orange juice
- 1 tbsp tomato puree
- 225g dried apricots
- 1 clove garlic, finely chopped
- 2 tbsp vegetable oil
- 1 onion, finely chopped
- 1 pinch ground cinnamon
- 1 tsp ground ginger
- 1 tsp turmeric
- 1 tsp ground cumin
- Salt and pepper to taste

INSTRUCTIONS

1. Heat the oil in a frying pan, and add the spices, garlic, and onion. Cook, stirring constantly, for 5 minutes until softening. Add the tomato puree and stock, then bring to the boil, stirring constantly.
2. Add the dried apricots and orange juice and a pinch of seasoning. Reduce the heat, cover loosely and simmer for 15 minutes until the juices have reduced slightly and the fruits have softened.
3. Add the turkey to the casserole, re-cover, and simmer for another 20 minutes. Serve with couscous mixed with freshly chopped coriander or with some basmati rice.

LAMB AND SPINACH CURRY

SERVES 6 | PER SERVING - CALORIES: 509, FAT: 32.1G, CARBOHYDRATES: 9.7G, PROTEIN: 46G

INGREDIENTS

FOR THE CURRY PASTE:

- 1 medium onion, chopped
- 3 spring onions
- 8 cloves garlic
- ½ tsp cayenne pepper
- 1 tsp ground pepper
- ½ tsp salt
- 1 tsp coriander seeds
- 2 tbsp paprika
- ½ tsp ground cinnamon
- 2 tsp cumin
- 1 tsp ground cardamom
- 1 handful spinach leaves

FOR THE CURRY:

- 2 tbsp sunflower oil
- 900g boneless leg of lamb, diced
- 1 bay leaf
- 2 medium tomatoes, roughly chopped
- 1 (400g) tin coconut milk
- 2 handfuls spinach leaves

INSTRUCTIONS

1. Preheat the slow cooker to the auto or low setting.
2. Blend all of the paste ingredients to create a smooth paste.
3. Put the oil in a wok, and cook the lamb until browned on all sides. Stir in the curry paste, and cook for a further 2 to 3 minutes. Transfer to the slow cooker.
4. Add the coconut milk, tomatoes, and bay to the slow cooker. Cook for 6 to 8 hours on low, or 3 to 4 hours on high.
5. Just prior to serving, remove the bay leaves then stir through two good handfuls of fresh spinach and cook until wilted. Serve immediately.

CHICKEN CURRY WITH CAULIFLOWER

SERVES 4 | PER SERVING - CALORIES: 390, FAT: 12.8G, CARBOHYDRATES: 16.1G, PROTEIN: 50.9G

INGREDIENTS

- 2 (400g) tin chopped tomatoes, drained
- 2 tbsp tomato puree
- 2 tbsp freshly grated ginger
- 1 tbsp curry powder
- ½ tsp sea salt, or to taste
- Freshly ground black pepper
- 1 small cauliflower, cored and cut into florets
- 675g skinless, boneless chicken thighs
- 1 onion, finely chopped
- 40g raisins
- 25g chopped freshly chopped coriander, for garnish (optional)

INSTRUCTIONS

1. Set the slow cooker on low.
2. Stir the tomatoes, puree, curry powder, ginger, and seasoning in the slow cooker. Stir through the raisins, onion, cauliflower, and chicken.
3. Cook for 4 to 5 hours on high, or 6 to 7 hours on low. Garnish with coriander.

MOROCCAN CHICKEN STEW

SERVES 8 | PER SERVING - CALORIES: 326, FAT: 9G, CARBOHYDRATES: 21.9G, PROTEIN: 36.3G

INGREDIENTS

- 950g chicken breast, cut into chunks
- 2 sweet potatoes, peeled and diced
- 3 medium carrots, peeled and diced
- 1 onion, sliced
- 400g tin chopped tomatoes
- 400g tin chickpeas, rinsed
- 1 tsp dried parsley
- ¼ tsp ground cinnamon
- ½ tsp ground cumin
- ½ tsp ground turmeric
- ½ tsp ground black pepper
- 1 tsp salt
- 2 cloves garlic, minced (optional)

INSTRUCTIONS

1. Place the onion, garlic, carrots, sweet potatoes, chickpeas, and chicken breast pieces into a slow cooker.
2. In a bowl, mix the cumin, turmeric, cinnamon, black pepper, parsley and salt, sprinkle over the chicken and vegetables. Add the tomatoes and stir.
3. Cook for 4 to 5 hours on high.

PEANUT CHICKEN

SERVES 4 | PER SERVING - CALORIES: 759, FAT: 44.6G, CARBOHYDRATES: 14.9G, PROTEIN: 75.9G

INGREDIENTS

- 180g spicy salsa
- 65g crunchy peanut butter
- 180ml light coconut milk
- 2 tbsp fresh lime juice
- 1 tbsp soy sauce
- 1 tsp sugar
- 2 tbsp freshly grated ginger
- 900g skinless chicken thighs
- 70g chopped peanuts, for serving
- 2 tbsp chopped coriander, for serving

INSTRUCTIONS

1. Mix the salsa, coconut milk, peanut butter, soy sauce, lime juice, sugar, and ginger in the slow cooker. Place the chicken thighs in the sauce, spoon mixture over chicken to coat.
2. Set the slow cooker on low. Cook for 8 to 9 hours. Garnish with peanuts and freshly chopped coriander before serving.

SWEET AND SOUR MEATBALLS

SERVES 6 | PER SERVING - CALORIES: 594, FAT: 35.7G, CARBOHYDRATES: 38.6G, PROTEIN: 28.9G

INGREDIENTS

- 400g tinned pineapple chunks in juice
- 1 green pepper, sliced
- 100g brown sugar
- 2 tbsp cornflour
- 2 tbsp soy sauce
- 2 tbsp lemon juice, or to taste
- 1.3kg bag frozen cooked meatballs, thawed

INSTRUCTIONS

1. Pour the pineapple chunks and their juice into a saucepan. Stir all the ingredients except the meatballs through the pineapple until the sugar and cornflour dissolve.
2. Cook for 10 minutes until thick.
3. Put the meatballs and pineapple in the slow cooker.
4. Cook for 2 hours on medium, mixing every 30 minutes.

CHICKEN AND COURGETTE PHO

SERVES 6 | PER SERVING - CALORIES: 189, FAT: 5.2G, CARBOHYDRATES: 15G, PROTEIN: 23.4G

INGREDIENTS

- 2.4L vegetable stock
- 340g boneless chicken breasts
- 170g sliced onion, separated into rings
- 2 tbsp oyster sauce
- 1 ½ tsp coconut sugar
- 1 tsp salt
- 1 tsp freshly ground black pepper
- 4 whole cloves
- ½ tsp minced ginger
- 2 whole star anise pods
- 600g bean sprouts
- 425g coarsely chopped bok choy cabbage
- 4 courgettes

INSTRUCTIONS

1. Combine vegetable stock, chicken breasts, onions, oyster sauce, coconut sugar, salt, pepper, cloves, ginger, and star anise in a slow cooker.
2. Cook on high until chicken breasts can be easily shredded with a fork, about 1 1/2 hour. Stir in the bok choy and bean sprouts. Continue cooking soup until vegetables are tender, about 1 hour.
3. Slice courgettes into thin noodles using a spiraliser or peeler.
4. Divide soup among 6 serving bowls. Top with courgette 'noodles'.

CORIANDER AND LIME CHICKEN

SERVES 6 | PER SERVING - CALORIES: 464, FAT: 17.4G, CARBOHYDRATES: 4.7G, PROTEIN: 68.7G

INGREDIENTS

- 450g salsa
- Packet of taco seasoning mix
- Juice of 1 lime
- 3 tbsp chopped coriander
- 1.4kg chicken breasts

INSTRUCTIONS

Place the salsa, taco seasoning, lime juice and coriander into a slow cooker; stir to combine. Add the chicken and stir to coat. Cover the cooker, set to high, and cook on high for 4 hours, or low for 6 to 8 hours. Shred chicken with 2 forks to serve.

HOISIN RIBS

SERVES 6 | PER SERVING - CALORIES: 928, FAT: 45.8G, CARBOHYDRATES: 55G, PROTEIN: 69G

INGREDIENTS

- 1.7kg pork ribs
- 2 tbsp tomato puree
- 125ml soy sauce
- 75ml white wine
- 4 cloves of garlic, crushed
- 225g caster sugar
- 235ml hoisin sauce
- ½ tsp Chinese five-spice powder
- 2 tsp chilli-garlic sauce
- Salt and ground black pepper to taste

INSTRUCTIONS

1. Preheat the oven on 180C. Put the ribs on a tray, and season with salt and pepper.
2. Bake until lightly browned, this should take about 30 minutes.
3. Stir the remaining ingredients in a bowl.
4. Once cooked, put the ribs in the slow cooker, and pour over the sauce.
5. Cook on low for about 8 hours, turning halfway through, until the ribs are tender.

SPICY PULLED BEEF

SERVES 16 | PER SERVING - CALORIES: 928, FAT: 45.8G, CARBOHYDRATES: 55G, PROTEIN: 69G

INGREDIENTS

- 1.5kg beef roasting joint
- 2x 400g tins chopped tomatoes with chillies
- 4 cloves garlic, chopped
- 1 onion, sliced into rings
- 125g jarred green chillies, chopped
- 260ml cold coffee
- 450ml beef stock
- 1 tsp chilli powder
- ½ tsp ground cumin
- Salt and pepper to taste
- 2 fresh jalapeno chilli peppers, sliced (optional)

INSTRUCTIONS

1. Put half of the onion in the slow cooker and put the beef on top.
2. Add the remainder of the ingredients and stir.
3. Cook on low until the beef is very soft, for around 6 to 10 hours.
4. Shred the beef and toss through the sauce.

FISH STEW WITH CHICKPEAS

SERVES 4 | PER SERVING - CALORIES: 454, FAT: 18.6G, CARBOHYDRATES: 28.2G, PROTEIN: 39.8G

INGREDIENTS

- 550g white fish fillets
- 125ml tomato passata
- 3 garlic cloves, crushed
- 3 tomatoes, cut into chunks
- 1 onion, finely chopped
- 400g tin of chickpeas, rinsed
- 1 or 2 tbsp oil
- 2 tbsp plain flour
- Freshly chopped parsley
- Salt, pepper, turmeric, and cumin to taste

INSTRUCTIONS

1. Fry the onion in the oil for 10 to 15 minutes until soft.
2. Mix the flour, spices, and seasoning in a bowl, and coat the fish in the flour mixture. Put the fish in the top of the slow cooker, then add the remaining ingredients.
3. Cook for 2 to 3 hours on low until the fish is opaque and flaky.

LAMB SHANK ROGAN JOSH

SERVES 2 | PER SERVING - CALORIES: 1132, FAT: 49G, CARBOHYDRATES: 64G, PROTEIN: 95G

INGREDIENTS

- 3 lamb shanks
- 400g tin diced tomatoes
- 220ml soured cream
- 320g carrots, sliced
- 400g whole new potatoes, peeled
- 1 large onion, cut into wedges
- 2 tbsp cornflour
- 1 tbsp plain flour
- 4 tbsp water
- ½ to 1 tsp chilli powder (depending on your tastes)
- 1 tsp ground coriander
- ½ tsp ground ginger
- 2 chicken stock cubes
- 4 whole cardamom pods, broken
- 250ml water
- Ground nutmeg, salt, and pepper to taste
- 250g button mushrooms, quartered (optional)

INSTRUCTIONS

1. Stir the sour cream and flour together until smooth, and set aside. In a separate small bowl, mix the cornflour and water to make a smooth paste.
2. Tip the water, stock, spices and tomatoes into a saucepan, and boil. Add the cornflour paste gradually, stirring constantly for 2 minutes. Remove from the heat, and fold in the soured cream and flour.
3. Put the onions in the slow cooker and put the lamb on top. Add the prepared tomato mixture. Add the remaining ingredients on top of the tomato mixture.
4. Cook for 8 hours on high.

MEATLESS CHILLI

SERVES 6 | PER SERVING - CALORIES: 220, FAT: 3G, CARBOHYDRATES: 26.6G, PROTEIN: 22G

INGREDIENTS

- 5 garlic cloves, minced
- 2 to 3 onions, diced
- 3 celery stalks, diced
- 2 carrots, diced
- 1 jalapeno chilli, minced
- 2 peppers, seeds removed and diced
- 2x 400g cans of chopped tomatoes
- 150g tomato puree
- 450g meat free mince
- 400g red kidney beans, drained
- 1 tbsp plain flour
- 1 tbsp cider or red wine vinegar
- 1 tbsp light brown soft sugar
- 1 tsp ground cumin
- 3 bay leaves
- 2 tsp dried oregano
- Chilli seasoning, to taste
- 250ml water

INSTRUCTIONS

1. Put everything in a slow cooker and stir. Cook on low for 8 to 10 hours
2. Serve with grated cheese and pasta.

LENTIL AND SAUSAGE STEW

SERVES 12 | PER SERVING - CALORIES: 429, FAT: 24.3G, CARBOHYDRATES: 24.2G, PROTEIN: 27.2G

INGREDIENTS

- 1 kg sausage, cut into 1cm pieces
- 1 carrot, chopped
- 1 stick celery, chopped
- 450g dried lentils
- 1 (400g) tin chopped tomatoes, drained
- 1L beef stock
- 600ml water

INSTRUCTIONS

1. Rinse the lentils, but do not soak. In the slow cooker, stir together the lentils, tomatoes, stock, water, carrot, sausage, and celery.
2. Cook on high for 3 hours, or for 6 to 7 hours on low. Stir well before serving.

PAPRIKA GOULASH

SERVES 8 | PER SERVING - CALORIES: 448, FAT: 16.9G, CARBOHYDRATES: 34.3G, PROTEIN: 40.1G

INGREDIENTS

- 175g tomato puree
- 350g egg pasta
- 1.25kg lean beef, cubed
- 3 onions, chopped
- 4 tbsp vegetable oil
- 3 cloves garlic, diced
- 4 tbsp smoked paprika
- 2 tsp salt
- 1 tsp ground pepper
- 375ml water
- 125ml soured cream and 8 sprigs fresh parsley (optional)

INSTRUCTIONS

1. Heat 1 tbsp of oil in a frying pan and cook the onions until soft. Stir in the garlic and cook for a minute. Put the onions and garlic in the slow cooker, put the lid on, and set the slow cooker on low.
2. Put the salt, pepper, and paprika in a bowl and stir. Evenly coat the meat cubes in the seasoning mix.
3. Heat 1 tablespoon of fresh oil in the pan and brown the beef. Add 2 tablespoons of water in between batches and scrape the brown bits from the pan. Tip the browned beef into the slow cooker and add a new tablespoon of oil in between batches.
4. Stir the remaining water and tomato puree into the slow cooker. Cook for 6 to 9 hours on low, or 4 to 5 hours on high.
5. Cook the pasta.
6. Serve the goulash and pasta with parsley and soured cream.

ROAST LEMON AND OREGANO CHICKEN

SERVES 8 | PER SERVING - CALORIES: 337, FAT: 14.9G, CARBOHYDRATES: 0.9G, PROTEIN: 47.2G

INGREDIENTS

- 1.3kg whole chicken
- 2 cloves of garlic, minced
- Few sprigs of fresh oregano
- Knob of butter
- Sprinkle of salt and pepper
- Sprinkle of dried mixed herbs
- 1 lemon

INSTRUCTIONS

1. Place a few sprigs of fresh oregano and the minced garlic inside the chicken's cavity.
2. Put the chicken in the slow cooker and rub with the butter. Add the salt, pepper, and dried herbs.
3. Grate some lemon rind over the chicken, then slice the lemon in half and squeeze the juice over the chicken. Put half of the lemon in the slow cooker.
4. Cook for 6 hours on low.

CABBAGE AND BEEF SOUP

SERVES 10 | PER SERVING - CALORIES: 211, FAT: 6.1G, CARBOHYDRATES: 19.3G, PROTEIN: 19.1G

INGREDIENTS

- 500ml water
- 450g minced beef
- 700g passata
- 375g chopped cabbage
- 2x 400g tins red kidney beans, drained
- ½ onion, chopped
- 1 ½ tsp ground cumin
- 1 tsp pepper
- 1 tsp salt
- 2 tbsp vegetable oil
- 4 beef stock cubes

INSTRUCTIONS

1. Cook the mince and onion in a frying pan with the oil until brown and the mince has crumbled. Drain fat, and transfer beef to a slow cooker. Add cabbage, kidney beans, water, passata, stock cubes, cumin, salt, and pepper. Stir to dissolve stock cubes, and cover.
2. Cook on low for 6 to 8 hours, or for 4 hours on high.

LAMB SHANKS IN RED WINE

SERVES 4 | PER SERVING - CALORIES: 274, FAT: 13.5G, CARBOHYDRATES: 8.8G, PROTEIN: 25G

INGREDIENTS

- 4 lamb shanks
- 2 mushrooms, sliced
- 2 sticks of celery, diced
- 1 onion, diced
- 1 carrot, sliced
- 100ml red wine
- 1 beef stock cube - dissolved in 150ml hot water
- 1 bay leaf
- 1 tbsp dark brown sugar
- ½ tsp salt
- ½ tsp ground black pepper
- 2 tbsp tomato puree
- 1 tbsp cornflour
- 2 tbsp olive oil

INSTRUCTIONS

1. Brown the lamb in a frying pan using the olive oil.
2. Put the vegetables and bay leaf in the slow cooker.
3. Put the lamb on top, and sprinkle with salt, pepper, and the sugar.
4. Stir the wine and tomato puree into the stock, then pour over the lamb.
5. Cook for 8 hours on low until the lamb is tender.
6. Take out the lamb and wrap in foil to keep warm.
7. Put the liquid in a saucepan and stir in the cornflour. Stir well over a low heat until the sauce thickens. Serve the shanks and vegetables with the sauce poured over.

PUMPKIN AND RED LENTIL CURRY SOUP

SERVES 8 | PER SERVING - CALORIES: 234, FAT: 3.4G, CARBOHYDRATES: 41.2G, PROTEIN: 12.1G

INGREDIENTS
- 1.5kg pumpkin
- 1 leek
- 300g red lentils
- 1.2 litres vegetable stock
- 2 tbsp curry paste

INSTRUCTIONS
1. Cut up the pumpkin and add to the slow cooker. Peel off skin if desired. Chop leek, add to slow cooker. Pour dried red lentils on top of pumpkin. Mix through. Add curry paste to vegetable stock, mix through and add liquid mix to vegetables. Mix through yet again.
2. Cook for 4 hours on high, or 8 hours on low. Mash the pumpkin with a potato masher at the end of the cook time

PUMPKIN CREAM SOUP

SERVES 8 | PER SERVING - CALORIES: 154, FAT: 8.1G, CARBOHYDRATES: 20.9G, PROTEIN: 3.6G

INGREDIENTS
- 750ml chicken stock
- 130ml double cream
- 2 small cinnamon sticks
- 1 onion, chopped
- 1 medium pumpkin, cubed
- 1 tbsp olive oil
- 2 bay leaves
- 1 sprig fresh thyme
- 1 sprig fresh sage
- 1 sprig fresh rosemary

INSTRUCTIONS
1. Heat the oil in a frying pan and cook the onion and pumpkin over a medium to high heat until browned. Tip into the slow cooker and add enough stock to submerge the pumpkin.
2. Place the herbs and cinnamon in a cheesecloth, and tie to create a bag. Place the bag in the slow cooker. Cover and cook on low for 4 hours.
3. Remove the herbs, then stir through the cream. Puree until smooth.

CHICKEN TAGINE

SERVES 8 | PER SERVING - CALORIES: 344, FAT: 10.5G, CARBOHYDRATES: 31.8G, PROTEIN: 30G

INGREDIENTS
- 8 boneless chicken thighs, cut into pieces
- 2 large onions, sliced
- 4 large carrots, sliced
- 65g dried apricots, chopped
- 60g dried cranberries
- 1 aubergine, cubed
- 175g couscous
- 2 tbsp olive oil
- 500ml chicken stock
- 2 tbsp tomato puree
- 2 tbsp lemon juice
- 2 tbsp plain flour
- 2 tsp garlic granules
- 1 ½ tsp each ground cumin and ginger
- 1 tsp cinnamon
- ¾ tsp black pepper
- Salt to taste
- 250ml water

INSTRUCTIONS
1. Cook the aubergine and chicken in the oil over a medium to high heat until browned. Remove from the heat.
2. Put the chicken, aubergine, onion, carrots, cranberries, and apricots in the slow cooker.
3. Mix the chicken stock, tomato puree, lemon juice, flour, and seasonings in a bowl. Tip into the slow cooker.

4. Cook on for 8 hours on low, or for 5 hours on high.
5. Prepare the couscous as per the packaging's instructions and serve alongside the tagine.

CHRISTMAS CASSEROLE

SERVES 6 | PER SERVING - CALORIES: 269, FAT: 15.9G, CARBOHYDRATES: 5G, PROTEIN: 25G

INGREDIENTS

- 500g cooked turkey
- 2 leeks
- 50g butter
- 2 tbsp red wine
- 2 cloves garlic
- 2 tbsp cream
- 2 tbsp olive oil
- 2 tbsp cranberry sauce
- 2 bay leaves

INSTRUCTIONS

1. Set the slow cooker on high. Melt the butter in a pan, and cook the leaks (seasoned with salt and pepper) until soft. Tip into the slow cooker.
2. Cut turkey into bite-sized pieces. Heat the oil in same pan and cook the garlic. Add the turkey when the garlic starts to sizzle. Stir fry for 10 minutes, add bay leaves and cranberry sauce then place on top of the leeks.
3. Pour over the red wine and turn the slow cooker down to low. Cook for 3 to 5 hours until cooked through. Stir in cream just before serving.

GREEN BEAN AND PEA RISOTTO

SERVES 4 | PER SERVING - CALORIES: 379, FAT: 11.1G, CARBOHYDRATES: 61.5G, PROTEIN: 8.1G

INGREDIENTS

- 750ml hot vegetable stock
- 250g risotto rice
- 130g frozen green beans
- 125g frozen peas
- 35g butter
- 2 tsp green pesto
- 2 cloves garlic, chopped
- 1 red onion, chopped
- 1 tbsp olive oil
- Salt and pepper, to taste
- Parmesan cheese, grated
- 1 handful rocket leaves

INSTRUCTIONS

1. Cook the onions in a frying pan in the oil and butter until starting to colour.
2. Add the rice and garlic, then stir whilst cooking for a minute.
3. Add 500ml of the stock, saving the rest for later. Season with salt and pepper, then bring to the boil.
4. Add to the slow cooker, then cook for 2 hours on low.
5. Heat the rest of the stock in a saucepan, then tip into the slow cooker. Also, add the pesto and stir everything together.
6. Place the vegetables on top of the rice. Cook for a further 30 minutes on low.
7. Serve and garnish with the parmesan and rocket.

LENTIL AND HAM SOUP

SERVES 6 | PER SERVING - CALORIES: 646, FAT: 23G, CARBOHYDRATES: 64.7G, PROTEIN: 44.4G

INGREDIENTS

- 600g red lentils, rinsed
- 1 ham shank (ham hock)
- 2 carrots, chopped
- 3 celery sticks, chopped
- 1 onion, chopped
- 2 cloves fresh garlic, chopped
- 4 tbsp butter
- Pinch nutmeg
- 1 bay leaf
- 125ml cream (optional)
- 1 tsp curry powder

INSTRUCTIONS

1. Put the ham shank into a large pot and fill with water up to the ham. Bring to the boil for ten minutes to take away the saltiness. Discard water and refill with fresh water. Tip the contents of the pan into the slow cooker, and cook for 3 to 4 hours on low.
2. Close to the end of the cook time, melt the butter in a pan. Cook the onions, celery and carrot for 15 to 20 minutes, stirring constantly. Stir in the garlic and fry for 2 minutes.
3. Take the ham out, and set aside the cooking water in a bowl. Transfer the vegetables to the pot the ham was cooked in and add all the remaining ingredients except the cream. Skim off any scum from the ham cooking water and taste the water for saltiness. If it is not too salty add enough of it to the soup pot so that the ingredients are just about covered. If it is too salty use less and top the stock up with fresh water.
4. Cook for a further hour until the lentils are soft. Remove the bay leaf, and blend until smooth. Break or shred the ham and stir into soup. Check seasoning. If using the cream, let the soup cool for 30 minutes or so then stir in the cream.

JAMBALAYA

SERVES 12 | PER SERVING - CALORIES: 214, FAT: 12G, CARBOHYDRATES: 3.3G, PROTEIN: 20.7G

INGREDIENTS

- 450g frozen cooked and peeled prawns
- 450g chicken breast fillets, cut into chunks
- 450g smoked pork sausage, sliced
- 2 (400g) tins chopped tomatoes
- 125g celery, chopped
- 1 large onion, chopped
- 1 large green pepper, chopped
- 2 tsp dried oregano
- 2 tsp dried parsley
- 2 tsp Cajun seasoning
- 1 tsp cayenne pepper
- ½ tsp dried thyme
- 250ml chicken stock

INSTRUCTIONS

1. Mix all of the ingredients excluding the prawns in the slow cooker.
2. Cook for 7 to 8 hours on low, or 3 to 4 hours on high. Stir in the prawns during the last 30 minutes of cook time.

THAI PORK WITH PEANUTS

SERVES 8 | PER SERVING - CALORIES: 196, FAT: 8.6G, CARBOHYDRATES: 8.8G, PROTEIN: 21.5G

INGREDIENTS

- 2 red peppers, seeded and sliced into strips
- 4 boneless pork loin chops
- 125ml teriyaki sauce
- 4 tbsp creamy peanut butter
- 2 tbsp rice vinegar
- 1 tsp crushed chillies
- 2 cloves garlic, finely chopped
- 50g spring onions, chopped
- 4 tbsp chopped roasted peanuts
- 2 limes, cut into wedges

INSTRUCTIONS

1. Grease the slow cooker. Place the pepper strips and pork chops into the slow cooker. Pour the teriyaki sauce, vinegar, crushed chillies, and garlic over the pork chops.
2. Cook for 8 to 9 hours on low until the pork is tender. Take out the pork and stir in the peanut butter. Put the pork back and cook for 10 minutes.
3. Pour into a serving dish and sprinkle with spring onions and peanuts to garnish. Decorate with lime wedges to serve.

INDIAN INSPIRED PULLED PORK

SERVES 8 | PER SERVING - CALORIES: 702, FAT: 54G, CARBOHYDRATES: 9.1G, PROTEIN: 46.7G

INGREDIENTS

FOR THE CURRY PASTE:

- 1 tbsp vegetable oil
- 1 onion, roughly chopped
- 6 cloves garlic, chopped
- 80g ginger, peeled and chopped
- 1 tbsp tomato purée
- 1 tbsp coriander seeds
- 1 tsp sea salt
- 1 tsp cumin seeds
- 1 tsp turmeric
- 1 tsp dried fenugreek
- 1 tsp mustard seeds
- 1 red chilli, roughly chopped (optional)

FOR THE PORK:

- 2 tbsp vegetable oil
- 2kg boneless pork shoulder
- 400ml coconut milk
- 1 onion, sliced
- 1 red pepper, sliced
- 1 yellow pepper, sliced
- 15g coriander, to serve
- Greek yoghurt, to serve (optional)
- Mango chutney, to serve (optional)
- Flatbreads, warmed to pack instructions, to serve

INSTRUCTIONS

1. Toast the coriander, cumin, and mustard seeds in a dry pan until they start popping. Leave to cool slightly, then crush in a pestle and mortar or using the end of a rolling pin.
2. Put the remaining paste ingredients and crushed spices in a blender, and blitz to a paste. Set aside.
3. Heat a tablespoon of oil in a frying pan. Brown the pork joint on all sides until golden all over
4. Set the pork joint aside and add the remaining oil to the frying pain. Fry the curry paste until fragrant, around 2 to 3 minutes. Tip in the peppers and onion, then stir well. Cook for another 2 or 3 minutes, then tip in the water and coconut milk. Bring to a simmer, then take the pan off the heat.
5. Tip the contents of the pan into the slow cooker, and sit the pork on top. Spoon some of the curry paste on top of the pork.
6. Cook for 5 hours on high. After an hour, turn the joint and baste with the sauce.
7. Stand for ten minutes, then shred the meat using two forks. Stir the sauce through and sprinkle with coriander to garnish.

PERSIAN CHICKEN STEW

SERVES 4 | PER SERVING - CALORIES: 523, FAT: 30G, CARBOHYDRATES: 36.8G, PROTEIN: 28.1G

INGREDIENTS

- 150ml chicken stock
- 150g natural yoghurt
- 800g chicken thighs on the bone
- 1 onion, sliced into rings
- 550g new potatoes, halved
- 100g dried dates
- 1 tbsp olive oil
- 25g walnut halves
- ½ tsp ground cinnamon
- ½ tsp ground ginger
- ½ tsp turmeric
- 2 tbsp harissa paste
- Steamed greens, to serve

INSTRUCTIONS

1. Toss the chicken in the spices.
2. Cook the onion in the oil for 2 minutes. Add the walnuts and cook for a minute.
3. Put the potatoes in a slow cooker. Add the chicken and then spoon in the sautéed onions and walnuts. Tip over the dates and pour in the stock.
4. Cook for 4 ½ to 5 hours on low.
5. Meanwhile, stir the Harissa paste into the yoghurt.
6. Serve the chicken on a bed of steamed greens such as kale with the spiced yoghurt on the side.

SOUTH INDIAN CHICKEN CURRY

SERVES 4 | PER SERVING - CALORIES: 364, FAT: 24G, CARBOHYDRATES: 8G, PROTEIN: 31.4G

INGREDIENTS

- 8 bone-in chicken thighs
- 1 large onion, diced
- 1 inch ginger, peeled and grated
- 100ml coconut milk
- 300g ripe tomatoes, chopped
- 3 garlic cloves, chopped
- 1 tbsp extra virgin olive oil
- 1 tbsp dried curry leaves
- 1 tsp turmeric
- 1 tsp paprika
- ½ tsp chilli powder
- 4 cardamom pods
- 1 tbsp garam masala
- 1 cinnamon stick
- 4 cloves
- Small handful coriander leaves
- Chapattis, to serve

INSTRUCTIONS

1. Put all ingredients except the coriander and coconut milk in the slow cooker. Season to taste. Cook for 3 ½ hours on low.
2. Stir in the coconut milk, and cook on high for 30 minutes. Sprinkle with chopped fresh coriander and serve with chapattis.

BEEF TAGINE

SERVES 4 | PER SERVING - CALORIES: 723, FAT: 15G, CARBOHYDRATES: 63.9G, PROTEIN: 87.4G

INGREDIENTS

- 1.3kg beef, cut into chunks
- 2 peppers, sliced
- 2 onions, sliced
- 800g chopped tomatoes
- 400g chickpeas, drained
- 1tbsp plain flour
- 1tbsp sunflower oil
- 2tbsp harissa paste
- 1 beef stock cube
- Handful dried apricots, halved
- 250g couscous

INSTRUCTIONS

1. Mix the flour with some seasoning and toss with the beef. Brown the beef in a frying pan in the oil in batches. Move the beef to a plate to rest once browned. Add the rest of the oil and cook the onion for 5 minutes until starting to soften. Tip in the peppers and stir through the harissa, then cook for a further minute.
2. Add the onions and beef to the slow cooker.
3. Crumble in the beef stock cube, and add the tomatoes, 200ml water, apricots, and chickpeas to the slow cooker. Cook for at least 6 hours on low, until the beef is tender. The meat should shred easily with two forks. If not, cook for a further 30 minutes and then check again.
4. Prepare the couscous, and season to taste.

THAI CHICKEN STEW

SERVES 4 TO 6 | PER SERVING - CALORIES: 276, FAT: 13G, CARBOHYDRATES: 9.3G, PROTEIN: 29.9G

INGREDIENTS

- 10 chicken drumsticks and thighs
- 1 x 400g tins coconut milk
- 125ml vegetable or chicken stock
- 1 tbsp vegetable oil
- 4 tbsp red curry paste
- 2 tbsp soft brown sugar
- 1 tbsp Worcestershire sauce
- 2 tbsp fish sauce
- Zest and juice of 2 limes
- Juice of half a lemon

INSTRUCTIONS
1. Over a medium heat, warm the oil in a pan. Season the chicken, then brown in the frying pan, working in batches. Place in the slow cooker once browned.
2. Fry the curry paste for 2 minutes, then stir in the Worcestershire sauce, lemon, and sugar. Let the sugar melt, stirring constantly. Pour in the coconut milk, fish sauce, lime zest and juice, and stock, then stir together. Tip into the slow cooker.
3. Cook on high for 4 hours, or low for 8 hours.

CHICKEN STROGANOFF
SERVES 4 | PER SERVING - CALORIES: 347, FAT: 17G, CARBOHYDRATES: 8.7G, PROTEIN: 41.1G

INGREDIENTS
- 4 large skinless chicken breasts
- 1 onion, chopped
- 1 x 300g pack closed cup mushrooms, halved
- 1 x 294g can condensed chicken soup
- 2 tbsp olive oil
- 150ml chicken stock (made with 1 stock cube)
- 1 tsp paprika
- 100ml soured cream
- 15g (1/2oz) chives, snipped

INSTRUCTIONS
1. Heat the oil in a frying pan, then add the chicken and onion. Cook for 5 until the chicken is browned, turning once, and stirring the onions frequently.
2. Put the chicken and onion in the slow cooker. Add the mushrooms, condensed soup, chicken stock, paprika and soured cream. Stir gently to combine all the ingredients and to coat the chicken. Cook for 5 to 6 hours on low. Scatter over the chives and serve with tagliatelle if you like.

CHINESE STYLE PORK
SERVES 4 | PER SERVING - CALORIES: 347, FAT: 17G, CARBOHYDRATES: 8.7G, PROTEIN: 41.1G

INGREDIENTS
- 1kg pork shoulder, cut into 5cm pieces
- 4 tbsp soy sauce
- 1 tbsp vegetable oil
- 2-inch piece ginger shredded into matchsticks
- 2 cloves garlic, sliced
- 2 red chillies, sliced
- 4 tbsp red wine vinegar
- 200ml sherry
- 50g soft brown sugar
- 150ml water

INSTRUCTIONS
1. Marinate the meat in 1 tbsp of the soy sauce. Heat the oil in a pan, and cook the ginger, garlic, and half of the chilli for 5 minutes.
2. Add the sherry, vinegar, remaining soy sauce, sugar, and water and heat until the sugar is dissolved. Put the pork in the slow cooker, and tip over the sauce. Cook on high for 4 hours, or low for 8 hours.
3. Skim off any excess oil. Remove the meat and strain the sauce through a fine mesh sieve.
4. Serve the meat and juice with rice noodles, chopped spring onions, red chilis, fresh coriander and toasted sesame seeds.

LAMB AND MANGO CURRY

SERVES 4 | PER SERVING - CALORIES: 710, FAT: 23G, CARBOHYDRATES: 91.3G, PROTEIN: 39.5G

INGREDIENTS

- 600g diced lamb shoulder
- 2 x 400g tins chopped tomatoes
- 3cm piece ginger, peeled and finely grated
- 2 red onions
- 2 garlic cloves, crushed
- 1 large mango, stoned, peeled, and cubed
- ½ tbsp vegetable oil
- 100g tikka curry paste
- 1 cinnamon stick
- 15g fresh coriander, leaves roughly chopped, stalks finely chopped
- 1 beef stock cube, made up to 250ml
- 320g basmati rice
- 120g 0% fat natural yoghurt, to serve

INSTRUCTIONS

1. In a large pan over a medium heat, warm the oil, then cook the onions until soft. Stir in the ginger and garlic and cook for another minute. Add the curry paste and cook for 2 minutes. Add the cinnamon, lamb, and 1 tablespoon of coriander stalks. Cook for 4-5 minutes to colour the lamb. Tip the contents of the pan, the tomatoes, and stock into the slow cooker. Season to taste, then cook for 4 hours on low.
2. Stir in the mango and most of the coriander leaves. Cook for a further 30 minutes. Cook the rice as per the package's directions. Scatter the curry with the remaining coriander leaves, then serve with the rice and yoghurt.

CHICKEN TIKKA MASALA

SERVES 4 | PER SERVING - CALORIES: 672, FAT: 38G, CARBOHYDRATES: 24G, PROTEIN: 63.5G

INGREDIENTS

- 1kg chicken drumsticks and thighs, skin removed
- 150ml natural yoghurt
- 1 jalapeño pepper, pierced
- 400g can chopped tomatoes
- 1 onion, sliced
- 3 garlic cloves
- 2 tbsp cornflour mixed with 2 tbsp water
- 100ml single cream plus a little extra to serve
- 1 tbsp coriander
- 1 tbsp cumin
- 1 tbsp brown sugar
- 2 tbsp flaked almonds
- 1 tbsp garam masala
- 2 tbsp freshly chopped coriander
- 1 tbsp grated fresh ginger
- 3 tbsp olive oil
- Cooked basmati rice and naan bread to serve

INSTRUCTIONS

1. Mix the coriander and cumin into the yoghurt, and season to taste. Add the drumsticks and thighs and toss until evenly coated.
2. Brown the chicken in batches in a saucepan using 1 tablespoon of the oil. Transfer to a plate and set aside.
3. Add the remaining oil to the pan, and cook the onions for 5 minutes, stirring regularly. Stir through the garlic, ginger, and garam masala, and cook for a further minute. Add the sugar and tomatoes.
4. Tip the contents of the pan, the jalapeno, and the chicken into the slow cooker, and cook on low for 2 to 3 hours.
5. Add the cornflour mix and stir until combined. Cook for a further 30 minutes until thick. Fold in the cream.
6. Garnish with the coriander, flaked almonds, and a swirl of cream.

RAMEN

SERVES 4 | PER SERVING - CALORIES: 803, FAT: 3G, CARBOHYDRATES: 51G, PROTEIN: 70G

INGREDIENTS

- 1L chicken stock
- 4 tbsp dark soy sauce
- 1 tbsp mirin
- 1 tsp dark brown sugar
- 3 garlic cloves
- 100g white miso paste
- 4cm ginger, peeled and grated
- 600g pork shoulder
- 200g mixed mushrooms
- Juice of 1 lime
- 2 pak choi, halved
- 2 spring onions, finely sliced
- 250g ramen noodles
- 4 soft-boiled eggs, halved

INSTRUCTIONS

1. In a jug, mix the stock, soy sauce, mirin, miso, and sugar until the sugar and miso have dissolved.
2. Put the ginger, garlic, pork, and mushrooms in the slow cooker, and tip over the stock. Cook on low for 6 hours.
3. Stir the lime juice into the ramen, breaking up any large pieces of pork. Season to taste.
4. Cook the noodles, then add the pak choi for the last minute.
5. Drain the noodles and pak choi and divide between 4 bowls. Ladle the ramen mixture from the slow cooker over the bowls, and top with spring onions and the egg.

PRAWN AND FENNEL RISOTTO

SERVES 4 | PER SERVING - CALORIES: 502, FAT: 12G, CARBOHYDRATES: 67G, PROTEIN: 23G

INGREDIENTS

- 300g risotto rice
- 1 large fennel bulb, sliced
- 2 tbsp olive oil
- 1 shallot, sliced
- 1 garlic clove
- 2 preserved lemons, chopped, seeds discarded
- 150ml white wine
- 1L vegetable stock
- 300g raw king prawns
- 40g Pecorino cheese, grated

INSTRUCTIONS

1. Fry the fennel in the oil for 5 minutes. Add the shallot and cook for another 5 to 8 minutes until almost cooked through. Tip in the garlic and rice, and fry, stirring constantly, until the edges of the rice are starting to become translucent.
2. Add the white wine, and bubble for about 30 seconds.
3. Add to the slow cooker and stir in the stock. Season to taste.
4. Cook on high 1 ¾ hours, then stir in the prawns and lemons. Cook for a further 10 minutes until the prawns are cooked.
5. Stir through the cheese and add a little extra stock if needed.

CHICKEN PICCATA

SERVES 4 | PER SERVING - CALORIES: 425, FAT: 31G, CARBOHYDRATES: 1G, PROTEIN: 30G

INGREDIENTS

- 550g chicken breast
- 125g unsalted butter
- 200ml white wine
- 250ml chicken stock
- 1 tbsp vegetable oil
- 3 lemons
- 2 tbsp capers

INSTRUCTIONS

1. Brown the chicken in the oil over a medium to high heat. Transfer the chicken to the slow cooker.
2. Slice one lemon and juice the other two. Put the lemon slices and chicken stock in the slow cooker. Season to taste. Cook on high until the chicken is cooked, around an hour.
3. In a pan, melt 75g of the butter, then pour in the wine, 60ml lemon juice, capers, and a splash of the liquid from the slow cooker. Reduce by half.
4. Take off the heat and stir in the rest of the butter. Season to taste, fold in the parsley, and serve with the chicken.

BLACK BEAN SOUP

SERVES 6 | PER SERVING - CALORIES: 294, FAT: 2G, CARBOHYDRATES: 55G, PROTEIN: 17G

INGREDIENTS

- 2 cloves of garlic
- 1 onion
- 2 carrots
- 2 celery stalks
- 450g black beans, uncooked
- 240ml salsa
- 1 tbsp chilli powder
- ½ tbsp ground cumin
- 1 tsp dried oregano
- 1L vegetable stock
- 480ml water

INSTRUCTIONS

1. Chop up the onion and celery, grate the carrots, and crush the garlic. Rinse the beans in a colander under cold water and pick out any stones.
2. Stir everything together in the slow cooker, and cook on high for 6 to 8 hours. Once the beans are soft, blend the soup until thick and creamy.

HAM AND BEAN SOUP

SERVES 8 | PER SERVING - CALORIES: 250, FAT: 3G, CARBOHYDRATES: 38G, PROTEIN: 17G

INGREDIENTS

- Half an onion
- 4 carrots
- 4 cloves of garlic
- 3 celery stalks
- 450g bean mix, uncooked
- 400g smoked ham chunks
- 2 bay leaves
- 1 ½ tsp dried thyme
- 1 ½ tsp dried oregano
- 1 ½ tbsp chicken stock powder

INSTRUCTIONS

1. The night before cooking, rinse the beans. Cover with twice the amount of water and refrigerate overnight.
2. Chop up the onion, carrot, celery, and garlic. Add to the slow cooker, and stir in the ham.
3. Drain the beans, and rinse again. Add the beans to the slow cooker and add the seasoning.
4. Pour in 1.4L of water and give everything a stir to distribute the seasoning.
5. Cook for 4 to 6 hours on high, or until the beans have softened. Season to taste.

BEEF WITH PRUNES

SERVES 6 | PER SERVING - CALORIES: 342, FAT: 10G, CARBOHYDRATES: 20.7G, PROTEIN: 36.8G

INGREDIENTS

- 1kg beef joint
- 1 red onion
- 2 onions, chopped
- 2 garlic cloves, chopped
- 150g pitted prunes
- 2-inch piece peeled ginger, finely chopped
- 250ml beef stock
- 250ml red wine
- 2 tbsp flour
- 2 tsp cumin powder
- 3 tbsp olive oil
- 2 tbsp honey
- 15g flat leaf parsley for serving

INSTRUCTIONS

1. Slice the beef into pieces and season. Brown the meat in the oil over a high heat. Take the beef out of the frying pan and set aside.
2. Add fresh olive oil, and cook the ginger, garlic, and onion for 8 minutes. Stir through the flour.
3. Cook the flour for 2 minutes, before mixing in the cumin, honey, prunes, stock, and red wine. Pour the mixture into the slow cooker over the beef.
4. Cook for 8 hours on low, or 4 hours on high. Regardless of temperature, do not lift the lid during the cook time as it could slow the process down.

DUCK AND POTATO MASSAMAN CURRY

SERVES 4 | PER SERVING - CALORIES: 356, FAT: 13G, CARBOHYDRATES: 22.9G, PROTEIN: 40.5G

INGREDIENTS

FOR THE CURRY PASTE:

- 1 tsp cumin seeds
- 2 tsp coriander seeds
- 1 star anise
- 3 peppercorns
- 1 red chilli, diced
- 3 garlic cloves
- 2.5cm (1in) piece galangal or root ginger, finely grated
- 2 tsp fish sauce
- 4 tsp palm sugar
- 1 lemongrass stalk, finely chopped
- 25g (1oz) peanuts, toasted
- 2g (1 tsp) salt
- ¼ tsp ground cloves
- ¼ tsp ground nutmeg
- pinch cinnamon
- small handful coriander

FOR THE CURRY:

- 4 duck legs
- 12 Charlotte potatoes, peeled
- 4 kaffir lime leaves
- 1 cinnamon stick
- 2 cardamom pods
- 400ml (14fl oz) coconut milk
- jasmine rice, to serve

INSTRUCTIONS

1. To make the Massaman paste, dry fry the coriander seeds, cumin seeds and peppercorns in a pan until fragrant. Remove, and crush using a pestle and mortar.
2. Add the shallot, star anise, garlic, chilli, ginger or galangal, and work into a paste. Add 1 tsp of the fish sauce, 2 tsp of the palm sugar and the remaining paste ingredients and continue until you have a thick paste. Set aside.
3. In a large frying pan, fry the duck on low to melt down all the fat under the skin (around 10 minutes). Drain the fat, increase the heat, and brown the duck. Place the duck, potatoes, kaffir lime leaves, cinnamon, and cardamom in a slow cooker.
4. Add a splash of oil to a hot pan, and fry the paste, stirring constantly to make sure it doesn't burn. When the flavours are fragrant, add the coconut milk. Mix well, making sure not to boil. Pour the liquid over the duck and add the sugar and remaining fish sauce. Cook on low for 6-7 hours.
5. Serve the duck, sauce, and potatoes with jasmine rice.

PORK VINDALOO

SERVES 6 | PER SERVING - CALORIES: 250, FAT: 11G, CARBOHYDRATES: 10G, PROTEIN: 28.3G

INGREDIENTS

- 750g pork shoulder steaks cut into pieces
- 2 medium onions chopped
- 6 small new potatoes halved
- 400g tin chopped tomatoes
- 100ml chicken stock
- 1 tbsp tomato puree
- 3 tbsp vegetable oil
- 1 cinnamon stick

FOR THE SPICE PASTE:

- 3 cloves garlic
- 1 inch ginger, peeled and chopped
- 3 tbsp cider vinegar
- 1 tsp cumin seeds
- 1 tsp turmeric
- 2tsp chilli powder or 2 dried chillies
- 1 tsp black peppercorns
- 3 cardamom pods

INSTRUCTIONS

1. Grind all the spices for the spice paste until fine. Put in a blender, and puree with the remaining paste ingredients.
2. Marinate and chill the meat in the paste for at least 2 hours.
3. Put the meat and potatoes in the slow cooker. Heat the oil, and fry the onions for 10 minutes. Season to taste.
4. Stir in the tomato puree, chopped tomatoes, and stock, then bring to the boil. Put the meat and cinnamon stick in the slow cooker. Cook for 8 hours on low, or 4 hours on high.
5. Serve with a swirl of yoghurt, fresh rice, and your favourite chutney.

SCANDINAVIAN INSPIRED SPICED MEATLOAF

SERVES 4 | PER SERVING - CALORIES: 367, FAT: 22G, CARBOHYDRATES: 10.6G, PROTEIN: 33.2G

INGREDIENTS

- 90g smoked bacon
- 250g pork mince
- 250g beef mince
- 1 large clove garlic
- 2 tsp Dijon mustard
- 1 tbsp tomato puree
- 1 onion, chopped
- 1 tbsp olive oil
- Pinch of ground cloves
- 1 tsp allspice
- Small bunch fresh parsley, chopped
- Small bunch dill, chopped
- 1 large egg, lightly whisked

FOR THE GLAZE:

- 80g tomato ketchup
- 1 tbsp Worcestershire sauce
- ½ tsp brown sugar

INSTRUCTIONS

1. Sauté the onion for 5 minutes. Stir in the spices and garlic, and cook for a couple minutes more.
2. Transfer the onion mix into a bowl and let it cool. Add the remaining ingredients to the bowl and combine by hand, scrunching the mixture.
3. Shape the mince by hand into a load, and add to the slow cooker. Stir together the glaze ingredients and pour over the top.
4. Cook for 6 hours on low.

THAI DUCK CURRY

SERVES 4 | PER SERVING - CALORIES: 494, FAT: 25G, CARBOHYDRATES: 34G, PROTEIN: 34.8G

INGREDIENTS

- 500g duck breast, skin removed, cut into chunks
- 400g waxy potatoes, cut into 2.5cm chunks
- 90g unsalted peanuts
- 6 shallots, peeled and quartered
- 3 ½ to 4 tbsp red curry paste
- 2 tbsp sunflower oil
- 1 red pepper, seeded and cut into chunks
- 400ml tin coconut milk
- 1 tbsp Thai fish sauce
- 1 tbsp dark brown sugar
- Thai Jasmine rice and 4 spring onions to serve

INSTRUCTIONS

1. Cook the peanuts in a dry frying pan or wok until toasted and set aside. Let the peanuts cool before chopping. Add the sunflower oil to the hot wok, and fry the curry paste, duck, and shallots until browned. Add the coconut milk and boil, then stir in the fish sauce and sugar. Add to the slow cooker, along with the peppers, potatoes, and about two thirds of the peanuts.
2. Cook for 8 hours on low, or 4 hours on high.
3. Scatter over the peanuts and spring onions, and serve with jasmine rice.

ASIAN-STYLE ROAST PORK

SERVES 6 | PER SERVING - CALORIES: 312, FAT: 8G, CARBOHYDRATES: 16.5G, PROTEIN: 34.8G

INGREDIENTS

- 900g pork leg steaks
- 3cm piece ginger peeled and finely chopped
- 3 garlic cloves sliced
- 2 long red chillies, seeded and sliced
- 1 tbsp vegetable oil
- 3 whole star anise
- 1 tbsp honey
- 250ml sherry
- 150ml hoisin sauce

INSTRUCTIONS

1. Season the meat. Heat the oil in a pan and brown the meat on all sides. Remove from the pan and then sauté the ginger, garlic and one of the chilis for 5 minutes. Pour in the hoisin, rice wine or sherry and star anise. Stir well.
2. Put the pork in the slow cooker and pour over the sauce. Cook for 8 hours on low, or 4 hours on high. Do not lift the lid while cooking as it will take longer.
3. Serve over rice with the remaining red chili and some chopped spring onions.

LAMB OSSO BUCCO

SERVES 6 | PER SERVING - CALORIES: 312, FAT: 8G, CARBOHYDRATES: 16.5G, PROTEIN: 34.8G

INGREDIENTS

- 800g lamb shoulder or leg cut into chunks
- 2 carrots
- 2 stalks of celery
- 2 medium onions
- 1 tin of chopped tomatoes
- 2 cloves garlic
- 250ml white wine
- 200ml beef stock
- 1 tsp fresh thyme
- 4 tbsp olive oil
- Flour to dust

FOR THE GREMOLATA:

- 15g chopped flat leaf parsley
- Zest of 1 lemon
- 1 garlic clove, chopped

INSTRUCTIONS

1. Season the lamb to taste, and dust with the flour. Heat a spoon of oil, and brown the meat, working in batches. Put the lamb in the slow cooker once browned.
2. Heat the remaining oil in the same pan, then fry the vegetables for 10 minutes. Tip in the stock, wine, and tomatoes. Boil for a couple minutes, then tip into the slow cooker. Cook for 8 hours on low, or 4 hours on high.
3. Sprinkle with parsley, lemon, and garlic to serve.

VEGETARIAN STEW

SERVES 4 | PER SERVING - CALORIES: 383, FAT: 21G, CARBOHYDRATES: 35.6G, PROTEIN: 14.5G

INGREDIENTS

- 1 onion, chopped
- 75g pine nuts, toasted
- 400g tin chopped tomatoes
- 400g tin cannellini beans, drained and rinsed
- 400g tin chickpeas, drained and rinsed
- 360g butternut squash, chopped into chunks
- 250g sweet mini peppers, seeded and halved
- 2 tbsp extra-virgin olive oil
- 10-12 basil leaves, shredded
- Vegetarian hard cheese or Parmesan, shaved, to serve (optional)

INSTRUCTIONS

1. Put the onion, butternut squash, peppers, beans, and chickpeas in the dish a slow cooker.
2. Pour over the chopped tomatoes then sprinkle with half the basil and season well. Stir, then cook for 4 hours on low.
3. Serve with the left over basil, nuts, parmesan, and a drizzle of olive oil.

BARBACOA BEEF

SERVES 10 | PER SERVING - CALORIES: 50, FAT: 3G, CARBOHYDRATES: 0.5G, PROTEIN: 4G

INGREDIENTS

- 1kg brisket, cut into large pieces
- 3 tbsp chipotle paste
- 1 red onion
- 2 garlic cloves
- Pinch of ground cloves
- 100ml cider vinegar
- 500ml low-salt chicken stock
- 3 bay leaves
- Juice of 2 limes
- 1 bunch coriander, roughly chopped

INSTRUCTIONS

1. Put everything in the slow cooker and set the brisket on top. Stir the sauce ingredients together and turn the beef over in the sauce a few times to coat.
2. Cook on high for an hour, then turn the heat down to low for a further 8 hours.
3. Serve with lettuce cups, jalapeños, and crème fraiche.

CHICKEN, POTATO AND LEEK CASSEROLE

SERVES 4 | PER SERVING - CALORIES: 268, FAT: 5G, CARBOHYDRATES: 23G, PROTEIN: 30G

INGREDIENTS

- 1 leek, roughly chopped
- 1 carrot, roughly chopped
- 1 onion, roughly chopped
- 350g new potatoes, roughly chopped
- 6 skinless, boneless chicken thighs, chopped
- 500ml chicken stock
- 4 tbsp vegetable gravy granules

INSTRUCTIONS

1. Put the vegetables and chicken in the slow cooker. Pour the stock over and around the chicken thighs, then mix in the gravy granules to thicken it up (the sauce will be quite thick – use less gravy if you prefer a runnier casserole).
2. Cook for 6 to 8 hours on low. Season well, then serve.

LAMB SHOULDER CURRY

SERVES 4 | PER SERVING - CALORIES: 624, FAT: 48G, CARBOHYDRATES: 11G, PROTEIN: 36G

INGREDIENTS

- 700g lamb chunks
- 350g Greek yoghurt
- 2 onions, chopped
- 5 cloves of garlic, crushed
- 5cm piece of ginger, grated
- 2 tbsp rapeseed or olive oil
- 1 green chilli, deseeded if you like
- 1 tbsp tomato purée
- 2 tbsp toasted flaked almonds
- 1 tsp cinnamon
- 2 tsp cumin
- 2 tsp garam masala
- 1 tsp chilli powder
- 1 small bunch coriander, chopped
- Rice, to serve

INSTRUCTIONS

1. Season the lamb and brown in batches using a little oil for each batch. Put the lamb in the slow cooker once cooked.
2. Fry the onions, stirring regularly, for around 10 minutes until tender. Mix in the ginger, garlic, spices, chilli and tomato purée and fry for another minute. Transfer to the slow cooker.
3. Add 200ml boiling water and stir. Cook for at least 6 hours on low.
4. Stir in the yoghurt, then cook for a further 30 minutes to 1 hour on low. Stir well before serving. Scatter the coriander and flaked almonds to serve.

BEEF CURRY

SERVES 4 | PER SERVING - CALORIES: 425, FAT: 30G, CARBOHYDRATES: 6G, PROTEIN: 32G

INGREDIENTS

- 800g beef, chunks
- 1 onion
- 5 garlic cloves
- 400ml coconut milk
- 5cm ginger, grated
- 4 cardamom pods
- 1 cinnamon stick
- 1 tbsp ground coriander
- 2 tsp ground cumin
- ½ tsp ground turmeric
- 1 tsp chilli powder
- 3 tbsp oil
- Small bunch coriander, chopped

INSTRUCTIONS

1. Brown the beef in a frying pan, then transfer to the slow cooker. Add the rest of the oil, then cook the onion until it softens. Stir in the garlic and ginger and cook for a minute.
2. Add the spices and cook until fragrant. Pour in the coconut milk, then simmer for a couple of minutes. Transfer to the slow cooker.
3. Cook for 4 hours on high, or 8 hours on low. Stir in the coriander just before serving.

PORK, CIDER AND SAGE HOTPOT

SERVES 6 | PER SERVING - CALORIES: 644, FAT: 35G, CARBOHYDRATES: 39G, PROTEIN: 35G

INGREDIENTS

- 4 tbsp olive oil
- 1kg diced pork shoulder
- 400g potatoes
- 400g sweet potatoes
- 20g butter, cubed
- 4 leeks, trimmed and sliced
- 4 garlic cloves, crushed
- 500ml dry cider
- 400ml chicken stock
- 2 bay leaves
- ½ small bunch parsley, finely chopped
- Small bunch sage
- 200ml single cream
- 3 tbsp plain flour

INSTRUCTIONS

1. Heat half of the oil in a pan, and brown the pork. Set aside.
2. Add another tablespoon of oil, then cook the leeks until soft. Add the garlic, and cook for a minute. Stir through the flour.
3. Add all the ingredients apart from the sage and butter to the slow cooker. Cook for 3 to 4 hours on medium.
4. Finally add the butter and sage leaves, then cook for an hour and a half on low.

AUBERGINES

SERVES 6 | PER SERVING - CALORIES: 269, FAT: 20G, CARBOHYDRATES: 11G, PROTEIN: 8G

INGREDIENTS

- 500g aubergines
- 300g tomatoes
- 60g sundried tomatoes
- 3 garlic cloves
- 1 tsp coriander seeds
- 1 red onion
- 1 small fennel bulb
- 4 tbsp olive oil

FOR THE DRESSING:

- Small bunch flat leaf parsley, chopped
- Small bunch basil, chopped
- Small bunch chives, chopped
- 2 tbsp olive oil
- Juice of 1 lemon
- 2 tsp capers

FOR THE TOPPING:

- 50g toasted flaked almonds
- 100g crumbled feta

INSTRUCTIONS

1. Put 2 tablespoons of oil with the onions in the slow cooker. Slice the aubergines and brush with the remaining oil. Put the aubergines, tomato, and fennel in the slow cooker. Add the coriander, and season to taste.
2. Cook on low for 6 to 8 hours. Blend the dressing ingredients until smooth.
3. Put the vegetables on a serving platter using a slotted spoon and drizzle over the dressing. Top with the feta cheese and flaked almonds.

BEEF BOURGUIGNON

SERVES 6 | PER SERVING - CALORIES: 497, FAT: 20G, CARBOHYDRATES: 14G, PROTEIN: 47G

INGREDIENTS

- 750ml bottle of red wine
- 1 ½ kg stewing or braising steak, cut into chunks
- 100g unsmoked bacon
- 6 small shallots or baby onions, quartered
- 300g closed cup mushrooms, quartered
- 2 onions
- 2 carrots
- 2 celery stalks
- 2 tbsp tomato purée
- 2 bay leaves
- 2 thyme sprigs or rosemary sprigs
- 1 tsp caster sugar
- 3 tbsp plain flour
- 1 beef stock cube
- 3 tbsp vegetable oil

INSTRUCTIONS

1. Season the meat. Brown the meat in a pan with 2 tablespoons of the oil. Transfer the cooked meat to a plate.
2. Fry the carrot, celery, and onion in the same pan until soft. Tip in the flour and herbs and cook for 2 minutes.
3. Add a splash of wine to a bowl, and mix in the stock, tomato puree, and sugar to create a paste. Tip the paste into the frying pan and mix in the leftover wine.
4. Bring the frying pan to a simmer and tip the contents into the slow cooker. Stir well and top up with water until the beef is covered if needed. Cook on low for 6 to 8 hours.
5. Thirty minutes before the end, heat the rest of the oil in a pan, and cook the bacon, shallots, and mushrooms until starting to caramelise. Tip into the slow cooker and cook on high for the last 30 minutes. If you want the gravy to be thicker, leave the lid off for this time.

CLASSIC CHICKEN CASSEROLE

SERVES 4 | PER SERVING - CALORIES: 382, FAT: 9G, CARBOHYDRATES: 30G, PROTEIN: 41G

INGREDIENTS

- 500ml chicken stock made with 2 cubes
- 700g chicken thighs, boneless
- 400g new potatoes, halved
- 250g mushrooms, quartered
- 15g dried mushrooms, soaked in 50ml boiling water
- 3 garlic cloves
- 2 celery sticks, diced
- 1 onion, chopped
- 2 carrots, diced
- ½ tbsp rapeseed or olive oil
- 1 ½ tbsp flour
- 2 tsp Dijon mustard
- 2 bay leaves
- Knob of butter

INSTRUCTIONS

1. Cook the onion in the oil and butter over a medium heat until the onion starts to soften and brown.
2. Put the flour and a seasoning in a bowl and cover the chicken with it.
3. Add the garlic and chicken to the pan, and fry until just starting to colour.
4. Put the chicken in the slow cooker, alongside with the potatoes, celery, carrots, mushrooms, chicken stock, Dijon mustard and bay.
5. Cook on for 7 hours on low, or 4 hours on high.
6. Discard the bay leaves and serve with a little mustard.

TERIYAKI CHICKEN

SERVES 4 | PER SERVING - CALORIES: 319, FAT: 7G, CARBOHYDRATES: 28G, PROTEIN: 35G

INGREDIENTS

- 680g boneless chicken thighs
- 160ml low-sodium soy sauce
- 3 tbsp rice vinegar
- 3 tbsp honey
- 3 tbsp brown sugar
- 1 garlic clove, minced
- 1 tbsp minced fresh ginger
- 2 tbsp water
- 1 tbsp cornflour
- Toasted sesame seeds, chopped spring onions and prepared rice to serve

INSTRUCTIONS

1. Put the chicken thighs in the slow cooker.
2. In a bowl, whisk together the rice vinegar, honey, soy sauce, brown sugar, garlic, and ginger, then pour over the chicken.
3. Cook for 2 hours on high, or 4 hours on low until the chicken is tender. Take the chicken out of the slow cooker, and shred. Sieve the cooking liquid, and tip into a saucepan
4. Make a paste from the water and cornflour. Add to the strained cooking liquid, whisk to incorporate, then heat, stirring constantly until the sauce thickens and bubbles. Continue cooking and stirring until glossy and thickened, 1 to 2 minutes. Remove from heat.
5. Stir the chicken through the sauce. Toss to coat. Garnish with spring onions and toasted sesame seeds, and enjoy with rice.

MOROCCAN LAMB STEW

SERVES 6 | PER SERVING - CALORIES: 488, FAT: 35G, CARBOHYDRATES: 7G, PROTEIN: 34G

INGREDIENTS

- 600ml hot beef stock or lamb stock
- 1kg lamb shoulder, chunks
- 90g pitted Kalamata olives
- 5 garlic cloves, crushed
- 2 tbsp olive oil
- 2 onions, sliced
- Thumb-sized piece ginger, peeled and grated or finely chopped
- 1 small, preserved lemon, skin only, finely chopped
- 1 lemon, zested, plus a squeeze of juice
- 1 tbsp tomato purée
- 1 tbsp honey
- 1 tbsp ground coriander
- 1 tbsp ground cumin
- 1 tsp ground cinnamon
- Pinch saffron (or turmeric, to add colour)
- Handful chopped mint, coriander, or parsley (or a combination)

INSTRUCTIONS

1. Brown the lamb in a frying pan over a medium to high heat using a tablespoon of olive oil. Add the remaining oil and fry the onion for 10 minutes until soft. Add in the ginger and garlic, then cook for a further couple of minutes. Add the spices, lemon, and tomato puree, then warm through and add to the slow cooker. Add a little water to the pan and scrape up any stuck bits. Add to the slow cooker with the stock. Cook for 6 to 8 hours on low.
2. Once the meat is tender, turn the heat up to high. Add the honey, lemon and olives and cook for 20-30 minutes. Top with the herbs and serve with couscous or rice.

MUSHROOM RISOTTO

SERVES 4 | PER SERVING - CALORIES: 346, FAT: 3G, CARBOHYDRATES: 67G, PROTEIN: 10G

INGREDIENTS

- 300g wholegrain rice
- 250g chestnut mushrooms, sliced
- 50g porcini
- 1 onion, finely chopped
- 1l vegetable stock
- 1 tsp olive oil
- Small bunch parsley, finely chopped
- Grated vegetarian parmesan-style cheese to serve

INSTRUCTIONS

1. Cook the onion in a frying pan with a little water until soft, around 10 minutes. Stir in the mushroom and cook until they start to soften.
2. Tip the stock into the saucepan and stir through the porcini. Bring the pan to a simmer and leave to soak. Add to the slow cooker, and stir in the rice. Sieve the stock and porcini into the saucepan.
3. Cook for 3 hours on high, stirring halfway through the cook time. Check the consistency, if needed, stir in an extra splash of stock. Season to taste, and serve with the parsley and parmesan.

PAELLA

SERVES 6 | PER SERVING - CALORIES: 517, FAT: 21G, CARBOHYDRATES: 46G, PROTEIN: 31G

INGREDIENTS

- 4 skinless, boneless chicken thighs, thickly sliced
- 240g chorizo ring, sliced
- 2 garlic cloves, crushed
- 1 onion, sliced
- 200g fresh or frozen raw king prawns, peeled
- 150g frozen peas
- 400g can chopped tomatoes
- 2 tbsp olive oil
- 1 tbsp sweet smoked paprika
- pinch of saffron (optional)
- 150ml white wine
- 300g paella rice
- 400ml chicken stock
- ½ small bunch of parsley, finely chopped
- Lemon wedges and crusty bread, to serve (optional)

INSTRUCTIONS

1. Turn the slow cooker on low. Heat the oil in a frying pan and cook the chorizo and chicken until golden brown, brown, around 10 minutes. Transfer to the slow cooker. Cook the onion in the same frying pan until starting to soften, then stir through the paprika, saffron, and garlic. Cook for two minutes, stirring constantly. Tip in the wine, and simmer until it reduces by half. Add to the slow cooker, then stir in the stock, tomatoes, and rice. Season with salt and pepper to taste. Cook on low for 1 ½ hours.
2. Stir through the peas and prawns, then cook for thirty minutes longer. Check to see if the rice is cooked; if not, cook for another 15-30 minutes.
3. Serve with the parsley, lemon wedges, and crusty bread.

PORK BELLY

SERVES 6 | PER SERVING - CALORIES: 540, FAT: 40G, CARBOHYDRATES: 4G, PROTEIN: 39G

INGREDIENTS

- 1 - 1.2kg pork belly, cut into 3 long strips, rind trimmed
- 2 onions, sliced
- 3 garlic cloves, crushed
- 3 tsp sea salt
- 1 tbsp soy sauce
- Thumb-sized piece root ginger, finely grated

INSTRUCTIONS

1. Stir the garlic, soy sauce, salt, and ginger together in a bowl, then rub into the pork belly. Put the onion in the bottom of the slow cooker and put the pork on top. Cook for 4 hours on high.
2. Take the pork out of the slow cooker and transfer to a frying pan along with a couple tablespoons of the cooking juices. Cook over a high heat, turning regularly, until the pork is browned, and the juices have evaporated. Serve with potatoes, vegetables, and gravy.

BUTTER CHICKEN

SERVES 4 | PER SERVING - CALORIES: 371, FAT: 19G, CARBOHYDRATES: 11G, PROTEIN: 36G

INGREDIENTS

- 500g skinless, boneless chicken thighs

FOR THE MARINADE:

- 220g natural yoghurt
- 1 to 2 tsp hot chilli powder
- 3 tsp paprika
- 2 tsp ground cumin
- 1 lemon, juiced

FOR THE CURRY:

- 250ml chicken stock
- 3 garlic cloves, crushed
- 1 large onion, diced
- 3 tbsp tomato purée
- 2 tsp ground fenugreek
- Thumb-sized piece ginger, grated
- 50g flaked almonds, toasted
- 2 tbsp butter, ghee, or vegetable oil
- 1 tsp garam masala
- 1 green chilli, deseeded and finely chopped (optional)

INSTRUCTIONS

1. Stir the marinade ingredients together and toss in the chicken. Cover, and chill for at least an hour, but ideally overnight.
2. In a large saucepan, warm the butter, oil, or ghee. Cook the chilli, onion, garlic, ginger, and seasonings for 5 to 10 minutes until slightly softened.
3. Tip in the spices and tomato puree, then cook for a couple minutes more. Stir in the chicken and stock, then transfer everything to the slow cooker. Cook for 6 to 7 hours on low.
4. Sprinkle with the almonds, then serve with your choice of rice, naan breads, chutneys.

CHICKEN CHASSEUR

SERVES 4 | PER SERVING - CALORIES: 485, FAT: 26G, CARBOHYDRATES: 15G, PROTEIN: 29G

INGREDIENTS

- 4 chicken thighs
- 225g chestnut mushrooms, halved
- 200g canned chopped tomatoes
- 400ml hot chicken stock
- 2 tbsp olive oil
- 1 onion, chopped
- 2 garlic cloves, sliced
- 200ml white wine
- 2 thyme sprigs
- 1 tbsp tomato purée
- 1 bay leaf
- Small handful of parsley, finely chopped, to serve
- Mash, jackets, pasta, or roast potatoes, to serve (optional)

INSTRUCTIONS

1. Turn the slow cooker on to low, and warm the oil in a pan over a high heat. Season the chicken and fry, skin-side down, for 4-5 minutes until crisp. Turn and fry for 3-4 minutes more until golden all over. Set aside.
2. Tip the onion into the same pan and fry for 10 minutes over a medium heat until starting to soften. Add the garlic and mushrooms and fry for 10 minutes more until the mushrooms are golden brown.
3. Tip the wine into the frying pan and reduce by half. Stir through the tomato puree, chopped tomatoes, and herbs. Season to taste and heat the contents to a simmer.
4. Tip the sauce into the slow cooker with the chicken on top.
5. Pour over the chicken stock until the chicken thighs are covered, adding a little more if needed. Cook for 6 to 8 hours until the sauce has thickened and the chicken is soft.
6. Set the chicken aside. Pour the sauce into a pan and simmer until reduced.

CHICKEN CURRY

SERVES 2 | PER SERVING - CALORIES: 345, FAT: 13G, CARBOHYDRATES: 24G, PROTEIN: 28G

INGREDIENTS

- 2 chicken legs, skin and fat removed
- 1 large onion, chopped
- 1 yellow pepper, chopped
- 400g can chopped tomatoes
- 3 tbsp mild curry paste
- 1 ½ tbsp finely chopped ginger
- 2 tsp vegetable stock powder
- 30g pack fresh coriander, leaves chopped
- Cooked brown rice, to serve

INSTRUCTIONS

1. Put everything excluding the chicken and coriander in the slow cooker and stir in 100ml water.
2. Add the chicken and submerge, then chill in the fridge overnight.
3. Cook for 6 hours on low until the chicken is cooked through. Stir in the coriander just before serving and enjoy with brown rice.

CHICKEN KORMA

SERVES 6 | PER SERVING - CALORIES: 511, FAT: 33G, CARBOHYDRATES: 10G, PROTEIN: 43G

INGREDIENTS

- 6 chicken breasts, cut into chunks
- 150ml double cream
- 300ml chicken stock
- Thumb-sized piece ginger, peeled
- 2 large onions, finely chopped
- 2 garlic cloves
- 2 tbsp tomato purée
- 2 tbsp vegetable oil
- 1 tsp paprika
- ¼-½ tsp chilli powder
- 2 tsp sugar
- 1 tsp ground coriander
- 1 tsp turmeric
- 1 tsp ground cumin
- 6 tbsp ground almonds

INSTRUCTIONS

1. Turn the slow cooker on to low. Blend the garlic, ginger, and onions with a little water to make a smooth paste. Brown the chicken over a medium to high heat, then set aside, and add the paste to the pan. Turn the heat down to medium and fry the paste for about 10 minutes until it has started to colour.
2. Mix the tomato puree, 1 tsp salt, sugar, and spices in the frying pan, and cook, stirring constantly, until aromatic. Put the chicken back in the pan and stir through the stock. Increase the heat until simmering, then transfer to the slow cooker. Cook on low for 5 to 6 hours.
3. Stir in the ground almonds and cream and cook for 10 to 15 minutes longer to thicken if needed. Serve with coriander and flaked almonds.

ROAST CHICKEN SOUP

SERVES 8 | PER SERVING - CALORIES: 352, FAT: 21G, CARBOHYDRATES: 4G, PROTEIN: 35G

INGREDIENTS

- 2L chicken stock
- 1 lemon, juiced
- 2 medium leeks, halved and sliced
- 1 onion, finely chopped
- 2 celery sticks, chopped
- 2 carrots, cut into pieces
- 1 whole medium chicken
- ½ small bunch of dill or parsley, finely chopped
- 1 bay leaf and 3 thyme sprigs, tied together

INSTRUCTIONS

1. Put the onion, celery, carrots, and leeks in the slow cooker, and nestle in the bundle of herbs. Put the chicken in next and pour over the chicken stock. Cook on low for between 6 and 8 hours.
2. Take the chicken out of the slow cooker and put on a plate. Shred the meat using two forks, then tip back into the slow cooker. Dispose of the bones. Stir through the lemon juice and season to taste.
3. Discard the herbs. Dish the soup up into bowls, and top with dill or parsley.

GOAN PULLED PORK

SERVES 6 | PER SERVING - CALORIES: 529, FAT: 24G, CARBOHYDRATES: 11G, PROTEIN: 65G

INGREDIENTS

- 2kg boneless pork leg or shoulder
- 225ml cider vinegar
- Thumb-sized piece ginger, shredded into very thin matchsticks
- 2 tbsp olive oil
- 1 large onion, halved and sliced
- 1 garlic bulb, cloves peeled
- 1 tbsp ground cumin
- 2 tbsp smoked paprika
- 2 tbsp ground coriander
- ½ to 1 tsp cayenne pepper

FOR THE SALAD:

- 3 carrots, shredded or coarsely grated
- 1 red onion, chopped
- 3 tomatoes, chopped
- Handful fresh coriander
- 1 lemon, juiced
- 1 tbsp olive oil

INSTRUCTIONS

1. Fry the onion, ginger, and garlic in a frying pan in the oil for 5 to 10 minutes. Stir in the spices, pour in the vinegar, and stir well. Tip into the slow cooker, and stir in a teaspoon of salt and a generous amount of black pepper. Add the pork joint, turn in the mixture to coat it, then arrange it in the pot so it is rind-side down. Put the lid on, then cook on low for 7 to 8 hours.
2. Meanwhile, make the salad. Mix the carrot with the onion, tomato, and coriander, then toss just before serving with the lemon juice and oil.
3. Trim the pork and skim all the fat from the juices, then shred the meat in the slow cooker. To serve, put some meat and salad on one side of a chapati, then top with the raita and chutney, fold over and eat with your hands.

HAM WITH STICKY GINGER GLAZE

SERVES 8 | PER SERVING - CALORIES: 363, FAT: 14G, CARBOHYDRATES: 31G, PROTEIN: 27G

INGREDIENTS

- 1 onion, thickly sliced
- 10 cloves, plus extra for studding
- 1 medium gammon joint
- 1.5 litre bottle ginger beer
- 1 tbsp English mustard
- 3 tbsp ginger preserve

INSTRUCTIONS

1. Put the onion and 10 cloves in the slow cooker and add the gammon on top. Pour in the ginger beer, then cook on low for 7 hours. The gammon is done when it is tender, but still holding its shape.
2. Heat the oven to 180C, and carefully remove the skin. Leave the fat. Score the fat in a diamond pattern, making sure that you do not cut into the meat itself. Stud each diamond with another whole clove.
3. Stir the mustard and ginger together, and brush over the gammon. Cook for 20 minutes.

EASY CHICKEN TIKKA

SERVES 4 | PER SERVING - CALORIES: 599, FAT: 43G, CARBOHYDRATES: 17G, PROTEIN: 33G

INGREDIENTS

- 8-12 boneless, skinless chicken thighs, each cut into 3 chunks
- 1 large onion, chopped
- Thumb-sized piece ginger, grated
- 1 tbsp tomato purée
- 2 garlic cloves, crushed
- 2 tbsp vegetable or rapeseed oil
- 3 tbsp tikka paste
- 100ml double cream
- 500ml passata
- 1 tbsp malt vinegar
- 1 tbsp light brown soft sugar
- 1 cinnamon stick
- 5 cardamom pods
- Handful chopped coriander

INSTRUCTIONS

1. Season the chicken and cook in batches over a high heat until browned. Put the chicken in the slow cooker once cooked. Stir in the garlic, ginger and onion, and fry for 2 to 3 minutes until soft. Add a little water, then scrape the stuck bits off the pan. Transfer to the slow cooker.
2. Add the rest of the ingredients, excluding the coriander and cream, then season to taste. Cook for 5 to 7 hours on low, or 4 to 5 hours on high.
3. Add the cream and check the seasoning, adding more vinegar, sugar or salt if needed. Cook for another 10-15 minutes until hot. Ladle between bowls and garnish with the coriander. Serve with rice, naan bread and lime wedges, if you like.

CAMPFIRE STEW

SERVES 6 | PER SERVING - CALORIES: 202, FAT: 8G, CARBOHYDRATES: 12G, PROTEIN: 21G

INGREDIENTS

- 600g gammon
- 400g tinned chopped tomatoes
- 3 cloves garlic
- 2 green peppers
- 1 onion, chopped
- 3 tbsp Worcestershire sauce
- 2 tins of baked beans
- 2 tbsp tomato puree
- ½ tsp chilli powder
- 4 tsp smoked paprika
- 2 tsp cumin

INSTRUCTIONS

1. Put all the ingredients excluding the peppers in the slow cooker. Cook for 6 hours on high, or 8 hours on low.
2. Add the peppers for the last hour.
3. When the meat is cooked, shred with two forks.
4. Stir together and serve.

CHILLI CON CARNE

SERVES 8 | PER SERVING - CALORIES: 281, FAT: 13G, CARBOHYDRATES: 18G, PROTEIN: 19G

INGREDIENTS

- 550g beef mince
- 400g can chopped tomatoes
- 2 x 400g can black beans, drained
- 1 large red pepper, sliced
- 1 onion, chopped
- 2 garlic cloves, grated
- 1 celery stick, chopped
- 3 tbsp tomato purée
- 400ml beef stock
- 2 or 3 tbsp chipotle chilli paste, depending on taste
- 3 tbsp olive oil
- 2 tsp dried oregano
- 1 tsp smoked paprika
- 2 tsp ground cumin
- 4 small squares dark chocolate
- Tortilla chips or cooked rice and soured cream to serve

INSTRUCTIONS

1. Set the slow cooker to low. Heat a tablespoon of oil in a frying pan and brown the mince. Transfer to the slow cooker.
2. Heat the remaining oil in the frying pan, and soften the celery, onion, and pepper, about 10 minutes. Stir in the garlic, cumin and paprika, and cook for a minute. Transfer to the slow cooker.
3. Stir in the oregano, chipotle paste, tomato purée, tomatoes, and stock. Season. Cook for between 6 and 8 hours.
4. Stir in the chocolate and beans during the final 30 minutes of cooking.

COLA GAMMON

SERVES 8 | PER SERVING - CALORIES: 329, FAT: 15G, CARBOHYDRATES: 16G, PROTEIN: 33G

INGREDIENTS

- 1.5-1.8kg unsmoked boneless gammon joint
- 1 stick celery, chopped
- 1 carrot, peeled and chopped
- 1 onion, peeled and quartered
- 2l full fat cola
- 1 cinnamon stick
- ½ tbsp peppercorns
- 1 bay leaf

FOR THE GLAZE:

- 150ml maple syrup
- 2 tbsp red wine vinegar
- 2 tbsp wholegrain mustard
- Pinch of ground cloves or five-spice

INSTRUCTIONS

1. Put the gammon in the slow cooker and pour over the cola. Add the carrot, onion, celery, cinnamon, peppercorns, and bay leaf.
2. Cook on low for 5 ½ hours until the gammon is soft, but still holds its shape. Top up with water during the cook time if needed to keep the gammon submerged.
3. Tip the liquid away, and let the gammon cool a little. Preheat the oven to 170C and place the gammon in a roasting tin. Cut away the skin leaving behind the fat and score the fat all over.
4. Stir together the glaze ingredients. Pour half over the exposed fat and bake for 15 minutes. Pour the remaining glaze over the top and cook for another 30 minutes.
5. Allow the gammon to rest for 10 minutes and spoon more glaze over the top.

HONEY MUSTARD CHICKEN THIGHS

SERVES 4 | PER SERVING - CALORIES: 332, FAT: 16G, CARBOHYDRATES: 11G, PROTEIN: 35G

INGREDIENTS

- 1 tbsp butter
- 8 chicken thighs
- 8 spring onions, cut into lengths
- 150ml chicken stock
- 1 tbsp Dijon mustard
- 2 tbsp honey
- 2 tbsp double cream or crème fraiche
- 100g frozen peas

INSTRUCTIONS

1. Brown the chicken in the butter in a frying pan over a medium to high heat. Make sure the skin picks up plenty of colour. Season to taste, and put the chicken in the slow cooker. Brown the spring onions and add them to the slow cooker as well. Stir in the honey, mustard, and stock, then cook on low for 4 hours.
2. Fold in the cream and frozen peas. Cook for another 15 minutes with the lid off to thicken the sauce. Re-crisp up the chicken skin under the grill if you like.

LAMB MADRAS CURRY

SERVES 2 | PER SERVING - CALORIES: 568, FAT: 19G, CARBOHYDRATES: 49G, PROTEIN: 43G

INGREDIENTS

- 2 lean lamb steaks, fat trimmed and diced
- 1 large onion, halved and sliced
- 400g can chopped tomatoes
- 80g curly kale
- 210g can chickpeas, undrained
- 30g red lentils
- 3 tbsp Madras curry paste
- 2 tsp vegetable stock powder
- 1 cinnamon stick
- 1 tsp cumin seeds
- 1 tbsp grated ginger
- Cooked rice to serve

INSTRUCTIONS

1. Put all of the ingredients and 100ml of water in the slow cooker. Put the lid on, and chill in the fridge overnight.
2. In the morning, stir the contents of the pot, and cook for 6 hours on low until tender. Serve with rice.

LAMB SHANKS WITH RED WINE GRAVY

SERVES 4 | PER SERVING - CALORIES: 547, FAT: 32G, CARBOHYDRATES: 15G, PROTEIN: 37G

INGREDIENTS

- 4 lamb shanks
- 250ml light red wine (such as pinot noir)
- 500ml stock, vegetable, chicken, or lamb
- 1 large onion, finely chopped
- 2 medium carrots, chopped
- 3 garlic cloves, peeled
- 2 tbsp olive oil
- 2 tbsp tomato purée
- 2 thyme sprigs
- 2 bay leaves
- 2 tbsp plain flour
- 1 bunch parsley, leaves chopped separately to the stalks

INSTRUCTIONS

1. Put half of the oil in a frying pan and brown the lamb on all sides. Transfer to the slow cooker once done, you may need to work in batches. Add the remaining oil and fry the onion until it softens and starts to become translucent. Add the flour and tomato puree and cook for another minute.
2. Add the red wine and increase the heat until it boils. Stir constantly until the sauce is smooth. Tip the mixture into the slow cooker. Add the stock, bring back to a boil, and transfer to the slow cooker.

3. Add the garlic, carrots, bay leaves, thyme, and parsley to the slow cooker, and cook for 8 hours on low. Turn the lamb over halfway through the cook time.
4. After 8 hours, the lamb should be tender. If the sauce seems thin, take out the vegetables and meat, then boil the sauce until it thickens to your preference.

LAMB TAGINE

● ●

SERVES 4 | PER SERVING - CALORIES: 649, FAT: 45G, CARBOHYDRATES: 17G, PROTEIN: 42G

INGREDIENTS
- 950g lamb, cut into chunks
- 3 medium carrots, chunks
- 1 large onion, chopped
- 30g dried cherries
- 1 sweet potato, chopped
- 1 tsp ground cumin
- 2 tsp ras-el-hanout
- 1 tbsp tomato purée
- ½ tsp honey
- 1 tbsp olive oil
- 1 chicken or lamb stock cube or stock pot
- ½ bunch coriander, chopped
- Couscous, to serve

INSTRUCTIONS
1. Brown the lamb in the oil over a medium to high heat. Tip it into the slow cooker once done. Cook the onion in the same frying pan for 5 minutes until starting to soften.
2. Tip in the carrots and spices and stir together. Add the tomato puree, 250ml of water, and the stock, and stir together, before tipping into the slow cooker.
3. Add the potato, cherries, honey, and another 500ml water to the slow cooker.
4. Cook for 8 hours on low, or 4 hours on high. Serve with a sprinkling of coriander and the couscous.

LASAGNE

● ●

SERVES 4 | PER SERVING - CALORIES: 448, FAT: 12G, CARBOHYDRATES: 46G, PROTEIN: 33G

INGREDIENTS
- 500g lean mince beef
- 400g can chopped tomatoes
- 2 garlic cloves, chopped
- 2 medium onions, finely sliced
- 4 celery sticks, finely diced
- 4 carrots, sliced
- 1 tbsp balsamic vinegar
- 1 tbsp fresh thyme leaves
- 2 tbsp tomato purée
- 2 tsp vegetable stock
- 2 tsp rapeseed oil
- 6 wholewheat lasagne sheets

FOR THE SAUCE:
- 400ml whole milk
- 50g wholemeal flour
- Generous grating of nutmeg
- 15g finely grated parmesan
- 1 bay leaf

INSTRUCTIONS
1. Cook the garlic, onion, celery, and carrots in the oil over a medium heat until they start to colour. Tip in the meat, stirring and breaking it up until it browns. Pour in the tomatoes, along with a quarter of a can of water. Stir in the balsamic vinegar, puree, stock, thyme, and lots of black pepper. Increase the heat to a boil, and simmer for 5 to 10 minutes.
2. Put half of the mince in the slow cooker, and top with 3 lasagne sheets. Add the remaining meat, and then the remaining lasagne. Cook on low whilst you make up the sauce.
3. Put the milk and flour in a saucepan over a low heat with the nutmeg and bay leaf and whisk continuously until it thickens. Cook for a couple minutes to cook the flour. Take out the bay leaf, and fold through the cheese. Spread the sauce on top of the lasagne and cook for 3 hours. Leave to stand for 10 minutes.

LEG OF LAMB WITH GRAVY

SERVES 6 | PER SERVING - CALORIES: 574, FAT: 37G, CARBOHYDRATES: 16G, PROTEIN: 43G

INGREDIENTS

- 1.3kg boneless leg of lamb, tied
- 2 tbsp olive oil
- 300ml lamb stock
- 2 red onions, cut into wedges
- 30g unsalted butter
- 2 tbsp plain flour
- 200ml red wine
- 2 garlic cloves, sliced
- 5 sprigs of rosemary
- 5 sprigs of thyme
- Mashed potatoes and steamed vegetables, to serve

INSTRUCTIONS

1. Brown the lamb in the oil over a medium to high heat. Set the slow cooker to low. Melt the butter in a saucepan until it foams, then stir in the flour. Whisk in the stock gradually until incorporated, add the wine and bring to the boil. Set aside.
2. Put the onion, garlic, thyme, and rosemary into your slow cooker and sit the lamb on top. Pour over the lamb gravy. Cook on low for 8 hours.
3. Remove the lamb and set, covered, on a plate. Strain the liquid into a pan and simmer until slightly thickened. Serve the lamb thickly sliced or shredded with mashed potatoes, green veg and the gravy.

MACARONI CHEESE

SERVES 4 | PER SERVING - CALORIES: 666, FAT: 31G, CARBOHYDRATES: 71G, PROTEIN: 25G

INGREDIENTS

- 350g macaroni pasta
- 600ml whole milk
- 50g soft cheese
- 50g butter, cubed
- 100g grated mature cheddar, plus extra to serve
- 20g parmesan or vegetarian alternative, plus extra to serve

INSTRUCTIONS

1. Rinse the pasta in boiling water and drain. Tip everything into the slow cooker and mix. Season to taste and cook for 1 hour on low. Stir the contents of the pan, then cook for a further 30 minutes until the pasta is soft and the sauce has reduced.
2. If needed, cook for a further 10 minutes with the lid off, or add a splash more milk. Serve with extra cheese.

TURKEY MEATBALLS

SERVES 4 | PER SERVING - CALORIES: 260, FAT: 5G, CARBOHYDRATES: 21G, PROTEIN: 29G

INGREDIENTS

- 500g tomato passata
- 450g mince turkey
- 2 celery sticks, finely diced
- 1 garlic clove, crushed
- 2 garlic cloves, thinly sliced
- 2 carrots, finely diced
- 1 onion, finely chopped
- Pinch paprika
- 2 tbsp chopped parsley
- 4 tbsp porridge oats
- 1 tbsp rapeseed oil

INSTRUCTIONS

1. In a frying pan, fry the celery, onion, garlic, and carrots in the oil for a minute. Stir in the passata and parsley, then tip into the slow cooker.
2. To make the meatballs, tip the mince into a large bowl. Add the oats, paprika, garlic and plenty of black pepper, and mix everything together with your hands. Divide the mixture into 20 lumps about the size of a walnut and roll each piece into a meatball. Spray or run a non-stick pan with a little oil and gently cook the meatballs until they start to brown. Add them to the tomato base and cook on low for 5 hours. Serve over rice or pasta if you like, or with a green salad.

PORK CASSEROLE

SERVES 4 | PER SERVING - CALORIES: 416, FAT: 21G, CARBOHYDRATES: 13G, PROTEIN: 41G

INGREDIENTS

- 4 pork shoulder steaks (about 750g), cut into large chunks
- 1 leek, chopped
- 1 carrot, chopped
- 1 tbsp vegetable or rapeseed oil
- 1 onion, chopped
- Bundle of woody herbs (bouquet garni) – we used 2 bay leaves, 3 sage leaves and 4 thyme sprigs, plus a few thyme leaves to serve
- 2 tsp cornflour
- 1 chicken stock cube
- 1 tbsp cider vinegar
- 2 tsp Dijon mustard
- 1 tbsp honey

INSTRUCTIONS

1. Heat the oil in a frying pan over a high heat. Season the pork, then add to the hot pan. Avoid overcrowding the meat – you may want to do this in batches. Cook the meat until browned, then transfer to the slow cooker. Add both the leeks and onions to the same pan, and cook for 2 minutes until they start to soften. Add a couple tablespoons of water, and scrape any stuck bits from the pan, then transfer to the slow cooker. Tip the stock, mustard, vinegar, herbs, and carrots into the slow cooker, and top up with enough water to submerge all the vegetables. Cook for 6 to 8 hours on low, or 5 to 6 hours on high.
2. In a saucepan, mix the cornflour and honey with 1-2 tsp of liquid from the slow cooker to make a smooth paste. Add 100ml more liquid, bring to a simmer until thickened, then stir back into the casserole. Serve with mash or dumplings, scattered with thyme leaves.

PORK FILLET WITH APPLES

SERVES 4 | PER SERVING - CALORIES: 344, FAT: 14G, CARBOHYDRATES: 18G, PROTEIN: 33G

INGREDIENTS

- ½ tbsp rapeseed oil
- 500g pork fillet, sliced into medallions
- 1 medium onion, finely chopped
- 3 eating apples
- 150ml low-salt chicken stock
- 1 tbsp Dijon mustard
- 4 sage leaves, finely sliced
- 2 tbsp half-fat crème fraiche

INSTRUCTIONS

1. Heat the slow cooker. Heat the oil in a pan and brown the pork on each side. Add the onion, and fry for a couple of minutes, before stirring in the mustard and stock. Transfer to the slow cooker.
2. Core and cut the apples into quarters, add them to the pot with the sage. Season with pepper. Cook for 4 hours on low, then stir through the crème fraiche.

PORK LOIN WITH WHITE WINE

SERVES 6 | PER SERVING - CALORIES: 597, FAT: 41G, CARBOHYDRATES: 9G, PROTEIN: 42G

INGREDIENTS

- 2kg pork loin, skin removed, and fat scored
- 250ml chicken or pork stock
- 150ml white wine
- 350g shallots
- 2 eating apples, such as Braeburns or Coxes, peeled, cored, and cut into wedges
- 2 garlic cloves
- 1 small celeriac, peeled, quartered, and cut into chunks
- 3 sprigs fresh thyme
- 1 tsp fennel seeds
- 1 ½ tbsp honey
- 1 tbsp Dijon mustard
- 2 tbsp rapeseed or olive oil

INSTRUCTIONS

1. Crush the garlic, thyme, and fennel, then add a tablespoon of oil and plenty of seasoning. Form into a paste. Rub the paste into the pork, and chill for a minimum of 2 hours, but ideally 24 hours.
2. Pour boiling water over the shallots, then set aside to cool until you can manage them. Cut off the root and remove the skins. Heat the rest of the oil in a frying pan and brown the shallots. Tip into the slow cooker once browned. Add the celeriac and apples, season to taste, and mix well.
3. Brown the pork in the same frying pan on all sides. Add the pork to the slow cooker. Tip the wine into the frying pan, bubble, and scrape the pan to pick up any stuck bits. Tip in the stock, mustard, and honey, stir for another minute, and then pour into the slow cooker. Cook on low for 5 to 6 hours, turning the pork halfway through the cook time.
4. Take out the pork and wrap it in foil. Let the pork stand for 10 minutes.

RATATOUILLE

SERVES 6 | PER SERVING - CALORIES: 162, FAT: 5G, CARBOHYDRATES: 17G, PROTEIN: 6G

INGREDIENTS

- 400g can plum tomatoes
- 2 large aubergines, cubed
- 6 large tomatoes, chopped
- 3 mixed peppers, chopped
- 3 courgettes, halved and chopped
- 1 red onion, sliced
- 2 garlic cloves
- 2 tbsp olive oil
- 1 ½ tbsp red wine vinegar
- 2 tsp brown sugar
- 1 tbsp tomato purée
- Few sprigs of thyme
- Small bunch of basil, chopped, plus extra to serve

INSTRUCTIONS

1. Cook the onion in a frying pan with the oil until it starts to soften and turn translucent. Add the garlic and cook for a further minute. Turn the heat up to medium to high and cook the aubergine for around 5 minutes until golden brown.
2. Cook the courgettes and peppers until just starting to soften, around 5 minutes. Stir through the vinegar, tomato puree, tomatoes, herbs, sugar, and salt, then bring to the boil.
3. Put everything in the slow cooker, then cook on low for 5 to 6 hours.

PORK SHOULDER

SERVES 8 | PER SERVING - CALORIES: 245, FAT: 9G, CARBOHYDRATES: 1G, PROTEIN: 34G

INGREDIENTS

- 1.5kg pork shoulder
- 2 tbsp olive oil
- 1 garlic bulb
- 250ml chicken stock
- 250ml white wine
- 4 bay leaves
- 2 sprigs of rosemary
- 1 tsp black peppercorns

SARA R. ADAMS

INSTRUCTIONS

1. Trim the fat from the pork. Season the pork with plenty of salt and pepper, then brown in the oil over a medium to high heat. Transfer the pork to the slow cooker. Add the remaining ingredients, then cook for 6 to 8 hours on low.
2. Take the pork out of the slow cooker, and shred. Take the herbs out of the slow cooker, and squeeze the garlic cloves out of their skins and back into the sauce. Put the meat back in the sauce and stir through before serving.

BEEF POT ROAST

SERVES 8 | PER SERVING - CALORIES: 470, FAT: 25G, CARBOHYDRATES: 12G, PROTEIN: 36G

INGREDIENTS

- 1.6 kg beef brisket
- 300ml beef stock
- 500ml red wine
- 1 onion, chopped
- 2 garlic cloves, crushed
- 3 sticks of celery, chopped
- 2 tbsp plain flour
- 2 tbsp sunflower oil
- 2 parsnips, chopped
- 3 carrots, chopped
- 2 tsp English mustard
- 2 bay leaves
- 80g button mushrooms

INSTRUCTIONS

1. Heat the oil in a pan. Dust the brisket with the plain flour, and season well.
2. Put the carrots, celery, parsnips, onions and mushrooms in the slow cooker, and set it on low.
3. Brown the beef, then add it to the slow cooker on top of the vegetables.
4. Add the garlic, mustard, and bay to the slow cooker, followed by the stock and wine. Cook for 7 hours.
5. Preheat the oven to 180C. Remove the beef, and roast for 20 minutes.
6. Whilst the beef roasts, transfer the cooking liquid to a pan and boil until it reduces.
7. Serve the beef with the vegetables, gravy, and roast potatoes.

PULLED CHICKEN

SERVES 8 | PER SERVING - CALORIES: 398, FAT: 17G, CARBOHYDRATES: 22G, PROTEIN: 37G

INGREDIENTS

- 10-12 boneless chicken thighs
- 250ml passata
- 100g barbecue sauce
- 2 tbsp chipotle or chilli paste
- 2 red onions, halved and sliced
- 2 garlic cloves, crushed
- 2 tsp paprika
- 2 tbsp vegetable or rapeseed oil
- 1 lime, juiced
- 1 tbsp light brown soft sugar

INSTRUCTIONS

1. Heat 1 tablespoon of oil over a high heat and brown the chicken. Transfer to the slow cooker once cooked. Add the remaining oil and fry the onions until they soften. Stir in the paprika and garlic and cook for a minute. Transfer to the slow cooker. Swirl 100ml of water around the frying pan, then add this to the slow cooker too.
2. Add the chilli paste, BBQ sauce, passata, sugar, and lime juice to the slow cooker, then season and stir. Cook for 6 to 8 hours on low. Shred the chicken, then serve with the sauce.

SWEET PULLED PORK

SERVES 8 | PER SERVING - CALORIES: 325, FAT: 21G, CARBOHYDRATES: 7G, PROTEIN: 27G

INGREDIENTS

FOR THE PORK:

- 2kg pork shoulder, skin removed
- 2 tsp oil
- 1 onion, sliced
- ½ tsp cinnamon
- 2 tsp smoked paprika
- 1 tbsp flour

TO COOK:

- 4 garlic cloves, crushed
- 160ml cloudy apple juice
- 1 tbsp black treacle
- 2 tbsp honey
- 3 tbsp apple cider vinegar
- 50g onion marmalade

TO SERVE:

- 160ml cloudy apple juice
- 3 tbsp apple cider vinegar
- 4 garlic cloves, crushed
- 2 tbsp honey
- 1 tbsp black treacle
- 50g onion marmalade

INSTRUCTIONS

1. Place the onion in the slow cooker. In a bowl, mix a teaspoon of salt, teaspoon of pepper, the smoked paprika, and the cinnamon. Put the flour onto a plate then rub the spice mixture over the pork.
2. Heat the oil and cover the pork in the flour before browning it in the hot pan. Once the meat is browned, transfer it to the slow cooker.
3. In a large jug combine all the ingredients for slow cooking the pork then pours over the meat. Cook for 8 hours on low.
4. Take the pork out, leaving the liquid in the slow cooker. Shred with two forks in a large bowl or tray, then stir through a ladle's worth of the liquid.
5. Coat the fennel and apple in the lemon juice, and season to taste. Serve in rolls with the pulled pork. Spread the rolls with a little English mustard and mayonnaise if you like.

BBQ RIBS

SERVES 4 | PER SERVING - CALORIES: 414, FAT: 24G, CARBOHYDRATES: 24.7G, PROTEIN: 23G

INGREDIENTS

- 1 ½kg meaty pork ribs
- 350g barbecue sauce
- 2 pork stock cubes
- 2 bay leaves
- 1 tsp coriander seed
- 1 tsp mustard seed
- 1 tsp peppercorn

INSTRUCTIONS

1. Put the pork, 4 tbsp barbecue sauce, stock, bay, coriander, mustard, and peppercorns in the slow cooker. Pour in enough water to cover the meat. Slow cook on low for 8 - 9 hours until very tender but not completely falling off the bone.
2. Preheat the oven to 200C and remove the ribs from the slow cooker using tongs. Handle them carefully as the meat will be very tender and may start to fall off. Baste with the remaining barbecue sauce and lay on a foil-lined oven tray. Cook for 20 – 30 minutes until starting to crisp on outside.

SIMPLE ROAST CHICKEN

SERVES 4 | PER SERVING - CALORIES: 497, FAT: 30G, CARBOHYDRATES: 7G, PROTEIN: 49G

INGREDIENTS

- 1 whole small or medium chicken
- 2 tbsp butter, softened
- 2 carrots, chopped
- 1 large onion, cut into thick slices
- 1 bay leaf

INSTRUCTIONS

1. Place the onion and carrot in the bottom of the slow cooker, and tip in 100ml of boiling water. Carefully pull the chicken skin away from the breast. Mix salt and pepper into the butter, and push under the skin. Add the bay leaf to the chicken cavity, then transfer to the slow cooker.
2. Cook for 5 hours on low, then check the chicken is cooked. Lift the chicken up so any trapped liquid comes out, then cook for a further 30 minutes on high. To brown the skin, cook the chicken in a roasting pan under the grill for a couple minutes.
3. Sieve the liquid to separate the vegetables and gravy.

EASY SAUSAGE CASSEROLE

SERVES 4 | PER SERVING - CALORIES: 449, FAT: 28G, CARBOHYDRATES: 27G, PROTEIN: 17G

INGREDIENTS

- 12 chipolatas, halved
- 4 carrots, cut into fat pieces
- 2 red onions, finely chopped
- 1 sweet potato, peeled and cut into chunks
- 400g tin tomatoes
- 1 celery stick, finely chopped
- 1-2 tbsp rapeseed oil
- 1 tbsp tomato purée or tomato and veg purée
- 1 thyme sprig
- 1 rosemary sprig
- 1 beef stock cube or stock pot

INSTRUCTIONS

1. Fry the celery and onions in the oil for around 5 minutes, then transfer to the slow cooker. Fry the carrots briefly and add them too.
2. Brown the sausages in the same frying pan. Make sure to get a good colour on the skins as they won't get any darker when added to the slow cooker. Put the sausages, sweet potato, and tomatoes in the slow cooker.
3. Put the purée in the frying pan and add 250ml boiling water, swirl everything around to pick up every bit of flavour and tip the lot into the slow cooker. Add the herbs, stock cube and some pepper. Do not add salt until the casserole is cooked as the stock can be quite salty. Cook for 4 hours on high or 8 hours on low.

SHEPHERD'S PIE

SERVES 4 | PER SERVING - CALORIES: 439, FAT: 10G, CARBOHYDRATES: 57G, PROTEIN: 23G

INGREDIENTS

- 1 tbsp olive oil
- 250g lean mince lamb or beef
- 650g potatoes, peeled and chopped
- 250g sweet potatoes, peeled and chopped
- 400g can lentils, or white beans
- 1 onion, chopped
- 3-4 thyme sprigs
- 2 carrots, finely diced
- 1 tbsp plain flour
- 1 tsp Worcestershire sauce
- 1 tbsp tomato purée
- 2 tbsp crème fraiche

INSTRUCTIONS

1. Heat the slow cooker if necessary. Heat the oil in a large frying pan. Cook the thyme and onions for a couple of minutes, stirring constantly. Add the carrots, and fry until they start to brown. Stir in the mince and fry for 1-2 minutes until no longer pink. Stir in the flour then cook for another 1-2 minutes. Add the tomato puree and lentils, season with pepper, and add the Worcestershire sauce. Add a little water if the mixture seems dry. Put everything in the slow cooker.
2. Meanwhile cook both lots of potatoes in simmering water for 12-13 minutes or until they are cooked through. Drain well and then mash with the crème fraiche. Add the mash to the slow cooker, and cook for 5 hours on low. Crisp up the potato topping under the grill if you like.

SPAGHETTI BOLOGNESE

SERVES 12 | PER SERVING - CALORIES: 295, FAT: 12G, CARBOHYDRATES: 13G, PROTEIN: 34G

INGREDIENTS

- 6 smoked bacon rashers, roughly chopped
- 1 ½kg lean minced beef
- 4 x 400g cans chopped tomatoes
- 4 tbsp olive oil
- 4 tbsp red wine vinegar
- 4 onions, chopped
- 8 garlic cloves, crushed
- 3 carrots, chopped
- 4 celery sticks, chopped
- 500g mushrooms, sliced
- 2 tbsp dried mixed herbs
- 6 tbsp tomato purée
- 2 bay leaves
- 1 tbsp sugar
- Large glass red wine (optional)
- Cooked spaghetti, and Parmesan to serve

INSTRUCTIONS

1. Brown the mince and bacon in the oil. Tip into the slow cooker once cooked.
2. Put everything in the slow cooker and stir. Cook for 6 to 8 hours on low. Take the lid off, and cook for a further hour on high to thicken the sauce.
3. Serve with cooked spaghetti and grated or shaved parmesan.

SPANISH CHICKEN

SERVES 6 | PER SERVING - CALORIES: 447, FAT: 27G, CARBOHYDRATES: 7G, PROTEIN: 34G

INGREDIENTS

- 12 chicken thighs, skin removed
- 225g chorizo picante, sliced
- 1 onion, halved and sliced
- 3 peppers, cut into chunks
- 150g drained pitted Spanish pimento stuffed green olives
- 300ml chicken stock
- 300ml dry white wine
- 2 tbsp olive oil
- 1 tbsp tomato purée

INSTRUCTIONS

1. Fry the onion in the oil until it starts to colour.
2. Transfer the onion to the slow cooker, and fry the chorizo and chicken until they start to colour.
3. Add the chicken, chorizo, onion, peppers, and olives to the slow cooker.
4. Pour the tomato puree, white wine, and stock into the pan. Scrape up any stuck bits, then tip this all in the slow cooker. Cook on low for 6 hours.

SPICED ROOT AND LENTIL CASSEROLE

SERVES 4 | PER SERVING - CALORIES: 333, FAT: 9G, CARBOHYDRATES: 44G, PROTEIN: 13G

INGREDIENTS

- 650ml hot vegan vegetable stock
- 3 carrots, peeled and sliced
- 530g parsnips, peeled and sliced
- 150g red lentils, rinsed
- 3 garlic cloves, crushed
- 1 onion, finely chopped
- 2 tbsp olive oil
- 1 tbsp smoked paprika
- 2 tbsp mild curry powder
- 2 bay leaves
- Lemon juice, to serve

INSTRUCTIONS

1. Set the slow cooker on low. Fry the onions in the oil for 10 minutes until soft, then add the parsnips and carrots and cook for 10 minutes more until the vegetables are golden. Add the spices and garlic, then fry for another 4 to 5 minutes until the spices are fragrant. Add a couple tablespoons of water if needed. Add to the slow cooker, then stir in the stock, bay, lentils, and seasoning.
2. Cook on low for 5 to 6 hours. Add salt, pepper, and lemon juice to taste.

BEEF STROGANOFF

SERVES 4 | PER SERVING - CALORIES: 988, FAT: 61G, CARBOHYDRATES: 76G, PROTEIN: 31G

INGREDIENTS

- 750g stewing steak, such as chuck, cut into strips
- 2 garlic cloves, crushed
- 2 onions, halved and sliced
- 200g chestnut mushrooms, halved
- 1 tbsp vegetable or rapeseed oil, plus a little more if needed
- 1 beef stock cube, or 1 tbsp liquid stock
- 1 tbsp Dijon mustard
- 50g butter
- 2 tsp cornflour
- 200g soured cream
- Small bunch parsley, chopped tagliatelle or mashed potato and a pinch of paprika, to serve

INSTRUCTIONS

1. Brown the beef in the oil over a high heat, transferring to the slow cooker once browned. Fry the onion and garlic in the same pan, then transfer to the slow cooker. Add a little water to the pan and scrape any stuck bits from the bottom. Tip everything into the slow cooker.
2. Pour the stock and mustard into the slow cooker, then season to taste. Add water to submerge the beef. Cook for 6 to 8 hours on low, or 5 to 6 hours on high.
3. Thirty minutes before the end, cook the mushrooms in the butter until they start to caramelise. Transfer to the slow cooker. In the pan, stir the cornflour into a ladle of liquid from the slow cooker to make a paste. Stir in another ladleful and bring to a simmer. Once thick, add this and the sour cream to the slow cooker. Cook on high for a further 20 minutes. Stir through the parsley and serve with pasta or mash.

THAI CHICKEN CURRY

SERVES 4 | PER SERVING - CALORIES: 473, FAT: 25G, CARBOHYDRATES: 13G, PROTEIN: 49G

INGREDIENTS

- 3 tbsp green Thai curry paste
- 400ml coconut milk
- 800g boneless chicken thighs, halved
- 1 aubergine, chopped
- 2 fresh lemongrass stalks, sliced
- Thumb-sized piece root ginger, sliced
- 6 lime leaves
- 1 tbsp brown sugar
- 1 tbsp fish sauce

INSTRUCTIONS

1. Gently fry the Thai green curry paste in a dry non-stick frying pan until fragrant then pour in the coconut milk. Stir until smooth, then take the pan off the heat.
2. Put everything excluding the coconut milk into the slow cooker.
3. Stir in the coconut milk, then cook for 6 to 8 hours on low.
4. Serve with rice and Thai basil.

TURKEY BREAST WITH WINE AND BACON

SERVES 8 | PER SERVING - CALORIES: 297, FAT: 12G, CARBOHYDRATES: 7G, PROTEIN: 35G

INGREDIENTS

- 16 rashers smoked streaky bacon
- 2 turkey breast fillets
- 500ml chicken stock
- 150ml dry white wine
- 2 carrots, sliced
- 15g dried porcini mushrooms
- 1 onion, halved and thickly sliced
- 2 tbsp fresh thyme leaves, plus extra to serve
- 1 tbsp sunflower oil
- 2 bay leaves
- 2 tbsp plain flour

INSTRUCTIONS

1. Lay a piece of string twice the length of the turkey on a board. Arrange another 4 lengths of string large enough to tie around the width of the turkey fillet across the first string, winding them around the first string once so they do not move much. Place 8 rashers of the bacon across the string, in the same direction as the 4 strings. Overlap the rashers slightly. Scatter with 1 tablespoon of the thyme and add a generous amount of black pepper.
2. Lay a turkey fillet on top of the bacon, and then wrap the bacon around it using the strings. Tie the strings snuggly, but not too tight. Cut any excess string off with scissors.
3. Brown the fillet in the oil in a frying pan, then place in the slow cooker. Repeat with the second turkey fillet.
4. Add the carrots and onions to the pan, and fry until starting to brown. Put the contents of the frying pan in the slow cooker, then add the mushrooms and bay. Lay the turkey on top. Tip the wine and stock into the frying pan, and quickly bring to the boil before pouring into the slow cooker. Cook on low for 3 to 4 hours.
5. Take out the turkey, then wrap in foil to keep warm. Stir the flour into 4 tablespoons of water to make a paste. Strain the liquid from the slow cooker into a saucepan, and whisk in the flour paste. Stir continuously until the sauce thickens to your tastes. Serve the turkey with the gravy, and vegetables of your choice.

VEGETABLE STEW WITH CHEDDAR DUMPLINGS

SERVES 6 | PER SERVING - CALORIES: 554, FAT: 33G, CARBOHYDRATES: 40G, PROTEIN: 18G

INGREDIENTS

- 400ml vegetable stock
- 2 x 400g cans butter or cannellini beans, drained and rinsed
- 220ml crème fraiche
- 220g baby carrots, scrubbed, trimmed, and halved if large
- 2 courgettes, cut into large chunks
- 3 garlic cloves, crushed
- 3 leeks, cut into thick slices
- 220g broad beans or peas
- 220g spinach
- 4 thyme, rosemary, or tarragon sprigs
- 2 tbsp olive oil
- 3 ½ tbsp plain flour
- 1 tbsp wholegrain mustard
- 1 bay leaf
- ½ small bunch of parsley, finely chopped, plus extra to serve

FOR THE DUMPLINGS:

- 50g vegetarian suet or cold butter, grated
- 100g mature cheddar
- 100g self-rising flour
- ½ small bunch of parsley, finely chopped

INSTRUCTIONS

1. Set the slow cooker to low. Fry the carrots in half of the oil until golden. Tip into the slow cooker.
2. Add the remaining oil, then cook the leaks with a little salt until they soften, about 5 minutes. Slowly add the stock, stirring constantly until smooth. Bring the frying pan to the boil and add everything to the slow cooker. Put the beans, herbs, and courgettes in the slow cooker, and top up with water if needed to submerge the vegetables. Cook for 4 hours.
3. Next, make the dumplings. Tip the flour and suet into a bowl and mix in the butter until evenly distributed. Add the parsley, cheese, cracked black pepper, and salt. Stir in 3 to 4 tbsp water and mix by hand to create a sticky dough. Divide into six and shape into balls.
4. Tip the beans, mustard, crème fraiche, and spinach into the slow cooker. Turn the slow cooker up to high. Add the dumplings, and cook for another 1 or 2 hours until the dumplings have doubled and are firm. Scatter across the parsley to serve.

VEGETABLE LASAGNE

SERVES 4 | PER SERVING - CALORIES: 325, FAT: 11G, CARBOHYDRATES: 36G, PROTEIN: 15G

INGREDIENTS

- 6 wholewheat lasagne sheets
- 2 tsp vegetable stock
- 1 large aubergine, sliced across length for maximum surface area
- 400g can chopped tomatoes
- 2 onions, sliced
- 1 red and 1 yellow pepper, roughly sliced
- 2 courgettes, diced
- 2 garlic cloves, chopped
- 1 tbsp rapeseed oil
- 2 tbsp tomato purée
- 15g fresh basil, chopped plus a few leaves
- 125g vegetarian mozzarella, chopped

INSTRUCTIONS

1. Fry the onions and garlic in the rapeseed oil over a medium to high heat for 5 minutes, stirring regularly until softened.
2. Add the courgettes, peppers, chopped tomatoes, tomato puree, vegetable stock, and basil.
3. Mix well, and fry for 5 minutes. Do not add any more liquid.
4. Slice one aubergine, and lay half of it into the slow cooker. Top with three lasagne sheets.
5. Top with a third of the ratatouille mix, then the rest of the aubergine, followed by the remaining lasagne. Finish with the leftover ratatouille.
6. Cook for 2 ½ to 3 ½ hours on high until the pasta is soft. Turn the slow cooker off.
7. Shred the mozzarella, and place over the top. Put the lid on and let it settle for 10 minutes until the cheese melts.
8. Serve with additional basil and rocket.

VEGETABLE CURRY

SERVES 4 | PER SERVING - CALORIES: 391, FAT: 22G, CARBOHYDRATES: 30G, PROTEIN: 11G

INGREDIENTS

- 1 red pepper, deseeded and sliced
- 175g peas, defrosted if frozen
- 200g butternut squash, cut into chunks
- 400ml can light coconut milk
- 1 small aubergine, halved and sliced
- 2 tsp vegetable stock powder
- 1 red chilli, deseeded and sliced
- 3 tbsp mild curry paste
- 1 tbsp finely chopped ginger
- 3 garlic cloves, sliced
- 1 lime, juiced, to taste
- 15g coriander, chopped

INSTRUCTIONS

1. Put everything apart from the peas and coriander in the slow cooker. Chill in the fridge overnight.
2. The next day, cook the curry on low for 6 hours. Finish by stirring through the peas and coriander; the temperature of the curry should heat the peas on its own.

TURKEY PHO

SERVES 4 | PER SERVING - CALORIES: 334, FAT: 6G, CARBOHYDRATES: 36G, PROTEIN: 33G

INGREDIENTS

FOR THE STOCK:

- 1 turkey or chicken carcass, meat removed
- 50g ginger, peeled and sliced
- 2 onions, halved
- 2-3 tbsp fish sauce
- 3 whole star anise
- 2 cloves
- ½ tbsp coriander seeds
- 2 cinnamon sticks
- 2 tbsp sugar

FOR THE PHO:

- 450g cooked and sliced turkey or chicken
- 220g rice noodles
- 100g beansprouts
- 2 red chillies, sliced
- 1 lime, cut into wedges
- Handful of Thai basil, mint, and coriander leaves, chopped
- Hoisin and sriracha to serve

INSTRUCTIONS

1. Fry the ginger and onion in a dry pan until coloured. Tip into the slow cooker and set on low. Add the spices, and cook for a couple minutes until fragrant, then transfer to the slow cooker.
2. Add 3 to 4 litres of water and the carcass to the slow cooker. Cook on low for 8 to 10 hours.
3. Sieve the stock, removing the spices and bones. Season to taste with the sugar and fish sauce.
4. Cook the noodles and divide between bowls. Add the meat and bean sprouts, then pour over the stock. Serve with herbs, chilli, lime wedges, and the sauces.

TUSCAN CHICKEN

SERVES 6 | PER SERVING - CALORIES: 528, FAT: 31G, CARBOHYDRATES: 12G, PROTEIN: 48G

INGREDIENTS

- 3 tbsp virgin olive oil
- 120ml low-salt chicken stock
- 120ml double cream
- 450g baby potatoes, halved
- 1 red pepper, sliced
- 950g chicken thighs, bone in
- 60g grated Parmesan
- 2 tbsp melted butter
- 1 tsp garlic powder
- 1 tsp dried oregano
- Salt and pepper to season

INSTRUCTIONS

1. Season the chicken with salt and pepper, then brown in a tablespoon of oil over a mediu around 3 minutes each side.
2. Meanwhile, in a large slow cooker, combine potatoes, pepper, broth, cream, Parmes spices. Season to taste, then put the chicken on top.
3. Cook on high for 3 to 4 hours, or low for 6 to 8 hours.
4. Garnish with parsley and more Parmesan, before serving.

CHICKEN AND BROCCOLI

SERVES 4 | PER SERVING - CALORIES: 550, FAT: 18G, CARBOHYDRATES: 26G, PROTEIN: 68G

INGREDIENTS

- 2 cloves of garlic
- 1 tsp ginger, minced
- 60ml low sodium soy sauce
- 60ml honey
- 2 tbsp rice wine vinegar
- 1 tbsp ketchup
- 1 tbsp Sriracha
- 1 tsp sesame oil
- 900g chicken breasts
- 1 tbsp cornflour
- 1 large broccoli, cut into florets

INSTRUCTIONS

1. Stir together the honey, sesame oil, ginger, ketchup, vinegar, Sriracha, soy sauce, and garlic in a bowl.
2. Season the chicken breast, then add to the slow cooker. Pour over the sauce mix and toss to combined.
3. Cook for 4 hours on low.
4. Mix the cornflour with 60ml of cold water to create a smooth paste. Mix in the paste and stir through the broccoli. Cook for an hour until the broccoli is tender.
5. Cut the cooked chicken into small pieces, then return to slow cooker and toss in the sauce.
6. Garnish with spring onions and sesame seeds and serve with rice.

BUFFALO CHICKEN WINGS

SERVES 6 | PER SERVING - CALORIES: 287, FAT: 11G, CARBOHYDRATES: 0.4G, PROTEIN: 43G

INGREDIENTS

- 900g chicken wings
- 240ml buffalo or chilli wing sauce
- Salt and pepper to season

INSTRUCTIONS

1. Put the chicken in the slow cooker.
2. Mix the buffalo sauce and seasonings together and pour over the chicken wings.
3. Cook on high until the chicken wings are cooked through, around 2 ½ to 3 hours.
4. Heat the grill. Place the chicken wings on baking trays and cook under the grill for 5 minutes until crispy.
5. Garnish with chives and serve with ranch dressing.

GARLIC AND PARMESAN CHICKEN

SERVES 4 | PER SERVING - CALORIES: 639, FAT: 33G, CARBOHYDRATES: 15.2G, PROTEIN: 68G

INGREDIENTS

- 3 tbsp extra-virgin olive oil
- 900g bone-in chicken thighs
- 450g baby potatoes, quartered
- 2 tbsp butter
- 5 garlic cloves, chopped
- 2 tbsp fresh thyme
- 2 tbsp grated Parmesan

RUCTIONS

Heat a tablespoon of oil over a medium to high heat. Season the chicken, then brown until golden.

2. In the slow cooker, toss the potatoes with the remaining oil, butter, thyme, parsley, garlic, and parmesan. Season to taste and add the chicken. Cook on high for 4 hours, or on low for 8 hours.

3. Garnish with Parmesan before serving.

CHEESE AND BACON POTATOES

SERVES 6 | PER SERVING - CALORIES: 258, FAT: 8.9G, CARBOHYDRATES: 20G, PROTEIN: 25G

INGREDIENTS

- 900g baby potatoes, quartered
- 260g grated cheese
- 2 cloves of garlic, sliced
- 8 rashers of cooked bacon
- 2 spring onions, chopped
- 1 tbsp paprika
- Salt and pepper to season
- Sour cream to drizzle

INSTRUCTIONS

1. Line a slow cooker with foil and spray with cooking spray. Tip in half of the potatoes, spring onion, cheese, bacon, garlic, and paprika. Season with salt and pepper. Repeat.

2. Cook for 5 to 6 hours on high. About 20 to 30 minutes before serving, top with remaining cheese and bacon.

3. Garnish with more green onions and drizzle with sour cream before serving.

CHICKEN ALFREDO

SERVES 6 | PER SERVING - CALORIES: 771, FAT: 51G, CARBOHYDRATES: 25.6G, PROTEIN: 51G

INGREDIENTS

- 900g chicken breasts
- 480ml double cream
- 240ml chicken stock
- 4 tbsp butter
- ½ tsp garlic powder
- 30g grated Parmesan
- 250g pasta
- Salt and pepper to season

INSTRUCTIONS

1. In a slow cooker, add chicken, heavy cream, butter, and broth. Stir in the garlic powder, and season to taste with salt and pepper.

2. Cook for 2 hours to 2 ½ hours on high until the chicken is cooked. Transfer to a plate and shred with two forks, then set aside.

3. Put the chicken back in, and stir through the sauce.

BUFFALO CHICKEN MEATBALLS

SERVES 6 | PER SERVING - CALORIES: 384, FAT: 15.7G, CARBOHYDRATES: 11.3G, PROTEIN: 46G

INGREDIENTS

- 900g minced chicken or turkey
- 90g breadcrumbs
- 1 egg
- 1 tbsp chives
- 1 tsp cayenne pepper
- Salt and pepper to season
- 5 tbsp unsalted butter, melted
- 7 tbsp buffalo or hot sauce
- 1 tsp Worcestershire sauce
- ½ tsp garlic powder

INSTRUCTIONS

1. Preheat oven to 200C and line a large tray with greaseproof paper. Coat the chicken in breadcrumbs, and then cover with the egg, garlic, cayenne, and chives. Season with salt and pepper.
2. Roll mixture into 20 meatballs, around two tbsp chicken per ball. Bake until firm, about 5 minutes. Put in the slow cooker.
3. In a medium bowl, mix melted butter with hot sauce and Worcestershire sauce. Whisk to combine and pour over meatballs. Cook for 2 hours on low.
4. Serve with a drizzle of blue cheese and chives for garnish.

COMFORTING CHICKEN NOODLES

SERVES 6 | PER SERVING - CALORIES: 281, FAT: 9.2G, CARBOHYDRATES: 16.1G, PROTEIN: 32.4G

INGREDIENTS

- 2.5 litres of chicken stock
- 650g chicken breasts
- 230g egg noodles
- 2 stalks of celery, sliced
- 3 carrots, peeled and sliced
- 1 onion, chopped
- 3 cloves of garlic, minced
- 1 bay leaf
- 4 tsp fresh rosemary
- 4 tsp fresh thyme
- Salt and pepper to season

INSTRUCTIONS

1. In a slow cooker, combine all the ingredients apart from the chicken, and pour over the stock.
2. Cook for 6 to 8 hours on low. Discard the herbs and bay and shred the chicken. Put the chicken back in the slow cooker and stir in the noodles.
3. Cook on low for 20 to 30 minutes until the noodles are al dente.

CHEESE, CHICKEN AND BROCCOLI SOUP

SERVES 6 | PER SERVING - CALORIES: 587, FAT: 30G, CARBOHYDRATES: 18G, PROTEIN: 58G

INGREDIENTS

- 900g chicken breasts
- 1.25 litres of chicken stock
- 340g baby potatoes, quartered
- 1 large head of broccoli, cut into florets
- 1 onion, chopped
- Salt and pepper to season
- 30g plain flour
- 240ml double cream
- 200g grated cheddar
- 40g grated Parmesan
- Sour cream to serve

INSTRUCTIONS

1. Put the onion, potatoes, broccoli, and chicken in the slow cooker, and pour over the stock.
2. Cook for 5 to 6 hours on low.
3. Take the chicken out of the slow cooker, and shred in a bowl.
4. Mix the cream and flour in a bowl and pour into the slow cooker. Stir to combine. Put the chicken back in the slow cooker and stir in the cheeses. Cook for 30 minutes on high until the cheese melts.
5. Season to taste.
6. Ladle into soup bowls and serve immediately. Garnish with sour cream and more cheese.

CREAMY TORTELLINI SOUP

SERVES 4 | PER SERVING - CALORIES: 447, FAT: 30G, CARBOHYDRATES: 27G, PROTEIN: 17G

INGREDIENTS

- 500g seasoned sausage, browned
- Half an onion, chopped
- 1 large carrot, chopped
- 1 stalk of celery, chopped
- 2 cloves of garlic, minced
- 1 crumbled chicken stock cube
- ½ tsp salt
- 375ml chicken stock
- 2 tbsp cornflour mixed in to 60ml of water
- 400g evaporated milk
- 200g tortellini or other pasta
- 60g baby spinach
- 90ml milk

INSTRUCTIONS

1. Put the carrots, onion, garlic, celery, seasonings, and sausages in the slow cooker. Sprinkle over the stock cube and pour over the stock. Cook on high for 4 hours, or low for 7 hours.
2. Uncover and skim any fat that is sitting on the top of the soup with a spoon, discard. Stir in the cornflour mixture with the evaporated milk. Add the tortellini and mix well. Cover again and cook on HIGH heat setting for a further 45 minutes until the soup has thickened, and the tortellini is soft and cooked through.
3. Add in the spinach, pressing the leaves down to completely submerse into the liquid. Cover again for a further 5-10 minutes until the leaves have wilted.
4. Pour in the milk gradually to reach your desired consistency. Season to taste.

SALSA, HONEY AND LIME CHICKEN TACOS

MAKES 12 MINI TACOS | PER SERVING (RECIPE ONLY) - CALORIES: 147, FAT: 3.1G, CARBOHYDRATES: 14G, PROTEIN: 16G

INGREDIENTS

- 950g chicken breast
- 120ml lime juice
- 120ml honey
- 250ml salsa
- 1 tbsp olive oil
- 1 ½ tsp chilli powder
- ½ tsp cumin
- ½ tsp black pepper
- 1 ½ tsp salt
- 1 tsp onion powder
- 1 tsp garlic powder
- ½ tsp smoked paprika
- Hot sauce to taste

INSTRUCTIONS

1. Rub the chicken breasts with olive oil and put in the slow cooker. Add the rest of the ingredients excluding the hot sauce. Cook on low for 6 to 7 hours until the chicken can be shredded.
2. Remove the chicken and leave it to rest for 5 minutes. Shred the chicken and put back in the slow cooker. Cook for another 20 to 30 minutes. Drain the excess liquid before serving.
3. Serve in tacos with toppings of your choice.

PORK LO MEIN

SERVES 6 | PER SERVING - CALORIES: 682, FAT: 26G, CARBOHYDRATES: 70G, PROTEIN: 39G

INGREDIENTS

- 900g boneless pork shoulder
- 270g broccoli florets
- 2 carrots, sliced
- 2 stalks of celery, diced
- 125g peas
- 150g canned sliced water chestnuts, drained
- 450g dried spaghetti

FOR THE SAUCE:

- 80ml reduced sodium soy sauce
- 3 cloves of garlic, minced
- 2 tbsp brown sugar
- 1 tbsp sambal oelek or fresh chilli paste
- 1 tbsp fish sauce
- 1 tbsp grated ginger
- 1 tsp sesame oil

INSTRUCTIONS

1. Whisk together soy sauce, garlic, brown sugar, sambal oelek, ginger, and sesame oil in the slow cooker. Tip in the pork. Cook for 7 to 8 hours on low, or 3 to 4 hours on high.
2. Take the pork out of the slow cooker, and shred. Put the pork back in the pot. Stir in broccoli, carrots, celery, snow peas and chestnuts. Cook on high for 15 to 30 minutes until tender.
3. Cook the pasta, then drain well.
4. Serve the pasta immediately topped with the pork mixture.

SALSA CHICKEN WITH QUINOA CASSEROLE

SERVES 6 | PER SERVING - CALORIES: 488, FAT: 25G, CARBOHYDRATES: 32G, PROTEIN: 32G

INGREDIENTS

- 400g cooked chicken, shredded
- 225g quinoa
- 425g black beans, rinsed and drained
- 425g canned sweetcorn, drained
- 350ml salsa
- 480g chicken stock
- 225g grated cheese
- 115g diced green chilli
- 150g cheese of your choice
- 1 tsp ground cumin
- ½ tsp salt
- ½ tsp fresh ground pepper

INSTRUCTIONS

1. Put all the ingredients in the slow cooker, excluding half of the cheese and chicken stock. Level out the top with a spatula.
2. Add the remaining stock and cheese over the top.
3. Cook on high for 4 hours, or on low for 6 to 8 hours.

CHICKEN GNOCCHI SOUP

SERVES 8 | PER SERVING - CALORIES: 615, FAT: 29G, CARBOHYDRATES: 57G, PROTEIN: 30G

INGREDIENTS

- 450g chicken breast
- 1 onion, chopped
- 1 stalk of celery, chopped
- 1 carrot, chopped
- 2 tsp dried basil
- 2 tsp Italian-style seasoning
- 1 tsp salt
- 1 litre chicken stock
- 3 tbsp cornflour dissolved in 2 tbsp water
- Two cans of evaporated milk
- 900g gnocchi
- 6 rashers of bacon
- 3 garlic cloves, minced
- 150g fresh baby spinach

INSTRUCTIONS

1. Place the chicken, onion, celery, carrot, seasonings, and broth in the slow cooker. Cook on low for 6 to 8 hours, or on high for 5 hours. Shred the chicken.
2. Add the cornflour mixture, evaporated milk, and gnocchi. Stir and cover for a further 45 minutes to an hour until the soup is thick and the gnocchi has softened.
3. Whilst the soup is thickening, cut the bacon into small pieces until crispy. Drain on paper towels and dry the pan. Add the spinach and sauté. Take off the heat, then stir into the slow cooker.
4. Add added water if the soup is too thick. Season to taste.

BEEF RAGU

SERVES 8 | PER SERVING - CALORIES: 375, FAT: 6G, CARBOHYDRATES: 52G, PROTEIN: 27.7G

INGREDIENTS

- 1 tsp olive oil
- 6 garlic gloves, crushed
- 680g steak chunks
- Salt and pepper to season
- 800g canned chopped tomatoes
- 60ml beef broth
- 1 carrot, chopped
- 2 bay leaves
- 2 sprigs of fresh thyme
- 450g pasta
- Parmesan, ricotta, and parsley to top

INSTRUCTIONS

1. Cook the garlic for 2 minutes in the oil over a medium heat until it starts to colour.
2. Season the beef to taste. Transfer to a slow cooker. Pour the tomatoes and broth over the beef and add the garlic from step one, carrots, bay leaves, and thyme.
3. Cook on low for between 8 and 10 hours, or on high for about 6 hours. Discard the herbs and shred the beef in the pot using 2 forks.
4. Cook the pasta, then drain and return to the saucepan. Add the sauce from the slow cooker, and stir well until the pasta and sauce are combined.
5. Divide among 8 bowls and top each with Parmesan, ricotta, and parsley. Serve immediately.

LOW-CALORIE VEGETABLE LASAGNE

SERVES 9 | PER SERVING - CALORIES: 351, FAT: 12G, CARBOHYDRATES: 52G, PROTEIN: 27.7G

INGREDIENTS

- 750g tomato pasta sauce
- 9 thick lasagne sheets
- 680g low-fat ricotta or cottage cheese
- 200g kale
- Pesto to taste
- 260g mozzarella
- Parmesan to top

INSTRUCTIONS

1. Grease the slow cooker. Spread a quarter of the tomato sauce on the bottom so the noodles do not stick.
2. Break apart the noodles to cover the bottom. Add a third of the vegetables, pesto, sauce, cheese, and ricotta, and then another layer of noodles. Repeat the layering twice. Finish with noodles on the top, with a small amount of sauce and extra cheese.
3. Cook on low for 5 to 7 hours, or high for 3 hours. Switch the slow cooker off, and let it stand for an hour.

ASIAN STYLE CHICKEN LETTUCE WRAPS

SERVES 6 | PER SERVING - CALORIES: 567, FAT: 8.3G, CARBOHYDRATES: 70G, PROTEIN: 50G

INGREDIENTS

- 900g minced chicken or turkey
- 3 garlic cloves, minced
- 1 red pepper, chopped
- Half an onion, chopped
- 120ml hoisin sauce
- 2 tbsp soy sauce
- Salt and pepper to season
- 225g canned sliced water chestnuts, drained and rinsed
- 315g cooked white or brown rice
- 3 spring onions, sliced
- 1 tbsp rice vinegar
- 1 ½ tsp sesame oil
- 2 heads of iceberg lettuce

INSTRUCTIONS

1. Break up the minced chicken into the slow cooker. Put the garlic, onion, and pepper in the slow cooker, and toss with the soy sauce, hoisin, salt, and pepper. Cook on low for between 2 and 3 hours.
2. Stir in the water chestnuts, rice, spring onions, rice vinegar, and sesame oil. Cook for a further 15 minutes until hot, then season with extra salt to taste.
3. Serve wrapped in iceberg lettuce leaves.

SHRIMP TACOS

SERVES 5 | PER SERVING - CALORIES: 115, FAT: 2.5G, CARBOHYDRATES: 5G, PROTEIN: 14G

INGREDIENTS

- 950g shrimp, peeled and tails off
- 120ml chunky salsa
- 400g can of chopped tomatoes
- 1 tsp minced garlic
- 1 pepper, chopped
- Half an onion, chopped
- ½ tsp chilli powder
- ½ tsp cumin
- ¼ tsp paprika
- 1 tbsp olive oil
- Sea salt and black pepper to serve

INSTRUCTIONS

1. Layer raw shrimp at the bottom of the slow cooker. Drizzle over the oil, and stir through the onion.
2. Drain the tomatoes, then pour over the shrimp. Stir together.
3. Add the pepper and the remainder of the ingredients and stir well.
4. Cook on low for 2 to 3 hours.
5. Serve with tortillas or taco shells.

CHILLI MACARONI

SERVES 8 | PER SERVING - CALORIES: 220, FAT: 6G, CARBOHYDRATES: 24G, PROTEIN: 16G

INGREDIENTS

- 550g lean minced beef
- 225g macaroni
- 2 cans of crushed tomatoes
- 4 garlic cloves, minced
- 1 onion, chopped
- Can of chilli beans in chilli sauce
- 450ml beef stock
- 1 tbsp chilli powder
- ½ tsp cumin
- Salt and pepper to taste

INSTRUCTIONS

1. Brown ground beef and drain grease. Add all of the ingredients excluding the pasta to the slow cooker.
2. Cook for 4 hours on high, or 8 hours on low. In the last 15 minutes of cooking stir in the uncooked pasta and cover. Stir and test to see if pasta is to your liking. If needed, cook the pasta further until it reaches the desired texture.
3. Serve immediately with desired toppings.

CHICKEN CACCIATORE

SERVES 8 | PER SERVING - CALORIES: 205, FAT: 6G, CARBOHYDRATES: 12G, PROTEIN: 27G

INGREDIENTS

- Cooking spray or extra virgin olive oil
- 10 chicken thighs, bone in
- 400g can of chopped tomatoes
- 250g mushrooms, sliced
- 5 garlic cloves
- Half a red pepper, chopped
- Half a green pepper, chopped
- Half an onion, chopped
- 2 bay leaves
- 2 sprigs fresh thyme
- Grated parmesan cheese to serve
- Salt and pepper to season

INSTRUCTIONS

1. Season the chicken. In a pan over a medium to high heat, drizzle in olive oil and brown the chicken. Transfer to a slow cooker.
2. Reduce the heat under the frying pan to medium and coat with more cooking spray or another drizzle of olive oil. Fry the onion and garlic until soft. Transfer to the slow cooker.
3. Add the tomatoes, peppers, mushrooms, thyme, and bay leaves to the slow cooker. Stir to combine.
4. Cook for 4 hours on high, or 8 hours on low.
5. Discard the bay leaf and transfer the chicken to a large plate or cutting board. Pull the chicken off the bones and shred the meat. Stir the chicken and parsley back into the slow cooker. Serve with pasta topped with Parmesan cheese.

TURKEY STUFFED GIANT PASTA

SERVES 8 | PER SERVING - CALORIES: 205, FAT: 6G, CARBOHYDRATES: 12G, PROTEIN: 27G

INGREDIENTS

- 1 litre tomato pasta sauce
- 950g minced turkey
- 28 giant pasta shells
- 3 cloves of garlic
- 1 red onion, diced
- ½ tbsp garlic powder
- 1 tbsp dried basil
- 1 tbsp dried parsley
- 1 tbsp dried oregano
- 1 tbsp avocado oil
- 375g ricotta
- 120g fresh diced spinach
- 85g mozzarella
- Salt and pepper to taste

INSTRUCTIONS

1. Heat the avocado oil in a pan over a high heat and fry the onions until softening. Add the garlic and cook for a further 30 seconds. Add the turkey and cook until no longer pink. Add the spinach and wilt, about 1 to 2 minutes.
2. In a bowl, mix the ricotta, turkey mixture, herbs, and seasonings. Stir to combine.
3. Stuff each shell with the mixture.
4. Put half of the pasta sauce in the slow cooker and put the shells on top. Pour in half of the remaining sauce, then another layer of the pasta shells. Finish with the rest of the sauce.
5. Cook for 3 hours on high, or 6 hours on low.
6. At the end of the cook time, sprinkle over the mozzarella. Let the pasta stand for 5 minutes until the cheese melts before serving.

LAMB KLEFTIKO
· ·

SERVES 4 | PER SERVING - CALORIES: 694, FAT: 43.6G, CARBOHYDRATES: 29.7G, PROTEIN: 31.6G

INGREDIENTS

- Juice of 1 lemon
- 100ml extra-virgin olive oil
- 175ml dry white wine
- ½ tsp black pepper
- 4 garlic cloves, peeled
- 2 tsp dried oregano
- 1 tsp ground cumin
- 4 lamb shanks
- 1 tsp sea salt
- 1 large tomato, quartered
- 1 cinnamon stick
- 750g potatoes, peeled and cut into bite-sized chunks

INSTRUCTIONS

1. Put the lemon juice, 2 tbsp oil, wine, pepper, garlic, oregano and cumin into a blender and whizz. Put the lamb in a bowl and pour over the marinade. Chill ideally overnight, but for a minimum of an hour.
2. Put the meat, marinade, salt, tomato, and cinnamon stick into the slow cooker. Cook on low for 6 to 8 hours, or high for 3 to 4 hours.
3. Once the lamb is cooked, brown the potatoes in 3 tablespoons of oil in a frying pan.
4. Remove the lamb from the slow cooker, put on a plate and cover tightly with foil.
5. Stir the potatoes into the slow cooker. Cook for a further hour until soft. Tip in the lamb and cook until heated through. Add extra seasoning if needed.
6. Serve with salad and crusty bread.

OXTAIL STEW WITH ORANGE, SZECHUAN
PEPPERCORNS AND STAR ANISE
· ·

SERVES 4 | PER SERVING - CALORIES: 693, FAT: 38.1G, CARBOHYDRATES: 2.8G, PROTEIN: 76G

INGREDIENTS

- 1.5kg oxtail, cut into pieces
- 5 garlic cloves, peeled and left whole
- Thumb-sized piece of ginger, skin-on and sliced into chunks
- 1 tsp Szechuan peppercorns
- 1 cinnamon stick
- 4 whole star anise
- 4 strips of orange peel
- 4 bay leaves
- 2 tbsp dark soy sauce
- 175ml red wine
- ½ tsp black pepper

INSTRUCTIONS

1. Heat the slow cooker to high or low, depending on desired cooking time.
2. Put everything in the slow cooker, and cover with boiling water. Do not add salt at this point.

3. Cook on low for 8 to 12 hours, or 4 to 6 hours on high. From time to time use a ladle to skim off any excess fat that might pool on top as the meat cooks.
4. Remove the oxtail pieces to a plate. Strain the juices, discarding the spices, ginger, and orange peel. Put the stock and oxtail back in the slow cooker, and season if needed.
5. Serve with rice and pak choi.

RED WINE, THYME AND ONION BRISKET

SERVES 8 | PER SERVING - CALORIES: 478, FAT: 31.6G, CARBOHYDRATES: 7G, PROTEIN: 36.4G

INGREDIENTS

- 1.5kg rolled beef brisket
- Groundnut oil to fry
- 2 onions, chopped
- 1 tbsp plain flour
- Glass of red wine
- 300ml chicken stock
- 2 tbsp Worcestershire sauce
- 8 sprigs of thyme
- 1 star anise
- 2 carrots, peeled and quartered
- 2 celery sticks, quartered

INSTRUCTIONS

1. Heat a dry pan over a high heat. Rub the brisket all over with oil and season, then brown in the hot pan. Transfer to the slow cooker.
2. Cook the onion in the same frying pan for 10 minutes or until turning golden.
3. Add the flour, then cook, stirring constantly, for a couple minutes. Slowly add in the wine, still stirring, followed by the stock and Worcestershire sauce. Tip the onion mixture on top of the beef, then add the thyme and star anise, and tuck in the carrots and celery.
4. Cook on high for 5 hours. Take out the brisket and put on a plate. Scoop out the carrot, celery and thyme, and discard.

GAMMON IN CIDER

SERVES 6 | PER SERVING - CALORIES: 419, FAT: 22.7G, CARBOHYDRATES: 6.2G, PROTEIN: 42.3G

INGREDIENTS

- 1.5kg gammon joint
- 1 stick of celery, halved
- 1 carrot, quartered
- 1 onion, quartered
- 1 tbsp black pepper
- 2 tbsp wholegrain mustard
- 1 tbsp runny honey
- 400ml dry cider

INSTRUCTIONS

1. Heat the slow cooker to low. Put the gammon joint in the slow cooker and add the vegetables around the sides. Add the peppercorns and cider.
2. Cook for 4 hours. Remove the gammon and cool a little. Discard the veg and cooking liquid.
3. Preheat the oven to 170C. When the skin has cooled slightly, carefully cut it away leaving the fat. Score the fat and sit the gammon in a foil-lined baking tray. Stir together the mustard and honey, and brush over the fat. Bake the gammon for 30 minutes until sticky.

SWEET AND SOUR CHICKEN FAKEAWAY

SERVES 6 | PER SERVING - CALORIES: 419, FAT: 22.7G, CARBOHYDRATES: 6.2G, PROTEIN: 42.3G

INGREDIENTS

- 1 to 2 tbsp olive oil
- 250ml chicken stock
- 550g chicken, diced
- 3 garlic cloves, crushed
- 1 green pepper, sliced
- 1 red onion, diced
- 1 red pepper, sliced
- Thumb-sized piece of ginger, grated
- 1 red chilli, deseeded and chopped
- 30g light brown sugar
- 2 tbsp apple cider vinegar
- 4 tbsp tomato ketchup
- 1 tsp cornflour
- 1 ½ tbsp soy sauce
- 1 spring onion, sliced (optional)

INSTRUCTIONS

1. Warm the oil over a medium heat and fry the chicken until golden brown.
2. Tip the chicken, ginger, chilli, garlic, onion, stock, sugar, ketchup and vinegar into the slow cooker. Cook on low for 6 hours.
3. Stir in the peppers and cook for 30 minutes longer.
4. Whisk together the cornflour and 1 tbsp of water in a small bowl, then add to the pan, stirring until thickened. Just before serving, add the soy sauce to taste, then sprinkle over the spring onions, if using.

CHILLI WITH CORNBREAD

SERVES 8 | PER SERVING - CALORIES: 689, FAT: 34.3G, CARBOHYDRATES: 50.3G, PROTEIN: 37G

INGREDIENTS

FOR THE CHILLI:

- 3x 400g tins of chopped tomatoes
- 400g tin of black beans, drained and rinsed
- 400g tin of kidney beans, drained and rinsed
- 800g beef mince
- 100ml beef stock
- 330ml lager
- 2 large onions, chopped
- 2 green chillies, chopped
- 1 tbsp celery salt
- 1 tbsp garlic salt
- 2 ½ tsp ground cumin
- 1 ½ tsp smoked paprika
- 1 tbsp mild chilli powder
- 1 tsp ground cinnamon
- ½ tsp ground allspice
- 2 bay leaves
- 2 tsp dried oregano
- 2 tbsp tomato puree
- 2 tbsp soft dark brown sugar
- 1 tbsp Worcestershire sauce
- 3 tbsp cider vinegar
- 25g dark chocolate

FOR THE CORNBREAD:

- 70g strong white bread flour
- 150g instant polenta
- 1 tbsp baking powder
- 1 tbsp caster sugar
- 3 eggs
- 375ml whole milk
- 75g unsalted butter, melted, plus extra to grease
- 100g mature cheddar, grated
- 6 pickled jalapeno slices from a jar

INSTRUCTIONS

1. Heat a large frying pan then fry the mince in batches making sure each batch is well browned with some crispy bits. Tip each batch into a slow cooker when finished.
2. Add all of the ingredients for the chilli apart from the beans to the slow cooker and stir. Cook for 4 hours on high, then fold in the beans and cook for 30 minutes.

3. Preheat the oven to 200C. Butter and line a 900g loaf tin with baking paper. Stir the dry ingredients in a bowl along with 1 ½ tsp salt. Beat the eggs with the melted butter and milk. Add the wet ingredients to the dry and mix. Stir in the cheddar and jalapeños. It will be quite thin but do not worry, the polenta soaks it all up in the oven.
4. Tip into a loaf tin and cook for 15 minutes. Reduce the temperature to 180C, and cook for 25 minutes until a skewer inserted in the middle comes out clean. Serve slices with the chilli – if you want to serve it warm, slice, then heat through in a hot oven, covered with foil, for 10 minutes.

CHORIZO AND PRAWN ORZO

SERVES 4 | PER SERVING - CALORIES: 449, FAT: 17.1G, CARBOHYDRATES: 41.5G, PROTEIN: 25.1G

INGREDIENTS

- 125g chorizo, diced
- 800ml chicken or vegetable stock
- 1 onion, chopped
- 1 stalk of celery, diced
- 5 garlic cloves, crushed
- 2 tbsp extra-virgin olive oil
- 125ml white wine
- 200g cherry tomatoes, quartered
- 200g orzo
- 400g raw peeled king prawns
- Handful of parsley, finely chopped
- 1 lemon to serve

INSTRUCTIONS

1. Turn the slow cooker on high. Put in the first eight ingredients, stir, then cook for 2 hours.
2. Stir in the pasta and scatter the prawns over the top. Cook until the pasta is soft and prawns are pink; around 20 to 25 minutes.
3. Stir in the chopped parsley with some seasoning and spoon into bowls. Serve with lemon wedges.

VEGETARIAN BLACK BEAN CHIPOTLE CHILLI

SERVES 4 | PER SERVING - CALORIES: 218, FAT: 7.3G, CARBOHYDRATES: 24.6G, PROTEIN: 8G

INGREDIENTS

- 2x 400g tins of black beans, rinsed
- 400g tin of chopped tomatoes
- 2 sticks of celery, diced
- 1 large red onion, half finely chopped, half thinly sliced
- 3 garlic cloves, finely sliced
- 1 cinnamon stick
- 1 tsp cumin seeds, toasted and ground
- 1 tsp smoked paprika
- 2 bay leaves
- 2 to 3 tsp chipotle chilli paste
- Juice of 1 lime
- 1 lime cut into wedges
- 2 tbsp olive oil
- Sour cream, tortillas, and chilli sauce to serve

INSTRUCTIONS

1. Heat the slow cooker to high or low, depending on desired cooking time.
2. In a frying pan, heat the oil and cook the cinnamon, bay, celery, garlic, onion, and green pepper for 10 minutes until soft.
3. Put the onion in a saucepan and cover with boiling water. Simmer for a minute and then drain. Mix in a pinch of salt and the juice of half a lime.
4. Stir in the spices, chilli paste, and tomatoes, then boil. Add the beans, mix well, and tip into the slow cooker.
5. Season to taste, and cook on low for 4 to 6 hours, or high for 1 to 2 hours. Check the seasoning, adding more salt and chilli to taste.
6. Serve the tortillas topped with the beans, soured cream, pickled red onions, coriander, and remaining lime wedges.

CHICKPEAS WITH DATES, TURMERIC, CINNAMON AND ALMONDS

SERVES 4 | PER SERVING - CALORIES: 370, FAT: 15.1G, CARBOHYDRATES: 39.7G, PROTEIN: 13.9G

INGREDIENTS

- 4 garlic cloves, finely chopped
- 2x 400g cans of chickpeas, rinsed and drained
- 400g tin of plum tomatoes
- 45g flaked almonds, toasted
- 100g pitted dates, halved
- 2 tbsp olive oil
- 1 tbsp grated ginger
- 1 tsp ground cumin
- 1 tsp ground coriander
- 1 tsp ground turmeric
- 1 cinnamon stick
- Juice of half a lemon, plus 2 strips of the zest
- Small bunch of coriander, chopped, with stalks and leaves separated
- Orange wedges and couscous to serve

INSTRUCTIONS

1. Heat the slow cooker to high or low, depending on desired cooking time.
2. Put half of the tomatoes and dates in a blender, and blitz to a puree. Tip into the slow cooker with the remaining tomatoes.
3. Put the oil, ginger, garlic, coriander stalks, lemon zest, spices and 100ml of water into the slow cooker. Season to taste. Cook on low for 4 to 6 hours, or high for 1 to 2 hours.
4. Mix through the dates and chickpeas and cook for a further 30 minutes. Add in the lemon juice and check the seasoning, adding more if desired. Take out the lemon zest.
5. Serve with a drizzle of olive oil, toasted almonds, and coriander. Enjoy with orange wedges and couscous.

CHICKPEA AND COCONUT DAHL WITH NAAN BREAD

SERVES 8 | PER SERVING - CALORIES: 859, FAT: 30.5G, CARBOHYDRATES: 107.9G, PROTEIN: 35.5G

INGREDIENTS

FOR THE DAHL:

- Sunflower oil
- 2 large onions, chopped
- 50g ginger, peeled and grated
- 1 tbsp ground cumin
- 1 tbsp ground coriander
- 1 tbsp nigella seeds
- 1 tbsp medium curry powder
- 1 tsp turmeric
- 300g red split lentils
- 500g dried split chickpeas (or chana dahl)
- 2x 400g tins of coconut milk

FOR THE NAAN:

- 7g fast-action dried yeast
- 100g natural yoghurt
- 500g strong white bread flour, plus extra to dust
- 1 ½ tsp fine salt
- Clarified butter or ghee

INSTRUCTIONS

1. Put all the dahl ingredients plus 800ml of water in the slow cooker. Cook for 3 ½ to 4 hours on high.
2. To make the naans, mix the yeast and yoghurt with 250ml warm water. Put the flour and salt in a bowl, then stir in the yeast until you have a dough. Knead for 10 minutes by hand, or 5 minutes with a mixer with dough hook, until the dough is smooth. Put into a clean bowl, cover with oiled clingfilm, and leave for 2 hours, or until doubled in size.
3. When the dough is ready, knead it briefly on a lightly floured worksurface. Cut into 8 pieces and roll each one out to an oval until they no longer spring back. Lay onto oiled baking sheets, cover with oiled clingfilm, and leave for 30 minutes until puffy.

4. Heat the oven to 240C/fan 220C/gas 9. Heat another baking sheet in the oven. Transfer the naans, two at a time, onto the hot baking sheet. Cook for 5-10 minutes until the dough starts to bubble and the bottom looks golden. Press them gently back down if they have domed too much.
5. Brush the naans with clarified butter or ghee, and scatter over some nigella seeds to serve.

COCONUT AND LENTIL CURRY

SERVES 6 | PER SERVING - CALORIES: 388, FAT: 18G, CARBOHYDRATES: 45G, PROTEIN: 17G

INGREDIENTS

- 315g dried brown lentils
- 2 tbsp ginger, chopped
- 1 tbsp cumin
- 1 tbsp coriander
- 1 tbsp turmeric
- 2x 400g cans of chopped tomatoes
- 1 garlic clove, chopped
- Half an onion, minced
- 400g can of coconut milk
- 2 to 3 tsp sea salt
- Bunch of fresh coriander, chopped
- Handful of cherry tomatoes

INSTRUCTIONS

1. Put the lentils, spices, tomatoes, garlic, onion, and 750ml of water in the slow cooker. Cook on low for 8 hours, or on high for 4 hours.
2. Stir in the coconut milk, sea salt, coriander, and cherry tomatoes. Add extra salt to taste if needed.
3. Serve on its own or with rice.

THAI CHICKEN SOUP

SERVES 4 | PER SERVING - CALORIES: 567, FAT: 16G, CARBOHYDRATES: 71G, PROTEIN: 31G

INGREDIENTS

- 2 medium carrots, chopped
- 1 red pepper, chopped
- ½ onion, chopped
- 2-inch piece of ginger, minced
- 4 garlic cloves, minced
- 4 tbsp red Thai curry paste
- 2 tbsp fish sauce
- 2 tbsp soy sauce
- 1 tbsp sugar
- 750ml chicken stock
- 4 boneless chicken thighs
- 2x 400g cans of coconut milk
- 1 lime
- 225g rice noodles, cooked

INSTRUCTIONS

1. Put everything excluding the lime, noodles, and coconut milk in the slow cooker. Stir, then cook for 8 to 10 hours on low.
2. Shred the chicken thighs, then return to the slow cooker. Stir in the coconut milk, then let stand for 15 minutes before serving.
3. Place the cooked noodles into soup bowls and top with the Thai chicken soup. Squeeze a little lime over to serve.

SARA R. ADAMS

POACHED SALMON WITH LEMON AND HERBS

SERVES 6 | PER SERVING - CALORIES: 359, FAT: 20.4G, CARBOHYDRATES: 4.5G, PROTEIN: 31.4G

INGREDIENTS

- 950g skin-on salmon
- 250ml white wine
- 480ml water
- 1 shallot, sliced
- 1 lemon, sliced
- 1 bay leaf
- 1 ½ tsp salt
- 1 ½ tsp black peppercorns
- Salt and pepper to taste
- 5 to 6 sprigs of fresh herbs, such as tarragon, dill, and/or Italian parsley
- Lemon wedges, sea salt, and olive oil to serve

INSTRUCTIONS

1. Mix the wine, water, lemon, shallots, herbs, bay, peppercorns, and salt in the slow cooker. Cook for 30 minutes on high.
2. Season the salmon with salt and pepper. Put skin-side down in the bottom of the slow cooker. Cook on low until the salmon is opaque and flaky. Start checking for desired doneness after 45 minutes to an hour and continue cooking until preferred doneness is reached. (Salmon can be held on the warm setting for several hours.)
3. Drizzle salmon with good-quality olive oil and sprinkle with coarse salt. Serve with lemon wedges.

SIDES

CHEESY SWEETCORN

SERVES 8 | PER SERVING - CALORIES: 367, FAT: 32.6G, CARBOHYDRATES: 6.2G, PROTEIN: 12.2G

INGREDIENTS

- 500g frozen sweetcorn
- 400g cream cheese, cubed
- 4 tbsp butter
- 3 tbsp water
- 3 tbsp milk
- 2 tbsp sugar
- 225g grated Cheddar cheese

INSTRUCTIONS

1. Put everything in the slow cooker and stir.
2. Cook on low for 3 to 4 hours.
3. Stir well before serving.

BAKED POTATOES

SERVES 4 | PER SERVING - CALORIES: 159, FAT: 3.7G, CARBOHYDRATES: 30.4G, PROTEIN: 3.5G

INGREDIENTS

- 4 baking potatoes, well-scrubbed and completely dry
- 1 tbsp extra-virgin olive oil
- 1 pinch coarse salt, to taste
- 4 pieces of aluminium foil

INSTRUCTIONS

Prick the potatoes with a fork several times, then rub potatoes with olive oil, sprinkle with salt and wrap tightly in foil. Stir in the potatoes. Cook on low for 7 ½ to 8 hours, or high for 4 ½ to 5 hours.

MUSHROOM WILD RICE

SERVES 12 | PER SERVING - CALORIES: 188, FAT: 8.5G, CARBOHYDRATES: 24.3G, PROTEIN: 4.6G

INGREDIENTS

- 525ml water
- 200ml beef stock
- 1 (400g) tin French onion soup
- 275g mushrooms, chopped
- 110g butter, melted
- 190g uncooked brown rice
- 160g uncooked wild rice

INSTRUCTIONS

In a slow cooker, combine all ingredients; stir well. Cook on low for 7 to 8 hours.

GLAZED CARROTS

SERVES 4 | PER SERVING - CALORIES: 171, FAT: 6.2G, CARBOHYDRATES: 30.2G, PROTEIN: 1G

INGREDIENTS

- 550g baby carrots
- 1 tbsp water
- 25g butter
- 6 tbsp orange marmalade
- Salt and pepper to taste

INSTRUCTIONS

Put all of the ingredients in the slow cooker and mix. Cook for 7 to 9 hours on low.

THAI GINGER AND COCONUT RICE

SERVES 4 | PER SERVING - CALORIES: 171, FAT: 6.2G, CARBOHYDRATES: 30.2G, PROTEIN: 1G

INGREDIENTS

- 450g Thai jasmine rice
- 3 shallots, thinly sliced
- 1 red chilli, seeded and minced
- 5cm piece root ginger, minced
- 400ml coconut milk
- 2 tbsp vegetable oil
- 1 clove garlic, minced
- 2 tbsp butter
- Zest of 1 lime
- 1 pinch ground nutmeg
- 2 bay leaves
- 200ml water
- Salt and pepper, to taste
- 1 bunch fresh coriander, chopped
- 3 tbsp chopped spring onion

INSTRUCTIONS

1. Preheat the slow cooker to auto or low setting. Fry the chilli, shallots, ginger, and garlic in the oil for 4 to 5 minutes until soft, but not brown. Add the butter, then stir through the rice for 2 to 3 minutes. Increase the temperature and add the lime, nutmeg, bay leaves and coconut milk and water. Season generously.
2. Transfer everything to the slow cooker. Cook for two hours, stirring half way through. To serve, stir through the fresh coriander and spring onions.

CHEESY SCALLOPED POTATOES

SERVES 6 | PER SERVING - CALORIES: 414, FAT: 18.4G, CARBOHYDRATES: 48.2G, PROTEIN: 15G

INGREDIENTS

- 4 large potatoes, thinly sliced
- 2 onions, finely diced or sliced in rings
- 3 cloves garlic, minced
- 300g cheese sauce
- 1 to 2 handfuls grated cheese of your choice
- Salt and pepper, to taste

INSTRUCTIONS

1. Mix the onion and garlic together in a bowl.
2. Spray the slow cooker with oil or brush a thin lining on - bottom and sides.
3. Put a layer of the potatoes in the slow cooker, then follow with a layer of onions and garlic. Repeat to use all of the vegetables.
4. Prepare the cheese sauce and pour this over your potatoes making sure they're all covered, then scatter grated cheese over and season to taste.
5. Cook on Low for 4 or 5 hours until the potatoes are tender, stirring halfway through.

REFRIED BEANS

SERVES 15 | PER SERVING - CALORIES: 140, FAT: 0.5G, CARBOHYDRATES: 25.5G, PROTEIN: 8.5G

INGREDIENTS

- 1 onion, peeled and halved
- 580g dry pinto beans, rinsed
- ½ fresh jalapeno, seeded and chopped
- 2 tbsp minced garlic
- 5 tsp salt
- 1 ¾ tsp fresh ground black pepper
- ¼ tsp ground cumin, optional
- 2 litres water, or as needed

INSTRUCTIONS

1. Put the onion, beans, garlic, jalapenos, salt, pepper, and cumin in the slow cooker. Pour in the water and combine. Cook on High for 8 hours, adding more water as needed and lowering the temperature to low if too much liquid is evaporating.
2. Once the beans have cooked, strain them, reserving the liquid. Mash the beans with a potato masher, adding the reserved liquid as needed to obtain desired consistency.

CRANBERRY SAUCE

SERVES 12 | PER SERVING - CALORIES: 84, FAT: 0G, CARBOHYDRATES: 20.2G, PROTEIN: 0.1G

INGREDIENTS

- 120ml orange juice
- 120ml water
- 100g soft brown sugar
- 100g caster sugar
- ¼ tsp ground cinnamon
- 350g fresh cranberries

INSTRUCTIONS

1. Combine orange juice, water, brown sugar, caster sugar and cinnamon in slow cooker; stir in cranberries. Cook on high for 3 hours, stirring once each hour.
2. Remove lid; stir well. Cook on high until sauce has thickened and most cranberries have popped, about 45 more minutes.

HOMEMADE TOMATO KETCHUP

SERVES 48 | PER SERVING - CALORIES: 24, FAT: 0G, CARBOHYDRATES: 5.2G, PROTEIN: 0.5G

INGREDIENTS

- 1.6L pureed tomatoes
- 125g granulated sugar
- 180ml white vinegar
- 120ml water
- 1 whole clove
- 1 tsp onion granules
- ½ tsp garlic powder
- ¼ tsp finely ground black pepper
- 1 ¾ tsp salt
- ¼ tsp mustard powder
- ¼ tsp celery salt

INSTRUCTIONS

1. Pour pureed tomatoes into slow cooker. Swirl water in the empty cans, and pour into the slow cooker. Add the vinegar, onion powder, garlic powder, sugar, salt, mustard powder, black pepper, celery salt, cayenne pepper, and clove. Whisk to combine.
2. Cook on high until the mixture reduces by half, around 10 to 12 hours.
3. Blend the ketchup using an immersion blender, around 20 seconds.
4. Sieve the ketchup to strain out any tomato skins and seeds.
5. Put the ketchup in a bowl and leave to cool before tasting. Add extra seasoning if needed.

WHITE BREAD

SERVES 10 | PER SERVING - CALORIES: 183, FAT: 0.5G, CARBOHYDRATES: 38.2G, PROTEIN: 5.4G

INGREDIENTS

- 500g strong white flour
- 7g sachet fast-action dried yeast
- ¼ tsp fine sea salt

INSTRUCTIONS

1. Put the flour, salt, and yeast in a bowl. Mix, and make a well in the middle. Measure 350ml warm water and pour most of it into the well. Mix the flour and water together with your fingers or a wooden spoon until combined into a slightly wet, pillowy, workable dough – add a splash more water if necessary.
2. Tip the dough out, and knead until smooth and stretchy. This can also be done in a tabletop mixer with a dough hook.
3. Shape the dough into a large, tight ball and sit the ball on a square of baking parchment. Use the paper to lift the dough into the slow cooker, and cook, covered, on high. Leave for 2 hours.
4. Lift the bread out using the parchment. The bottom should be crusty, and the top should be springy, but not soft.
5. Bread will not get a strong crust in the slow cooker. You can either let the bread cool, or bake for 5 to 10 minutes at 220C to get a crisp crust.

CHEESY CREAMED VEGETABLES

SERVES 8 | PER SERVING - CALORIES: 370, FAT: 34G, CARBOHYDRATES: 7G, PROTEIN: 6G

INGREDIENTS

- 50g butter
- ½ tbsp olive oil
- 1 onion, thinly sliced
- 400g cavolo nero
- 3 leeks, sliced
- 100ml stock
- 400ml double cream
- 1 heaped tsp Dijon mustard
- Generous grating of nutmeg
- 40g grated parmesan or vegetarian alternative

INSTRUCTIONS

1. Heat the slow cooker on low and heat the butter and oil in a frying pan. Add the onion and fry for 5 minutes over a low heat until softFry the onion in the butter and oil for 5 minutes until soft.
2. Add the cavolo nero to the pan and fry for a further 5 minutes until beginning to wilt. Tip into the slow cooked with the leeks, stock, and 300ml of the cream.
3. Cook on low, stirring occasionally for 3 hours.
4. Stir through the remaining cream, mustard, nutmeg, and cheese before serving.

RED CABBAGE WITH APPLES

SERVES 8 | PER SERVING - CALORIES: 137, FAT: 3G, CARBOHYDRATES: 22G, PROTEIN: 2G

INGREDIENTS

- 1kg red cabbage
- 2 white onions, chopped
- 4 Granny Smiths apples, peeled, cored, and chopped
- Zest of 1 orange or 2 clementines
- 2 tsp ground mixed spice
- 100g light brown soft sugar
- 3 tbsp cider vinegar
- 200ml dry cider
- 25g butter

INSTRUCTIONS

1. Heat the slow cooker on low. Peel the outer leaves from the cabbage and discard. Quarter the cabbage, remove the stem, and slice thinly.
2. Put a layer of cabbage in the slow cooker, then top with some onions, apples, spices, sugar, zest, and seasoning. Continue to create layers until you have used up these ingredients. Season to taste.
3. Pour over the vinegar, cider, and butter. Cook for 4 to 5 hours.

SPICED GINGER BEER CABBAGE

SERVES 6 | PER SERVING - CALORIES: 165, FAT: 8G, CARBOHYDRATES: 18G, PROTEIN: 3G

INGREDIENTS

- 1kg red cabbage
- 1 red onion, sliced
- 2 large eating apples, each sliced into six wedges
- Thumb-sized piece of ginger, peeled and finely grated
- 50g butter
- 100ml chicken or vegetable stock
- 300ml alcoholic ginger beer
- ½ tbsp light brown soft sugar
- 2 tsp coriander seeds, crushed
- 1 star anise
- 2 tbsp cider vinegar

INSTRUCTIONS

1. Heat the slow cooker to low. Tip everything into the slow cooker, and season generously. Stir well, then cook for 5 hours.
2. Take off the lid, turn the slow cooker to high and cook for another hour to reduce the liquid. Taste for seasoning and serve in a warmed bowl.

CREAMY WILD RICE

SERVES 12 | PER SERVING - CALORIES: 130, FAT: 3.5G, CARBOHYDRATES: 22G, PROTEIN: 4G

INGREDIENTS

- 310g uncooked wild rice
- 1 onion, chopped
- ½ tsp salt
- ½ tsp ground sage
- ¼ tsp pepper
- Can of cream of celery soup
- Can of cream of mushroom soup
- 540ml water
- 3 tbsp chopped parsley

INSTRUCTIONS

1. Rinse the rice in cold water. In the slow cooker, mix the rice and remaining ingredients excluding the parsley.
2. Cook for 8 to 9 hours on low, and stir through the parsley to serve.

CRUNCHY LEMON VEGETABLES

SERVES 4 | PER SERVING - CALORIES: 100, FAT: 3G, CARBOHYDRATES: 16G, PROTEIN: 2G

INGREDIENTS

- 450g mixed frozen cauliflower, carrots, and peas
- 100g cornflakes, crushed
- 1 tbsp butter
- ¼ tsp pepper
- ¼ tsp grated lemon peel

INSTRUCTIONS

1. Thaw the vegetables and put them in a slow cooker with the butter, pepper, lemon peel, and 250ml water. Cook on low for around 2 hours until soft.
2. Remove the vegetables with a slotted spoon. Toss in the cornflakes to serve.

HERBY POTATOES AND PEPPERS

SERVES 14 | PER SERVING - CALORIES: 70, FAT: 0G, CARBOHYDRATES: 16G, PROTEIN: 2G

INGREDIENTS

- 900g potatoes, cut into small chunks
- 1 green pepper, cut into strips
- 1 red pepper, cut into strips
- 2 cloves of garlic, chopped
- 120ml water
- 1 ½ tsp salt
- 1 tsp dried basil leaves
- 1 tsp dried oregano leaves
- Can of chopped tomatoes

INSTRUCTIONS

1. Put the potatoes, peppers, and garlic in the slow cooker.
2. Pour the water over the vegetables, and top with the remaining ingredients, adding the tomatoes last.
3. Cook for 4 to 6 hours on high.

BALSAMIC ROOT VEGETABLES

SERVES 8 | PER SERVING - CALORIES: 209, FAT: 5.5G, CARBOHYDRATES: 38.7G, PROTEIN: 2.9G

INGREDIENTS

- 2 onions, cut into wedges
- 225g baby potatoes, cut into quarters
- 450g parsnips, peeled and chopped
- 450g sweet potatoes, cut into chunks
- 450g ready-to-eat carrots
- 3 tbsp vegetable oil
- 2 tbsp balsamic vinegar
- 1 tbsp honey
- ½ tsp pepper
- 1 tsp salt

INSTRUCTIONS

1. Spray the slow cooker with non-stick cooking spray. Place the parsnips, carrots, onions, and potatoes in the bottom.
2. In a bowl, combine the remaining ingredients. Pour mixture evenly over vegetables.
3. Cook on high for 4 hours.

CAULIFLOWER CHEESE

SERVES 6 | PER SERVING - CALORIES: 260, FAT: 17G, CARBOHYDRATES: 12G, PROTEIN: 12G

INGREDIENTS

- 900g cauliflower, separated into florets
- 2 tbsp water
- 300ml cheese sauce
- 120ml milk
- ½ tsp salt
- ¼ tsp pepper
- 225g grated cheese

INSTRUCTIONS

1. Grease the slow cooker, then line with foil. Spray the foil with cooking spray too.
2. In large microwavable bowl, place cauliflower and water. Cover tightly with microwavable plastic wrap. Microwave on high 4 minutes or until cauliflower is partially cooked; drain.
3. Meanwhile, in saucepan, mix the cheese sauce, milk, salt, and pepper. Cook the mixture over a medium heat, stirring until smooth. Remove from heat; stir in cheese until melted. Add cauliflower; toss to coat. Tip into the slow cooker.
4. Cook on low for 3 hours.

GLAZED ROOT VEGETABLES

SERVES 9 | PER SERVING - CALORIES: 120, FAT: 2G, CARBOHYDRATES: 25G, PROTEIN: 2G

INGREDIENTS

- 2 sweet potatoes, cut into chunks
- 4 medium parsnips, cut into chunks
- 6 medium carrots, sliced
- 2 red onions, cut into wedges
- 1 ½ tbsp balsamic vinegar
- 3 tbsp honey
- 1 tbsp olive oil
- 5 tsp chopped fresh thyme
- 1 tsp salt
- ½ tsp pepper

INSTRUCTIONS

1. Grease the slow cooker. Add the carrots, onions, and parsnips. Add a layer of sweet potatoes.
2. In small bowl, mix honey, oil, 2 teaspoons of the thyme, the salt and pepper. Pour over vegetables; stir to coat.
3. Cook for 4 to 5 hours on low. Stir through the vinegar just before serving, and sprinkle with the remaining thyme.

SIMPLE LEMON RISOTTO

SERVES 12 | PER SERVING - CALORIES: 230, FAT: 7G, CARBOHYDRATES: 30G, PROTEIN: 9G

INGREDIENTS

- 1.4L hot chicken stock
- 2 shallots, finely sliced
- 2 cloves garlic, chopped
- 450g uncooked arborio rice
- 4 tbsp butter
- 240ml white wine
- 1 tsp chopped fresh thyme
- ½ tsp ground pepper
- ½ tsp salt
- 2 tsp grated lemon peel
- 1 tbsp fresh lemon juice
- 90g grated Parmesan

INSTRUCTIONS

1. Spray the slow cooker with cooking spray. In a frying pan, melt 2 tablespoons of butter over a medium heat. Fry the garlic and shallots for a couple minutes until soft.
2. Add rice; cook 2 to 3 minutes, stirring frequently, until edges of kernels are translucent. Stir in the wine. Cook about 3 minutes longer, stirring constantly, until wine is absorbed. Tip the rice into the slow cooker.
3. Pour the stock, thyme, salt, and pepper into the slow cooker.
4. Cook for 2 hours on high. Stir in cheese, the remaining butter, lemon peel and lemon juice. Serve immediately.

WILD RICE WITH VEGGIES

SERVES 12 | PER SERVING - CALORIES: 140, FAT: 4G, CARBOHYDRATES: 25G, PROTEIN: 4G

INGREDIENTS

- 315g uncooked wild rice
- 2 medium carrots, chopped
- 1 large onion, chopped
- 150g chopped dried cherries
- 100g pine nuts
- 200g chopped celery
- 840ml vegetable stock
- 1 tbsp butter
- 2 tsp fresh thyme
- ½ tsp salt
- ¼ tsp pepper

INSTRUCTIONS

1. Grease the inside of the slow cooker. Mix all the ingredients in except the nuts and cherries.
2. Cook for 5 to 6 hours on low.

3. Fry the pine nuts in a dry pan for 5 to 7 minutes until brown.
4. Just before serving, stir the cherries and toasted pine nuts through the rice.

FESTIVE CRANBERRY RICE
SERVES 6 | PER SERVING - CALORIES: 260, FAT: 7G, CARBOHYDRATES: 45G, PROTEIN: 9G

INGREDIENTS
- 315g uncooked rice
- 1 tbsp butter
- ½ tsp salt
- ¼ tsp pepper
- 4 spring onions, sliced
- 800ml vegetable stock
- 115g canned sliced mushrooms, undrained
- 80g almonds
- 60g dried cranberries

INSTRUCTIONS
1. Put all of the ingredients except the almonds and cranberries in the slow cooker.
2. Cook for 4 to 5 hours on low.
3. Cook the almonds in a dry pan until they start to colour, 5 to 7 minutes and start to become fragrant.
4. Fold the cranberries and almonds into the slow cooker, and cook for a further 15 minutes.

SWEET POTATOES WITH APPLE SAUCE
SERVES 6 | PER SERVING - CALORIES: 350, FAT: 13G, CARBOHYDRATES: 60G, PROTEIN: 3G

INGREDIENTS
- 900g sweet potatoes, peeled and cut into cubes
- 360g apple sauce
- 130g brown sugar
- 3 tbsp butter
- 1 tsp ground cinnamon
- 60g toasted chopped nuts

INSTRUCTIONS
1. Put the slow cookers in low. Mix the remaining ingredients except the nuts, and spoon over the potatoes.
2. Cook for 6 to 8 hours on low.
3. Sprinkle with the nuts to serve.

CIDER AND MAPLE BRUSSEL SPROUTS
SERVES 12 | PER SERVING - CALORIES: 90, FAT: 4G, CARBOHYDRATES: 13G, PROTEIN: 3G

INGREDIENTS
- 900g Brussel sprouts
- 1 red onion, chopped
- ½ tsp salt
- ¼ tsp pepper
- 60ml apple cider
- 60ml melted butter
- 60ml maple syrup
- 1 tbsp fresh thyme

INSTRUCTIONS
1. In the slow cooker, combine the Brussel sprouts and onion. Season, then tip in the cider.
2. Cook for 3 to 3 ½ hours on low.
3. In a small bowl combine melted butter, maple syrup, and thyme. Pour over sprouts in cooker, stirring to combine. If desired, garnish with additional fresh thyme leaves.

ROASTED ROOT VEGETABLES

SERVES 12 | PER SERVING - CALORIES: 73, FAT: 2G, CARBOHYDRATES: 12G, PROTEIN: 1G

INGREDIENTS

- 225g new potatoes, halved
- 230g beetroot, cut into chunks
- 440g butternut squash, cut into chunks
- 230g turnips, cut into chunks
- 1 red onion, cut into thin wedges
- 150g baby carrots
- 2 tbsp olive oil
- ½ tsp salt
- ½ tsp pepper
- 8 garlic cloves, peeled
- Chopped fresh parsley

INSTRUCTIONS

1. Mix all the vegetables in a bowl, and drizzle with the olive oil. Season to taste. Tip the content of the bowl in the slow cooker.
2. Cook for 3 to 4 hours on high. Sprinkle on the parsley.

ORANGE GLAZED CARROTS AND PARSNIPS

SERVES 10 | PER SERVING - CALORIES: 159, FAT: 4G, CARBOHYDRATES: 31G, PROTEIN: 2G

INGREDIENTS

- 450g parsnips, cut into chunks
- 950g carrots, sliced
- 2 tbsp fine orange peel
- 70g orange marmalade
- ½ tsp salt
- 1 tbsp tapioca starch
- ¼ tsp ground black pepper
- 3 tbsp fresh parsley
- 3 tbsp butter
- 120ml vegetable stock
- 60ml white wine
- 240ml orange juice

INSTRUCTIONS

1. Put the carrots and parsnips in a bowl. In a small bowl combine orange juice, marmalade, broth, wine, tapioca, salt, and pepper. Pour over carrot mixture, toss to coat.
2. Cook for 8 to 10 hours on low. Stir in the orange peel, parsley, and butter for the last 30 minutes.

RICE WITH PECANS AND CHERRIES

SERVES 15 | PER SERVING - CALORIES: 169, FAT: 5G, CARBOHYDRATES: 27G, PROTEIN: 5G

INGREDIENTS

- 1.2L chicken stock
- 500g rice
- 2 carrots, grated
- 125g canned sliced mushrooms, drained
- 2 tbsp butter
- 2 tsp dried marjoram, crushed
- ¼ tsp salt
- ¼ tsp black pepper
- 75g dried cherries
- 2 spring onions, chopped
- 50g coarsely chopped toasted pecans

INSTRUCTIONS

1. Combine the stock, uncooked rice, carrot, mushrooms, melted butter, marjoram, salt, and pepper in the slow cooker.
2. Cook for 5 to 6 hours on low.
3. Turn off the slow cooker. Stir in the cherries, spring onions, and pecans. Let stand, covered, for 10 minutes before serving.

THAI VEGETABLE MEDLEY

SERVES 8 | PER SERVING - CALORIES: 60, FAT: 2G, CARBOHYDRATES: 9G, PROTEIN: 2G

INGREDIENTS

- 1 courgette, halved lengthwise and cut into slices
- 225g summer squash, halved and cut into slices
- 250g button mushrooms, quartered
- 1 red pepper, cut into slices
- 2 medium leeks, cut into slices
- 2 cloves of garlic, minced
- 2 tbsp vegetable or chicken broth
- 2 tbsp Thai red curry paste
- 80ml coconut milk
- 1 tbsp grated ginger
- Small bunch of chopped basil leaves

INSTRUCTIONS

1. In the slow cooker, combine the courgette, squash, mushrooms, pepper, leeks, and garlic. In a bowl, whisk together the stock and curry paste, then drizzle over the vegetables.
2. Cook for 3 hours on low. Mix in the ginger and coconut milk. Add the basil just before serving.

VANILLA BUTTER BRUSSEL SPROUTS WITH POMEGRANATE SYRUP

SERVES 8 | PER SERVING - CALORIES: 171, FAT: 10G, CARBOHYDRATES: 18G, PROTEIN: 5G

INGREDIENTS

- 900g Brussel sprouts
- 750ml chicken stock
- 2 cloves garlic, minced
- 3 tbsp butter
- 2 tsp vanilla extract
- 1 tsp salt
- ½ tsp black pepper
- 4 to 6 bacon rashers, cooked and roughly chopped
- 60g chopped pecans, toasted
- Pomegranate syrup or sauce to drizzle

INSTRUCTIONS

1. Put the Brussel sprouts in the slow cooker and cover with the stock and garlic. Cook for 2 to 2 ½ hours on high until tender. Drain the sprouts and return to the cooker.
2. Beat the butter with the vanilla and seasoning, then tip over the sprouts. Drizzle with pomegranate syrup or sauce, and top with bacon and pecans.

CAULIFLOWER AND BROCCOLI IN CHEESE SAUCE

SERVES 10 | PER SERVING - CALORIES: 177, FAT: 12G, CARBOHYDRATES: 10G, PROTEIN: 8G

INGREDIENTS

- 225g broccoli
- 450g cauliflower
- 450g cheese sauce
- 175g grated Swiss cheese
- 1 large onion, chopped
- 1 tsp dried thyme
- ¼ tsp black pepper

INSTRUCTIONS

1. In the slow cooker, combine broccoli, cauliflower, pasta sauce, Swiss cheese, onion, thyme, and pepper.
2. Cook for 6 to 7 hours on low, or for 3 to 3 ½ hours on high.

SWEET POTATOES WITH ORANGE, SAGE, AND BACON

SERVES 10 | PER SERVING - CALORIES: 189, FAT: 4G, CARBOHYDRATES: 36G, PROTEIN: 4G

INGREDIENTS

- 1.8kg sweet potatoes, peeled and cut into slices
- 120ml orange juice
- 3 tbsp brown sugar
- 1 ½ tsp salt
- ½ tsp dried sage
- ½ tsp dried thyme
- 2 tbsp butter
- 4 slices bacon, cooked and crumbled

INSTRUCTIONS

1. Put the slices of potato in the slow cooker. Mix the orange juice, sugar, salt, thyme, and sage together in a bowl. Pour over sweet potato slices; toss to coat. Dot with butter.
2. Cook on high for 2 ½ to 3 ½ hours, or on low for 5 to 6 hours. Before serving, stir to coat with orange juice mixture and sprinkle with crumbled bacon.

GARLIC MASHED POTATOES

SERVES 8 | PER SERVING - CALORIES: 189, FAT: 4G, CARBOHYDRATES: 36G, PROTEIN: 4G

INGREDIENTS

- 1.5kg baby potatoes, quartered
- 3 garlic cloves, minced
- 4 tbsp butter
- 60ml water
- Salt and pepper
- 80ml sour cream
- 60ml milk
- 1 tsp dried rosemary
- 1 ½ tsp dried oregano
- 1 tbsp chives to garnish

INSTRUCTIONS

1. Grease the slow cooker. Add potatoes, butter, garlic, and water to slow cooker. Season with salt and pepper. Cook for 3 hours on high.
2. Once potatoes are tender, add sour cream, milk, and spices. Mash the potatoes, and season to taste.
3. Sprinkle over the chives to serve.

CHEESY SPINACH

SERVES 8 | PER SERVING - CALORIES: 247, FAT: 15.6G, CARBOHYDRATES: 10.3G, PROTEIN: 17.4G

INGREDIENTS

- 3 tbsp butter
- 330g cottage cheese
- 225g cubed cheese
- 550g frozen chopped spinach, thawed and dried
- 50g plain flour
- 1 tsp salt
- 3 large eggs

INSTRUCTIONS

Stir all the ingredients together in a greased slow cooker. Cook for an hour on high, then turn the heat down to low and cook for 4 to 5 hours.

CHILLI GRATED SWEET POTATOES WITH BACON

SERVES 10 | PER SERVING - CALORIES: 695, FAT: 44.8G, CARBOHYDRATES: 41G, PROTEIN: 32G

INGREDIENTS

- 1.5kg sweet potatoes, peeled and grated
- 500g smoked bacon, cooked, and chopped
- 2 shallots, chopped
- 1 onion, chopped
- 450g grated mixed cheese
- 225g cream cheese
- 2 tsp chilli powder
- ½ tsp paprika
- 3 tbsp finely chopped fresh parsley
- ½ tsp salt
- 1 tsp ground pepper
- 2 tbsp olive oil
- 240ml sour cream and 2 tbsp maple syrup to serve

INSTRUCTIONS

1. Heat the oil over a medium to high heat in a frying pan. Cook the onion until soft, about 4 to 6 minutes.
2. Put the onion mix in a bowl, and stir in the parsley and seasonings. Add sweet potatoes and cheeses, mixing well. Fold in the chopped bacon.
3. Put everything in the slow cooker. Sprinkle with paprika. Cook on low for 4 to 5 hours.
4. Mix the remaining ingredients in a bowl, and serve over the potatoes.

CORN ON THE COB

SERVES 6 | PER SERVING - CALORIES: 77, FAT: 1G, CARBOHYDRATES: 16G, PROTEIN: 2G

INGREDIENTS

- 6 to 8 ears of corn on the cob
- Olive oil
- Salt and pepper
- Butter

INSTRUCTIONS

1. Husk the corn, and brush with oil. Season to taste.
2. Add 160ml cold water to the slow cooker, add in the corn.
3. Cook on high for 3 to 4 hours. Butter the corn before serving.

GREEN BEANS WITH BACON

SERVES 8 | PER SERVING - CALORIES: 148, FAT: 9G, CARBOHYDRATES: 12G, PROTEIN: 5G

INGREDIENTS

- 8 bacon rashers
- 900g rinsed and trimmed green beans
- Half an onion, diced
- 1 potato, diced
- 360ml chicken stock
- Salt and pepper to taste

INSTRUCTIONS

1. Cook the bacon until crisp, and chop into pieces.
2. Add the onions and cook until soft.
3. Grease the slow cooker, and tip in the onion, beans, bacon, and bacon fat.
4. Add in the diced potato, chicken stock, and season to taste.
5. Cook for 6 to 8 hours on low, or 3 to 4 hours on high.

SWEET POTATO WEDGES

SERVES 6 | PER SERVING - CALORIES: 303, FAT: 8G, CARBOHYDRATES: 55G, PROTEIN: 4G

INGREDIENTS

- 1.4kg sweet potatoes
- 55g salted butter, melted
- 240ml orange juice
- 2 tbsp brown sugar
- ¼ tsp salt
- ¼ tsp nutmeg
- 1 tsp cinnamon

INSTRUCTIONS

1. Wash and dry the potatoes, then cut into wedges. Put in the bottom of the slow cooker.
2. Pour over the butter and orange juice, then sprinkle over the sugar, cinnamon, salt, and nutmeg.
3. Toss the wedges in the mixture, then cook on low for 6 hours, or high for 4 hours.

EASY JASMINE RICE

SERVES 6 | PER SERVING - CALORIES: 34, FAT: 0G, CARBOHYDRATES: 25G, PROTEIN: 1G

INGREDIENTS

- 210g Jasmine rice
- Pinch of sea salt
- 315ml water
- 1 tbsp butter (optional)

INSTRUCTIONS

1. Rinse the rice well until the water is clear. Transfer to the slow cooker, and sprinkle in salt.
2. Tip the water over the rice, and add the butter, if using.
3. Cook for 2 to 2 ½ hours on low.

BALSAMIC BRUSSEL SPROUTS

SERVES 6 | PER SERVING - CALORIES: 133, FAT: 5G, CARBOHYDRATES: 19G, PROTEIN: 5G

INGREDIENTS

- 900g Brussel sprouts
- 2 tbsp olive oil
- 120ml balsamic vinegar
- 1 to 2 tbsp light brown sugar
- Salt and pepper to taste

INSTRUCTIONS

1. Put the Brussel sprouts and olive oil in the slow cooker. Season to taste.
2. Cook on high for 1 to 2 hours, or low for 3 to 4 hours.
3. Whilst the sprouts cook, make the balsamic reduction by simmering the balsamic vinegar and brown sugar in a saucepan. Simmer until the sauce reduces.
4. Serve the Brussel sprouts drizzled with the balsamic reduction.

BEANS AND POTATOES WITH BACON

SERVES 10 | PER SERVING - CALORIES: 116, FAT: 4G, CARBOHYDRATES: 17G, PROTEIN: 5G

INGREDIENTS

- 650g green beans, trimmed and chopped
- 8 bacon rashers, chopped
- 4 potatoes, peeled and cubed
- 1 onion, sliced
- ¼ tsp pepper
- ½ tsp salt
- 60ml chicken stock

INSTRUCTIONS

1. Cook the bacon until crisp. Drain the bacon on paper towels, reserving 1 tablespoon of the drippings. Refrigerate the bacon until later.
2. Put the everything else in the slow cooker, and stir through the reserved bacon dripping. Cook on low for 6 to 8 hours. Stir in the bacon and heat through.

ITALIAN STYLE MUSHROOMS

SERVES 6 | PER SERVING - CALORIES: 99, FAT: 8G, CARBOHYDRATES: 6G, PROTEIN: 3G

INGREDIENTS

- 450g fresh medium mushrooms
- 1 large onion, sliced
- 60ml butter, melted
- 2 tsp Italian herb mix

INSTRUCTIONS

In the slow cooker, layer the mushrooms and onion. Combine the melted butter with the herbs and pour over the vegetables. Cook on low for 4 to 5 hours until the vegetables are tender.

MAPLE AND WALNUT SWEET POTATOES

SERVES 12 | PER SERVING - CALORIES: 298, FAT: 5G, CARBOHYDRATES: 62G, PROTEIN: 4G

INGREDIENTS

- 8 medium sweet potatoes
- 120g chopped walnuts
- 60g light brown sugar
- 50g dried cherries, chopped
- 120ml maple syrup
- 60ml apple cider
- ¼ tsp salt

INSTRUCTIONS

1. Peel and cut the potatoes in half, then crosswise into slices. Place in the slow cooker. Add the brown sugar, cherries, syrup, cider, salt, and two thirds of the walnuts. Toss to combine.
2. Cook on low for 5 to 6 hours until the potatoes are tender. Sprinkle over the rest of the walnuts.

SAUSAGE STUFFING

SERVES 16 | PER SERVING - CALORIES: 261, FAT: 13G, CARBOHYDRATES: 28G, PROTEIN: 8G

INGREDIENTS

- 250ml chicken stock
- 125ml white wine
- 225g fresh mushrooms, chopped
- 475g seasoned sausage meat
- 100g dried cranberries
- 2 onions, finely chopped
- 2 garlic cloves, minced
- 6 stalks of celery, chopped
- 4 tbsp butter
- 1 tbsp sage
- 1 loaf French bread, cut into cubes

INSTRUCTIONS

1. Break up the sausage meat and cook until no longer pink, then set aside. Melt the butter in the same pan over a medium heat, and cook the mushrooms, celery, and onion for 3 minutes. Stir in the garlic and cook for another minute.
2. Stir the sausage through the vegetables, add the bread and sage, and toss to combine. Add the contents of the pan, wine, stock, and cranberries. Cook for 2 to 3 hours on low.

MASHED POTATOES

SERVES 12 | PER SERVING - CALORIES: 339, FAT: 16G, CARBOHYDRATES: 43G, PROTEIN: 7G

INGREDIENTS

- 2.2kg potatoes, peeled and quartered
- 225g cream cheese
- 240ml sour cream
- 1 tsp onion powder
- 4 tbsp butter
- 1 ½ tsp salt
- ¼ tsp garlic powder
- ¼ tsp white pepper
- 1 egg

INSTRUCTIONS

1. Boil the potatoes for 20 to 30 minutes, then drain and mash until smooth.
2. Beat in the other ingredients, then allow to cool. Put the potatoes in the slow cooker.
3. Cook for 3 to 4 hours on low, stirring once or twice.
4. If needed, add extra cream or milk during the cooking time for a softer consistency.

ROASTED BEETROOTS

SERVES 12 | PER SERVING - CALORIES: 65, FAT: 2G, CARBOHYDRATES: 11G, PROTEIN: 2G

INGREDIENTS

- 10 whole beetroots
- 5 tsp olive oil

INSTRUCTIONS

1. Clean the beetroots and trim the roots leaving about 1 inch of the tops.
2. Place each beetroot on a small square of foil, and drizzle with about ½ tsp olive oil. Bring the corners of the foil up and twist around to seal. Repeat with all the beetroots.
3. Put the beetroots in the slow cooker. Cook on high for 3 to 4 hours until tender.

CHEESY PEPPERS AND SWEETCORN

SERVES 6 | PER SERVING - CALORIES: 121, FAT: 2G, CARBOHYDRATES: 8G, PROTEIN: 6G

INGREDIENTS

- Non-stick cooking spray
- 450g frozen sweetcorn
- Half a red pepper, diced
- Half a green pepper, diced
- 3 spring onions, finely diced
- 60ml water
- 60ml whole milk
- 2 tsp cornflour
- 30g crumbled blue cheese
- ½ tsp black pepper
- ¼ tsp salt
- 50g grated cheddar

INSTRUCTIONS

1. Grease the slow cooker. Stir in the peppers, onions, sweetcorn, and water.
2. Cook for 1 ½ hours on high.
3. In a bowl, mix the cornflour and milk until smooth. Stir into the slow cooker, then cook for 10 minutes longer until the sauce starts to thicken.
4. Stir in the blue cheese, black pepper, and salt. Serve in bowls dusted with grated cheddar.

ROASTED TOMATOES

SERVES 4 | PER SERVING - CALORIES: 121, FAT: 2G, CARBOHYDRATES: 8G, PROTEIN: 6G

INGREDIENTS

- 2 large tomatoes, halved
- 1 tbsp balsamic vinegar
- 2 tsp olive oil
- 2 cloves of garlic, minced
- 1 tsp dried basil
- ½ tsp dried oregano
- ¼ tsp dried rosemary
- ¼ tsp salt
- 90g breadcrumbs
- 2 tbsp grated Parmesan
- Small handful of fresh basil, chopped

INSTRUCTIONS

1. Grease the inside of the slow cooker. Add the tomatoes, cut side facing up. Mix the remaining ingredients excluding the breadcrumbs and parmesan together, then spoon over the tomatoes.
2. Cook for 2 hours on low, or 1 hour on high.
3. Cook the breadcrumbs over a medium to high heat in a dry pan until browned, then take off the heat and stir in the parmesan.
4. Serve the tomatoes with a drizzle of cooking liquid, sprinkled with the breadcrumbs, and garnished with fresh basil.

BUTTERED MAPLE SWEET POTATO MASH

SERVES 10 | PER SERVING - CALORIES: 192, FAT: 9G, CARBOHYDRATES: 27G, PROTEIN: 2G

INGREDIENTS

- 1.6kg sweet potato, cut into chunks
- 60ml apple juice
- 2 tbsp maple syrup
- 6 tbsp unsalted butter
- 1 tsp black pepper
- 1 ¼ tsp salt
- Cooking spray

INSTRUCTIONS

Grease the inside of the slow cooker, then add all of the ingredients. Cook for 3 ½ hours on low. Mash the potatoes to achieve the desired consistency, adding extra butter if needed.

SCALLOPED POTATOES WITH HAM

SERVES 16 | PER SERVING - CALORIES: 167, FAT: 4G, CARBOHYDRATES: 25G, PROTEIN: 8G

INGREDIENTS

- 350g cheese sauce
- Can of cream of mushroom soup
- 240ml semi-skimmed milk
- 10 medium potatoes, peeled and sliced thinly
- 500g cooked, cubed ham
- 2 onions, chopped
- 1 tsp paprika
- 1 tsp pepper

INSTRUCTIONS

1. Combine the milk with the soup and sauce. In a greased slow cooker, layer half of the potatoes, ham, onions, and soup mixture. Repeat layers. Sprinkle over the pepper and paprika.
2. Cook on low for 8 to 10 hours.

CHEESY BROCCOLI

SERVES 10 | PER SERVING - CALORIES: 159, FAT: 11G, CARBOHYDRATES: 11G, PROTEIN: 6G

INGREDIENTS

- 550g frozen broccoli, partially thawed
- Can of cream of celery soup
- 175g grated cheddar cheese
- Half an onion, chopped
- ½ tsp Worcestershire sauce
- ¼ tsp pepper
- 120g breadcrumbs
- 2 tbsp butter

INSTRUCTIONS

1. In a bowl, mix the broccoli, soup, onion, two thirds of the cheese, Worcestershire sauce, and pepper. Pour into a greased slow cooker. Add the breadcrumbs and butter to the top.
2. Cook on high for 2 ½ to 3 hours. Sprinkle over the rest of the cheese, and cook for 10 minutes longer.

SPINACH AND RICE

SERVES 8 | PER SERVING - CALORIES: 159, FAT: 11G, CARBOHYDRATES: 11G, PROTEIN: 6G

INGREDIENTS

- 1L chicken stock
- 500g frozen chopped spinach, thawed and dried
- 420g uncooked rice
- 225g cream cheese
- 210g grated cheddar cheese
- 2 tbsp butter
- 2 garlic cloves, minced
- 1 onion, finely chopped
- 1 tsp pepper
- 1 tsp salt
- ¼ tsp dried thyme
- 60g breadcrumbs
- 50g grated Parmesan

INSTRUCTIONS

1. Melt the butter in a saucepan, and cook the onion until soft, 4 to 6 minutes. Stir in the thyme and garlic and cook for a minute. Pour in the stock and bring to a simmer. Remove from heat. Stir in spinach, cream cheese, salt, and pepper until blended. Transfer everything to the slow cooker and mix in the rice.
2. Cook on low for 3 to 4 hours until most of the liquid has been absorbed. Top with cheddar cheese. Leave the dish to stand, covered, for 20 minutes. Sprinkle the breadcrumbs and Parmesan on top before serving.

SNACKS

BOILED PEANUTS

SERVES 12 | PER SERVING - CALORIES: 621, FAT: 53G, CARBOHYDRATES: 17G, PROTEIN: 28G

INGREDIENTS

- 1.3kg green peanuts
- 65g salt
- 1.4 litres water

INSTRUCTIONS

1. Rinse the peanuts in water until it runs clear.
2. Put everything in the slow cooker.
3. Cook for 12 hours on high, checking occasionally to see if more water is needed.
4. Cook for a further 6 to 8 hours on low. Serve straight from the slow cooker, straining off the brine.

SWEET AND SPICY STICKY CHICKEN WINGS

SERVES 8 | PER SERVING - CALORIES: 514, FAT: 16.8G, CARBOHYDRATES: 21.5G, PROTEIN: 66G

INGREDIENTS

- 2-inch piece of ginger, peeled and chopped
- 4 garlic cloves, peeled and chopped
- 150g dark brown sugar
- 60ml soy sauce
- 1 tsp Sriracha sauce
- ¼ tsp cayenne pepper
- 1.8kg chicken wings, halved at the joint and wingtips removed
- 60ml water
- 60ml tomato paste

INSTRUCTIONS

1. Blitz the ginger, garlic, 1 tablespoon of the soy sauce, ½ tsp Sriracha, cayenne pepper, and a third of the sugar. Pulse until a paste is formed.
2. Toss the chicken wings in the paste and place in the slow cooker.
3. Cook on low for 3 to 4 hours, then take the wings out using a slotted spoon. Drain on paper towels and discard any leftover liquid.
4. Let the wings cool for 20 minutes.
5. Preheat the grill.
6. Set a wire rack inside a tray and spray with non-stick cooking spray.
7. In a bowl, whisk together the water, tomato paste, remaining brown sugar, soy sauce, Sriracha, and cayenne pepper.
8. Coat the wings using half of the sauce. Place the winds skin-side up on the prepared rack.
9. Cook under the grill until the wings have lightly charred, around 10 to 15 minutes. Turn the wings and brush over the sauce, then cook for 3 to 5 minutes.
10. Flip the wings and brush with sauce one more time, before grilling for a final 2 minutes.

EASY CHOCOLATE FUDGE

MAKES 36 SQUARES | PER SQUARE - CALORIES: 120, FAT: 6G, CARBOHYDRATES: 14G, PROTEIN: 2G

INGREDIENTS

- 375g can condensed milk
- 250g milk chocolate
- 250g dark chocolate
- 1 tsp vanilla extract
- 100g brown sugar
- Vegetable oil to grease

INSTRUCTIONS

1. Mix everything together with a pinch of salt in the slow cooker. Cook for an hour on low, stirring well every 15 minutes until thick and smooth. Scrape off any blobs of fudge that start getting stuck.
2. Oil a 20cm square tin, and line with baking parchment. Pour the mixture into the tin and chill for 4 hours before slicing into 36 squares.

CHEESE FONDUE

SERVES 8 | PER SERVING (FONDUE ONLY) - CALORIES: 408, FAT: 27.8G, CARBOHYDRATES: 3.5G, PROTEIN: 25.3G

INGREDIENTS

- 350g grated Emmental cheese
- 350g grated Gruyere cheese
- 3 tbsp cornflour
- 2 tsp ground mustard
- 360ml white wine
- Salami, fresh baguettes, or boiled new potatoes for dipping

INSTRUCTIONS

1. Toss the cheeses, cornflour, and mustard together in a bowl until thoroughly mixed.
2. Boil the wine over a medium heat. Add the cheese mixture gradually, stirring between additions until all the cheese has been incorporated and has melted.
3. Pour in the fondue mixture and set the slow cooker on low. Stir regularly to stop the cheese sticking.

HOT WINGS

SERVES 8 | PER SERVING - CALORIES: 420, FAT: 23.7G, CARBOHYDRATES: 1.9G, PROTEIN: 47.6G

INGREDIENTS

- 8 tbsp butter
- 1 tbsp dried oregano
- 1 tbsp onion powder
- 1 tbsp garlic powder
- 2 tbsp soy sauce
- 2 tbsp tomato paste
- 150ml hot sauce
- 1.3kg chicken wings
- 1 tsp granulated sugar

INSTRUCTIONS

1. Melt the butter and put in the slow cooker. Tip in the onion powder, oregano, soy sauce, tomato paste, hot sauce, and garlic powder. Whisk together until combined.
2. Add the wings and coat in the sauce. Cook on high for 4 hours.
3. Just before the chicken wings are done, heat the oven to 220C. Put the wings on a baking tray, and cook for 30 minutes until crisp.
4. Transfer the liquid from the slow cooker to a saucepan, and heat over a medium heat. Mix in the sugar, stirring until dissolved. Bring to the boil, then simmer for 10 minutes until the sauce is thick.
5. Remove the wings from the oven and toss the wings in the sauce.

CHILLI CHICKEN DRUMSTICKS

SERVES 6 | PER SERVING - CALORIES: 615, FAT: 20G, CARBOHYDRATES: 9.9G, PROTEIN: 93.7G

INGREDIENTS

- 120ml low-sodium soy sauce
- 120ml chicken stock
- 60ml Thai sweet chilli sauce
- 2 tbsp Sriracha
- 2 tbsp brown sugar
- Juice of 1 lime
- 1" fresh ginger, peeled and grated
- 3 cloves of garlic, crushed
- 2kg chicken drumsticks
- 2 spring onions, sliced thinly
- 1 tsp sesame seeds to garnish

INSTRUCTIONS

1. In a bowl, mix the soy sauce, chilli sauce, Sriracha, chicken stock, brown sugar, and lime juice. Stir in ginger and garlic.
2. Put the drumsticks in a resealable bag. Pour over marinade and seal. Marinate 30 minutes up to overnight.
3. Tip into the slow cooker, and cook on high for 3 to 4 hours, or low for 5 to 6 hours.
4. When drumsticks are tender and cooked through, preheat the grill on high. Transfer drumsticks to a large foil-lined baking sheet and cook under the grill until golden and crisp, 3 to 5 minutes.
5. Serve with a garnish of spring onions and sesame seeds.

BOURBON BBQ CHICKEN WINGS

SERVES 8 | PER SERVING - CALORIES: 269, FAT: 8.4G, CARBOHYDRATES: 11.5G, PROTEIN: 32.6G

INGREDIENTS

- 240ml BBQ sauce
- 2 tbsp bourbon
- Salt and pepper
- 900g chicken wings

INSTRUCTIONS

1. Place chicken wings in a large slow cooker.
2. Season with salt and pepper.
3. Cover and cook on high until cooked through, 2 1/2 to 3 hours.
4. Heat the grill. Tip the wings onto trays, and grill until crispy, 5 minutes.
5. Serve with barbecue sauce.

PARMESAN AND GARLIC CHICKEN WINGS

SERVES 8 | PER SERVING - CALORIES: 318, FAT: 17.4G, CARBOHYDRATES: 1.1G, PROTFIN: 38G

INGREDIENTS

- 900g chicken wings
- 55g butter, melted
- 4 garlic cloves, minced
- 2 tbsp dried parsley
- 130g grated parmesan
- Salt and pepper

INSTRUCTIONS

1. Place chicken wings in a large slow cooker.
2. Mix the garlic, parsley and 90g of the parmesan into the butter, and season. Pour mixture over chicken wings and stir to coat.
3. Cook on high for 2 ½ to 3 hours.
4. Preheat the grill. Line two baking trays with greaseproof paper, and tip on the chicken wings. Sprinkle with the remaining parmesan and grill for around 5 minutes until crispy.

CHINESE INSPIRED CHICKEN WINGS

SERVES 8 | PER SERVING - CALORIES: 258, FAT: 9.5G, CARBOHYDRATES: 8.5G, PROTEIN: 33.5G

INGREDIENTS

- 950g chicken wings
- 75g brown sugar
- 4 garlic cloves, minced
- 60ml low-sodium soy sauce
- 1 tsp cayenne pepper
- 2 tsp ground ginger
- 1 tbsp cornstarch
- 1 tsp ground black pepper
- Salt to taste
- 2 tbsp sesame seeds to serve

INSTRUCTIONS

1. Place chicken wings in a large slow cooker.
2. In a large bowl, mix the soy sauce, brown sugar, garlic, ginger, cayenne pepper, and black pepper. Season with salt, then add cornflour and stir until mixed. Toss the chicken in the mix.
3. Cover and cook on high until cooked through, 2 1/2 to 3 hours.
4. Preheat the grill. Line two baking sheets with greaseproof paper and pour the wings onto them. Grill until crispy, 5 minutes.
5. Serve with the sesame seeds.

APRICOT, HONEY AND MUSTARD SAUSAGE BITES

SERVES 8 | PER SERVING - CALORIES: 115, FAT: 4.3G, CARBOHYDRATES: 16.4G, PROTEIN: 3.5G

INGREDIENTS

- 8 sausages
- 80g apricot preserve or jam
- 8 dried apricots, quartered
- 1 small onion, chopped
- 2 tbsp honey
- 1 tbsp mustard
- 1 tbsp water
- ½ tsp fresh thyme

INSTRUCTIONS

1. Cut each sausage into eight slices (giving 64 slices in total).
2. In the slow cooker, mix the apricot preserve, dried apricots, onion, honey, mustard and water. Add the sausage and stir to coat.
3. Cook for 1 ½ to 2 hours on high, or 3 to 4 hours on low. Stir through the thyme just before serving.

JAMMY BBQ MEATBALLS

SERVES 10 | PER SERVING - CALORIES: 258, FAT: 11G, CARBOHYDRATES: 28.3G, PROTEIN: 8.8G

INGREDIENTS

- 900g frozen meatballs
- 500g jam or sauce of your choice
- 500g BBQ sauce

INSTRUCTIONS

1. Stir the sauces in the slow cooker. Add the meatballs and stir until they are coated with the sauce.
2. Cook on low for 3 to 4 hours, or high for 2 to 3 hours.

   Tip:

   This recipe works great with cranberry sauce, apple sauce, or grape jam.

TURKEY AND CRANBERRY MEATBALLS

MAKES 60 MEATBALLS | PER MEATBALL - CALORIES: 43, FAT: 0.6G, CARBOHYDRATES: 4.8G, PROTEIN: 4.6G

INGREDIENTS

- 1 egg
- 60g breadcrumbs
- 50g dried cranberries
- Half an onion, finely chopped
- 1 tsp salt
- ½ tsp garlic powder
- ½ tsp ground cloves
- 900g minced chicken or turkey
- 450g cranberry sauce

INSTRUCTIONS

1. Preheat the oven to 170C, and grease a tray.
2. In a bowl, mix the mince, breadcrumbs, cranberries, onion, salt, garlic powder, cloves, and egg. Shape into 60 meatballs.
3. Bake the meatballs for 15 minutes on the prepared baking tray.

4. Add the cranberry sauce and meatballs to the slow cooker. Cook for 2 to 3 hours on low, or 1 to 1 ½ hours on high.

STICKY GINGER CHICKEN WINGS

SERVES 6 | PER SERVING - CALORIES: 752, FAT: 24.8G, CARBOHYDRATES: 28.2G, PROTEIN: 99G

INGREDIENTS
- 2kg chicken wings
- 60ml honey
- 240ml garlic teriyaki sauce
- 2 tbsp grated fresh ginger
- 3 tbsp fresh lime juice
- ½ tsp lime zest
- 3 cloves of garlic, sliced

INSTRUCTIONS
1. Preheat the grill. Place the wings on a lightly greased tray and cook for about 14 minutes until browned.
2. Put the wings in the bottom of the slow cooker and tip over the remaining ingredients. Cover and cook on low for 4 hours.

PORK NACHOS

SERVES 16 | PER SERVING - CALORIES: 593, FAT: 4.7G, CARBOHYDRATES: 91.4G, PROTEIN: 42.9G

INGREDIENTS
- 1.7kg boneless pork loin
- 1kg cooked rice
- 1kg canned black beans, drained
- 330ml beer
- 5 garlic cloves, quartered
- 1 tsp dried oregano
- 2 tsp ground cumin
- 2 red chillies, chopped
- ¾ tsp salt
- 2 tbsp tomato paste
- 2 tbsp fresh lime juice
- Tortilla chips

INSTRUCTIONS
1. Make slits on the outside of the pork, and stuff with garlic. Stir together the cumin, oregano, and salt then sprinkle on the pork. Put the pork in the slow cooker.
2. Combine the beer, chillies, lime juice, and tomato paste in a bowl. Pour over the pork, and cook for 6 to 8 hours on high.
3. Shred the pork with two forks.
4. Toss the shredded pork in around 150ml of the cooking liquid.
5. Make a layer of tortilla chips on a serving platter, then spoon across rice, beans, meat, and toppings of your choice.

CHOCOLATE AND COCONUT FONDUE

SERVES 8 | PER SERVING - CALORIES: 890, FAT: 39G, CARBOHYDRATES: 59G, PROTEIN: 10G

INGREDIENTS
- Non-stick cooking spray
- 340g semi-sweet dark chocolate
- 275g dark chocolate
- 325g milk chocolate
- 340g evaporated milk
- 240ml hot strong brewed coffee
- 425g coconut milk
- 2 tsp vanilla

INSTRUCTIONS
Grease the inside of the slow cooker. Stir everything into the slow cooker. Cook for 3 hours on low, stirring frequently.

CHOCOLATE COVERED PEANUT CLUSTERS

MAKES 60 CLUSTERS | PER CLUSTER - CALORIES: 120, FAT: 9.8G, CARBOHYDRATES: 5.2G, PROTEIN: 4.7G

INGREDIENTS

- 450g dry roasted peanuts
- 450g unsalted dry roasted peanuts
- 500g chocolate of your choice
- 275g salted cashews
- 1 tsp vanilla extract

INSTRUCTIONS

1. Add the peanuts and chocolate to the slow cooker. Cook on low for 2 hours then stir well. Add the cashews and vanilla, stirring well to coat.
2. Drop the mixture in spoonsful onto greaseproof paper. Leave to stand until cool and firm.

TOMATO BEEF NACHOS

SERVES 20 | PER SERVING - CALORIES: 107, FAT: 3.4G, CARBOHYDRATES: 3.7G, PROTEIN: 14.5G

INGREDIENTS

- 950g minced beef
- 1 can pinto beans in tomato sauce
- 1 ½ tbsp brown sugar
- 1 tbsp cider vinegar
- 2 tsp ground coriander
- 1 tsp cayenne pepper
- 2 tbsp chilli powder
- 2 tsp ground cumin
- 2 tsp dried oregano
- ¾ tsp salt
- Tortilla chips, cheddar, lettuce, and sour cream to serve

INSTRUCTIONS

1. Combine the beef, pinto beans, chilli powder, sugar, cumin, coriander, oregano, and cayenne pepper in the slow cooker. Cook for 4 to 6 hours on low until the meat crumbles. Stir in vinegar and salt.
2. Serve with tortilla chips, cheese, lettuce, and sour cream.

CANDIED NUTS

SERVES 12 | PER SERVING - CALORIES: 327, FAT: 31G, CARBOHYDRATES: 11G, PROTEIN: 6G

INGREDIENTS

- 55g butter
- 75g icing sugar
- 1 ½ tsp ground cinnamon
- ¼ tsp ground ginger
- ¼ tsp ground allspice
- 175g pecans
- 175g walnuts
- 125g unblanched almonds

INSTRUCTIONS

1. In a greased slow cooker, mix the butter, sugar, and spices. Add the nuts and toss to coat.
2. Cook on low for 2 to 34 hours until the nuts are crisp, stirring once during the cooking time.
3. Transfer the nuts to greaseproof paper to cool, and store in an airtight container.

PIZZA FONDUE

SERVES 16 | PER SERVING - CALORIES: 69, FAT: 3G, CARBOHYDRATES: 6G, PROTEIN: 5G

INGREDIENTS

- 850g tomato pasta or pizza sauce
- 240g mozzarella, grated
- 50g Parmesan, grated
- ¼ tsp garlic powder
- 2 tsp dried oregano
- 1 tsp onion powder

INSTRUCTIONS

Stir everything into the slow cooker. Cook on low for 4 to 5 hours until cooked through.

SWEET AND SPICY PEANUTS

SERVES 12 | PER SERVING - CALORIES: 284, FAT: 20G, CARBOHYDRATES: 22G, PROTEIN: 10G

INGREDIENTS

- 350g salted peanuts
- 65g sugar
- 40g brown sugar
- 2 tbsp hot water
- 2 tbsp butter
- 1 tbsp Sriracha
- 1 tsp chilli powder

INSTRUCTIONS

1. Put the peanuts in the bottom of the slow cooker. In a bowl, stir together the sugar, water, butter, chilli sauce, and chilli powder, then tip over the peanuts. Cook on high for 1 ½ hours, stirring once half way through.
2. Spread on aluminium foil to cool, and store in an airtight container.

DESSERTS

SWEET RICE PUDDING

SERVES 6 | PER SERVING - CALORIES: 200, FAT: 4G, CARBOHYDRATES: 32G, PROTEIN: 8G

INGREDIENTS

- 1 tsp butter
- 1 litre of semi-skimmed milk
- 200g wholegrain rice
- Small grating of nutmeg or cinnamon
- Honey, toasted almonds, and fruit to serve

INSTRUCTIONS

1. Butter the slow cooker all over the base and halfway up the sides. Heat the milk to simmering point. Mix the rice with the milk, and pour into the slow cooker. Add a grating of nutmeg or cinnamon. Cook for 2½ hours on High and stir once or twice if you can.
2. Serve with honey, almonds, or fruit if you like.

STICKY TOFFEE PUDDING

SERVES 8 | PER SERVING - CALORIES: 625, FAT: 32G, CARBOHYDRATES: 76G, PROTEIN: 6G

INGREDIENTS

- 220g self-raising flour
- 2 eggs
- 200g pitted dates, chopped
- 250g light brown sugar
- 300ml double cream
- 100g butter, plus extra to grease
- 1 tsp vanilla extract
- 1 tsp bicarbonate of soda
- 4 tbsp treacle
- Vanilla ice cream to serve

INSTRUCTIONS

1. Cover the dates with 150ml of boiling water in a bowl. Let the dates soak for 30 minutes. Butter a 1 litre pudding dish, and line with baking paper.
2. Put half of the butter, half the treacle, vanilla extract, 75g of sugar, and the cream in a pan. Cook over a medium heat, stirring constantly, until the sugar dissolves. Turn up the heat, and cook for a couple minutes longer. Whisk in the salt. Tip a third of the sauce into the bottom of the pudding dish.
3. Beat the butter with the eggs, treacle, and sugar. Stir in the bicarbonate of soda, salt, and flower. Stir through the dates and the liquid they soaked in. Spoon the mixture into the pudding dish, and smooth across the top. Leave a 1cm gap. Cover the pudding with a double layer of greaseproof paper and foil, making a pleat in the middle to let the pudding expand. Secure with string.
4. Set the slow cooker to low. Put in the slow cooker, and pour boiling water in to come halfway up the side. Cook for 7 to 8 hours. Serve with the leftover sauce and ice cream.

APPLE BREAD PUDDING

SERVES 6 | PER SERVING - CALORIES: 589, FAT: 32.5G, CARBOHYDRATES: 70.3G, PROTEIN: 7.5G

INGREDIENTS

- 375g apples, peeled, cored, and diced
- 10 slices of crusty bread, cubed
- ½ tsp ground cinnamon
- ½ tsp ground nutmeg
- Pinch of salt
- 100g dark brown sugar
- 120g butter, melted

SARA R. ADAMS

INSTRUCTIONS

Place apples into the crock of a slow cooker. In a bowl, mix the bread, spices, and sugar. Put on top of the apples and pour over the melted butter. Cook for 3 hours on low.

BLACK FOREST CAKE

SERVES 10 | PER SERVING - CALORIES: 379, FAT: 17.6G, CARBOHYDRATES: 56.2G, PROTEIN: 3.5G

INGREDIENTS

- 120g butter
- 430g canned crushed pineapple, drained and juice reserved
- 500g cherry pie filling or topping
- 500g chocolate cake mix

INSTRUCTIONS

1. Melt the butter and stir in the juice. Set aside.
2. Put the pineapple in the bottom of the slow cooker and spoon the pie filling over the top. Empty the dry cake mix into the top of the slow cooker. Stir the butter and pineapple juice together again and pour over the top of the cake mix.
3. Cook for 3 hours on low. Spoon the dessert into bowls and let cool about 5 before eating. Serve with vanilla ice cream.

CHOCOLATE ORANGE PUDDING

SERVES 6 | PER SERVING - CALORIES: 498, FAT: 27G, CARBOHYDRATES: 55.1G, PROTEIN: 7.3G

INGREDIENTS

- 175g caster sugar
- 175g butter, softened
- 175g self-raising flour
- 35g cocoa powder
- 3 eggs
- 2 tbsp milk
- ½ tsp vanilla extract
- 2 tbsp orange liqueur
- 1tsp baking powder
- Zest of 2 oranges

INSTRUCTIONS

1. Set the slow cooker on high, and grease six ramekins. In a bowl, beat the sugar and butter together until fluffy. Beat in the eggs one at a time until pale. Fold in the milk and vanilla, then add the liqueur and orange zest. Mix well.
2. Mix in the baking powder, cocoa, and flour.
3. Divide the batter between the ramekins, then cover each with pleated greaseproof paper secured with foil and string.
4. Put the puddings in the slow cooker over four layers of greaseproof paper. Pour in boiling water to come halfway up the sides of the ramekins. Cook for 90 minutes.
5. Take the ramekins out of the slow cooker, and remove the greaseproof paper and foil. Turn out onto a serving plate.

CRÈME CARAMEL

SERVES 6 | PER SERVING - CALORIES: 157, FAT: 4.5G, CARBOHYDRATES: 27.2G, PROTEIN: 3.7G

INGREDIENTS

- 600ml full fat milk
- 160g caster sugar
- 2 eggs
- 4 egg yolks
- 1 vanilla pod, seeded and split lengthways
- 55ml water

INSTRUCTIONS

1. Preheat the slow cooker to low. Grease six 150ml ramekin dishes. In a saucepan, mix the milk and vanilla together. Bring to a simmer, then remove from the heat. Let the mix cool for 45 minutes. Discard the vanilla pod.
2. Put half of the sugar in a separate small saucepan and add the water. Bring to a boil, and cook for 10 to 15 minutes until the sugar browns. Divide between the 6 ramekins.
3. In a bowl, mix the rest of the sugar, egg yolks, and eggs. Whisk until creamy and light. Whisking continuously, pour the cooled milk into the eggs. Once smooth, divide between the ramekins. Cover the ramekins with foil tied with string.
4. Put the ramekins in the slow cooker and pour in boiling water to halfway up the sides. Cook for 3 hours.
5. Take the ramekins out, and cool at room temperature for between 2 and 3 hours, then, cool in the fridge overnight. Invert over a serving plate.

PEANUT BUTTER FUDGE CAKE

SERVES 8 | PER SERVING - CALORIES: 601, FAT: 30.9G, CARBOHYDRATES: 76.3G, PROTEIN: 13.8G

INGREDIENTS

- 220g plain flour
- 275g chunky peanut butter
- 125g soft brown sugar
- 1 tsp bicarbonate of soda
- 1 tsp baking powder

- ¼ tsp salt
- 2 tbsp boiling water
- 3 tbsp melted butter
- 150g caster sugar
- 175g dark chocolate chips

- 175g soured cream
- 35g cocoa powder
- 200ml whole milk, warmed
- 1 tsp vanilla

INSTRUCTIONS

1. In a bowl, mix the baking powder, bicarbonate of soda, brown sugar, and salt into the flour. In another bowl, whisk the peanut butter, butter, soured cream and boiling water. Stir flour mixture into peanut butter mixture until fully combined, then stir in chocolate chips.
2. Generously grease the ceramic dish of your slow cooker; pour in cake mixture.
3. Whisk the caster sugar, milk, cocoa powder, and vanilla until smooth. Pour over the cake mix.
4. Cook on high for about 1 ½ to 2 hours on high until the cake starts to pull away from the sides and the edges appear solid.

CRÈME BRULÉ

SERVES 4 | PER SERVING - CALORIES: 461, FAT: 42G, CARBOHYDRATES: 17.4G, PROTEIN: 4.8G

INGREDIENTS

- 4 large egg yolks
- 50g caster sugar

- ¼ tsp salt
- 2 tsp vanilla extract

- 400ml double cream
- 4 tsp caster sugar for topping

INSTRUCTIONS

1. Whisk together yolks, 50g sugar, salt, and vanilla in a bowl, then gently whisk in cream. Pour mixture through a sieve into a measuring jug.
2. Line the bottom of an oval slow cooker with a folded piece of kitchen roll to create a level surface so ramekins will not slide around. Put 4 ramekins on the kitchen roll. Pour water in the slow cooker to come halfway up the sides of the ramekins.
3. Pour custard evenly into ramekins. Drape kitchen roll over the slow cooker, then put the lid on top. Cook on low until custard is set but jiggles slightly, about 2 hours.

4. Transfer ramekins to a rack to cool completely, about 45 minutes. Chill custards, uncovered, until cold, at least 3 hours.
5. Sprinkle 1 teaspoon of sugar evenly over each ramekin. Brown the sugar with a culinary blowtorch (or place under a hot grill under sugar has caramelised); serve immediately.

COCONUT CAKE

SERVES 8 | PER SERVING - CALORIES: 652, FAT: 47G, CARBOHYDRATES: 52.8G, PROTEIN: 7.5G

INGREDIENTS

CAKE
- 125ml coconut oil
- 120ml coconut milk
- 225g caster sugar
- 120g unsalted butter
- 250g plain flour
- 3 eggs
- 1 tsp baking powder
- ¼ tsp salt

ICING
- 120g toasted coconut flakes
- 180g icing sugar
- 125g cream cheese
- 70g unsalted butter
- ½ tsp vanilla
- ¼ tsp salt

INSTRUCTIONS
1. Beat the butter with the coconut oil and sugar, and add the eggs one at a time, beating well after each.
2. Mix the flour, salt, and baking powder together in a bowl. Gradually tip the flour into the butter until just combined.
3. Grease the slow cooker, and line the bottom with greaseproof paper. Tip the cake batter in evenly. Put pieces of kitchen roll over the top of the slow cooker and put the lid on top. Cook on high for 1 to 1 ½ hours.
4. Take off the lid and paper towel. Using gloves, take the bowl out of the slow cooker and let cool for a minimum of 10 minutes. When cool enough to handle, carefully turn the cake onto a plate and leave to cool fully.
5. Beat the butter and cream cheese until light. Mix in the icing sugar gradually, then beat in the vanilla and salt.
6. Ice the cake and top with the toasted coconut.

MANGO RICE PUDDING

SERVES 6 | PER SERVING - CALORIES: 321, FAT: 16G, CARBOHYDRATES: 40.7G, PROTEIN: 6G

INGREDIENTS
- 150g pudding rice
- 400ml coconut milk
- 500ml semi-skimmed or whole milk
- 60g caster sugar
- 6 cardamom pods, seeds removed and crushed (optional)
- 425g tin mango slices, drained and diced
- 1 lime, zested and juiced
- 20g toasted flaked almonds

INSTRUCTIONS
1. Put the pudding rice in a pan over low-medium heat with the coconut milk, milk, sugar, and cardamom (if using).
2. Simmer, then transfer to the slow cooker and cook for 1 to 2 hours on low, stirring frequently. Set aside for 10 minutes to cool slightly. it will look a little loose when you remove it from the oven but will thicken as it cools.

3. Spoon into serving bowls and top with the diced mango and lime zest. Squeeze over a little lime juice and top with the almonds to serve.

APPLE CRUMBLE

SERVES 4 | PER SERVING - CALORIES: 519, FAT: 29G, CARBOHYDRATES: 63.9G, PROTEIN: 5.9G

INGREDIENTS

- 5 Granny Smith apples, peeled, cored and each cut into 8 wedges
- 1 tsp ground cinnamon
- 1 orange, zested and half juiced
- 60g rolled oats
- 50g walnut pieces
- ½ tsp ground ginger
- 75g plain flour
- 85g light muscovado sugar
- 90g unsalted butter, melted

INSTRUCTIONS

1. Put the slices of apple in a slow cooker. Sprinkle over the ground cinnamon, orange zest and 1 tbsp juice and mix.
2. Pulse the walnuts and oats in a food processor until the texture is like coarse breadcrumbs then tip into a bowl.
3. Stir the ginger, flour and sugar into the oat and walnut mixture then add the butter and mix well.
4. Spoon the crumble mix over the apples, covering them all. Lay two sheets of kitchen paper on top of the crumble. Cook on low for around 3 ½ hours.
5. Remove the kitchen paper and cook for the last 10 minutes with the lid just slightly ajar.

CARAMEL BREAD PUDDING

SERVES 8 | PER SERVING - CALORIES: 544, FAT: 41G, CARBOHYDRATES: 36.2G, PROTEIN: 9G

INGREDIENTS

- 2 large eggs, plus 2 large egg yolks
- 230ml double cream
- 125g salted caramel sauce
- 35g unsalted butter
- 1 tsp vanilla extract
- 120g dark chocolate, chopped
- 120g pecans, chopped
- 8 pack butter brioche rolls, broken into 3cm pieces
- 2 tbsp dark rum (optional)

INSTRUCTIONS

1. Grease the slow cooker. Heat the cream with half of the caramel sauce in a pan until bubbling. Stir well and take off the heat. In a bowl, whisk the eggs with the egg yolks, salt, vanilla, and dark rum (if using). Slowly pour the cream into the eggs, whisking continuously.
2. Stir the brioche, chocolate, and pecans into the eggs. Leave for 5 minutes, then stir again to make sure everything is evenly combined.
3. Tip into the slow cooker, and cook on low for 1 ½ hours.
4. Heat the rest of the sauce in a pan, then divide the pudding between bowls and serve with the sauce.

GIANT CHOCOLATE AND SULTANA COOKIE

SERVES 10 | PER SERVING - CALORIES: 376, FAT: 16G, CARBOHYDRATES: 54G, PROTEIN: 5.5G

INGREDIENTS

- 150g butter, room temperature
- 75g light muscovado sugar
- 100g caster sugar
- 2 eggs
- 1 tbsp vanilla
- 340g plain flour
- ½ tsp baking powder
- ¼ tsp salt
- 100g dark chocolate chips
- 50g sultanas, raisins, or currants

INSTRUCTIONS

1. Beat together the butter, two sugars, eggs, and vanilla extract till light and fluffy.
2. In another bowl, mix the flour with the salt and baking powder.
3. Next stir the flour mixture into the butter mixture. I kneaded it together till it all came together like biscuit dough. Sides of the bowl should clean when it is the right consistency.
4. Stir in the choc chips and sultanas and make sure they are evenly distributed.
5. Grease your slow cooker bowl with butter, and cut grease proof paper to fit the base and put it in. Grease the top of the paper too.
6. Spoon the dough into the slow cooker bowl and flatten/press into the sides.
7. Slow cook for 3 hours on low, with lid on. You may need to switch to high for the last 30 minutes.
8. For the last 30 minutes leave the lid half open.
9. Leave the cookie to cool for half an hour.
10. Turn the cookie out on to a cooling rack, remove the grease proof paper for the bottom, and slice to serve.

CHOCOLATE CHIP SCONES

SERVES 10 | PER SERVING - CALORIES: 194, FAT: 8G, CARBOHYDRATES: 26.9G, PROTEIN: 3.7G

INGREDIENTS

- 225g self-raising flour
- Pinch of salt
- 55g butter, cubed
- 30g caster sugar
- 150ml milk
- 100g chocolate chips

INSTRUCTIONS

1. Stir the sugar and salt into the flour. Rub the butter into the flour until it resembles breadcrumbs.
2. Stir in the milk, and bring it together to form a dough.
3. Stir in the chocolate chips or other filling.
4. Bring it together gently and form it into a round. Score the top with a knife where you will cut the individual triangles.
5. Line your slow cooker pot and put the dough in gently.
6. Lay a tea towel over the slow cooker and put the lid on top. Cook for 1 ½ hours on high.
7. Leave to cool, then slice into triangles to serve.

LEMON CAKE

SERVES 8 | PER SERVING - CALORIES: 479, FAT: 23.8G, CARBOHYDRATES: 62G, PROTEIN: 6.1G

INGREDIENTS

- 240ml sour cream
- 250g sugar
- 75g polenta
- 250g plain flour
- 175g butter, softened
- 1 tsp bicarbonate of soda
- 1 tsp baking powder
- ½ tsp salt
- 1 tsp vanilla extract
- 1 tbsp grated lemon zest
- 1 ½ tsp poppy seeds
- 2 eggs

FOR THE GLAZE:

- 3 tbsp lemon juice
- 130g icing sugar

INSTRUCTIONS

1. Line the slow cooker with greaseproof paper.
2. In a bowl, mix the flour, bicarbonate of soda, baking powder, polenta and salt.
3. In another bowl, beat the sugar and butter. Add the eggs and beat for another 2 minutes.
4. With the mixer on low, mix in the sour cream, lemon zest, vanilla extract, and poppy seeds.
5. Gradually mix in the flour.
6. Pour the batter into the slow cooker. Cook on high for 2 ¼ to 2 ½ hours until set in the middle. Let the cake cool on a rack.
7. In a small bowl, beat the lemon juice and icing sugar together until smooth, then drizzle over the cake.

CHOCOLATE CHIP COOKIE BARS

SERVES 16 | PER SERVING - CALORIES: 333, FAT: 15.4G, CARBOHYDRATES: 45.7G, PROTEIN: 3.3G

INGREDIENTS

- 225g salted butter, melted
- 440g brown sugar
- 3 tsp vanilla extract
- 2 eggs
- ¼ tsp salt
- 250g plain flour
- 180g chocolate chips of your choice

INSTRUCTIONS

1. Line a slow cooker with aluminium foil to create a foil bowl.
2. In a bowl, mix the melted butter and brown sugar together until smooth. Add in vanilla extract and eggs and stir again until smooth. Stir in salt and flour until well combined.
3. Pour batter into the bottom of a foil lined slow cooker. Sprinkle chocolate chips on top. Secure a paper towel under the lid of the slow cooker.
4. Cook on high 2 ½ to 3 hours until set in the middle. Use the aluminium foil to remove the cookies from the slow cooker. Leave to cool for at least an hour.

COFFEE CAKE

SERVES 10 | PER SERVING - CALORIES: 411, FAT: 19G, CARBOHYDRATES: 56G, PROTEIN: 6G

INGREDIENTS

- 315ml milk
- 150ml vegetable oil
- 2 eggs
- 320g brown sugar
- 350g plain flour
- 1 tsp salt
- 2 tsp baking powder
- ½ tsp bicarbonate of soda
- 1 ½ tsp ground cinnamon
- 1 tsp white vinegar
- Chopped nuts to serve (optional)

INSTRUCTIONS

1. Mix the sugar, salt, and flour together, then stir in the oil until clumpy.
2. Fold the baking powder, cinnamon, and bicarbonate of soda into the flour. Place milk, oil, eggs, and vinegar in a measuring cup and whisk until the eggs are beaten, then add to the flour mixture and stir until combined (mixture may be slightly lumpy).
3. Grease the inside of the slow cooker and tip in the batter.
4. If using, sprinkle the chopped nuts on top of the batter.
5. Cook the cake on high for 1 ½ to 2 ½ hours.

CHOCOLATE FUDGE
SERVES 16 | PER SERVING - CALORIES: 65, FAT: 3G, CARBOHYDRATES: 9G, PROTEIN: 1G

INGREDIENTS

- 170g milk chocolate chips
- 60ml double cream
- 80ml honey
- 45g white chocolate chips
- 1 tsp vanilla

INSTRUCTIONS

1. Add milk chocolate chips, heavy whipping cream, and honey to the slow cooker. Cook for an hour on high.
2. Pour over the white chocolate chips and mix until melted. Stir in vanilla.
3. Pour into a foil-lined dish or box. If desired, sprinkle coarse sea salt over chocolate. Allow to cool completely (1-3 hours). Cut into squares.

STICKY CARAMEL PUMPKIN CAKE
SERVES 12 | PER SERVING - CALORIES: 426, FAT: 17G, CARBOHYDRATES: 66G, PROTEIN: 5G

INGREDIENTS

- 4 eggs
- 1 can of pumpkin puree
- 265g sugar
- 240g butter
- 250g plain flour
- 1 tsp ground cinnamon
- 2 tsp baking powder
- 1 tsp bicarbonate of soda
- ½ tsp salt
- Caramel sauce to serve

INSTRUCTIONS

1. Grease the inside of your slow cooker with oil or non-stick cooking spray.
2. Stir the baking powder, bicarbonate of soda, salt, and cinnamon into the flour in a bowl.
3. In a separate bowl, beat the sugar into the butter until fluffy.
4. Add the eggs, one at a time. Mix well after each egg.
5. Add the pumpkin and blend until well mixed.
6. Gradually add the flour mixture and beat at a low speed until smooth.
7. Level the top of the cake with a spatula.
8. Cook the cake on high for 2 hours.
9. Let the cake stand for about 10 minutes, before inverting onto a rack and then again onto a serving plate.
10. Drizzle caramel sauce over the cake to serve.

PEACH COBBLER

SERVES 6 | PER SERVING - CALORIES: 287, FAT: 6G, CARBOHYDRATES: 57G, PROTEIN: 4G

INGREDIENTS

FOR THE PEACHES:
- 500g peaches, peeled and sliced
- 50g light brown sugar
- ½ tsp ground cinnamon

FOR THE TOPPING:
- 200g powdered pancake mix
- 50g light brown sugar
- 50g granulated sugar
- ½ tsp ground cinnamon
- ¼ tsp ground nutmeg
- 2 tsp vanilla extract
- 120ml semi-skimmed milk

INSTRUCTIONS
1. Grease the slow cooker.
2. In a bowl, toss the peach ingredients together. Spread the peaches in the bottom of the slow cooker.
3. In another bowl, combine the topping ingredients, and stir thoroughly until smooth. Tip over the peaches.
4. Line the top of the slow cooker with kitchen towels to stop the condensation leaking into the cobbler.
5. Cook on low until the middle is set, 3 to 4 hours.

CARAMEL FLAN

SERVES 6 | PER SERVING - CALORIES: 376, FAT: 9G, CARBOHYDRATES: 65G, PROTEIN: 11G

INGREDIENTS
- 400g sweetened condensed milk
- 360ml milk
- 3 eggs
- 1 tsp vanilla extract
- 12 tbsp caramel sauce
- Whipped cream to serve

INSTRUCTIONS
1. Whisk the condensed milk, vanilla, eggs, and milk until smooth. Keep whisking until you cannot feel the heaviness of the sweetened condensed milk on the bottom of the bowl.
2. Put 2 tbsp of caramel in the bottom of each ramekin, and swirl to coat the sides.
3. Tip the milk mixture into the ramekins and fill to the inner lip.
4. Put the filled moulds in the slow cooker.
5. Put about an inch of water in the slow cooker around the ramekins.
6. Cover and cook on high for 1 hour 45 minutes. The flans are ready when they begin to puff slightly on the edges. The centre should jiggle, but not be liquid.
7. Take the ramekins out and let them cool in the fridge for a minimum of 3 hours.
8. Turn out onto a plate, and serve with cream.

BLACKBERRY COBBLER

SERVES 8 | PER SERVING - CALORIES: 274, FAT: 7G, CARBOHYDRATES: 49G, PROTEIN: 4G

INGREDIENTS

BLACKBERRY LAYER:
- 430g blackberries
- 1 tbsp cornflour
- 2 tbsp salted butter, melted
- 50g sugar

COBBLER LAYER:

- 240ml milk
- 160g sugar
- 160g plain flour

- ½ tsp salt
- 1 ½ tsp baking powder
- 1 tsp vanilla extract

- 2 tbsp salted butter, melted

TOPPING:

- 1 tbsp sugar

- ¼ tsp cinnamon

INSTRUCTIONS

1. Mix the ingredients for the blackberry layer in the slow cooker.
2. In a medium bowl, add the dry cobbler ingredients and stir. Add the vanilla, milk, and melted butter, and stir until combined.
3. Pour the batter over the blackberries.
4. Mix the topping ingredients together, and sprinkle over the top of the cobbler.
5. Cook for 2 ½ hours on high. Serve with ice cream or whipped cream.

BERRY GRANOLA CRISP

SERVES 5 | PER SERVING - CALORIES: 243, FAT: 7G, CARBOHYDRATES: 42G, PROTEIN: 6G

INGREDIENTS

- 360g raspberries
- 300g blueberries

- 1 tbsp lemon juice
- 180g granola

INSTRUCTIONS

1. Grease the slow cooker.
2. Add the berries, then drizzle over the lemon juice.
3. Sprinkle the granola over the berries evenly.
4. Place a paper towel over the slow cooker and then cover with the lid.
5. Cook on low for 1 hour and 45 minutes.
6. Serve with ice cream or whipped cream.

CRANBERRY AND PEACH COBBLER

SERVES 8 | PER SERVING - CALORIES: 357, FAT: 14G, CARBOHYDRATES: 55G, PROTEIN: 7G

INGREDIENTS

FOR THE FRUIT LAYER:

- 825g canned peaches in syrup

- 400g cranberry sauce

- 2 tbsp brown sugar

FOR THE COBBLER:

- 230g dry pancake mix
- 240ml milk

- 1 egg
- 75g melted butter

- 2 tbsp sugar

FOR THE TOPPING:

- 2 tbsp sugar

- ¼ tsp cinnamon

INSTRUCTIONS

1. Grease the slow cooker.
2. In a medium-sized bowl stir together the peaches in syrup, cranberry sauce and 2 tablespoons brown sugar. Pour this peach/cranberry mixture into the slow cooker.

3. In a another medium-sized bowl mix together the pancake mix, milk, egg, melted butter and 2 tablespoons of sugar until smooth. Spread this cobbler topping mixture evenly over the peach/cranberry mixture

4. Mix the cinnamon into the sugar in a bowl. Sprinkle this cinnamon sugar mixture over the cobbler evenly.

5. Cook for 2 ¼ hours on high. Serve warm with vanilla ice cream.

SPICED APPLES WITH BARLEY

SERVES 4 | PER SERVING - CALORIES: 168, FAT: 2G, CARBOHYDRATES: 28G, PROTEIN: 6G

INGREDIENTS
- 75g pearled barley
- 2 apples
- ½ tsp cinnamon
- Grated zest of 1 large orange
- 4 tbsp natural yoghurt
- Small grating of fresh nutmeg

INSTRUCTIONS
1. Heat the slow cooker if necessary. Put the barley and 750ml boiling water into the slow cooker. Peel and core the apples so you have a hole the size of a pound coin in each one. Cut each apple in half.

2. Stand the apples skin side down on the barley. Mix the cinnamon, nutmeg, and orange zest, and sprinkle them over the apples.

3. Cook for 2 hours on low. Serve with the natural yoghurt.

CHEESECAKE WITH HAZELNUTS AND BLACKBERRIES

SERVES 10 | PER SERVING - CALORIES: 612, FAT: 39G, CARBOHYDRATES: 52G, PROTEIN: 10G

INGREDIENTS
- 3 large eggs
- 750g full-fat cream cheese
- 250g light muscovado sugar
- 225g oat biscuits
- 200g blackberries
- 200ml soured cream
- 100g hazelnuts
- 50g butter, melted, plus extra for greasing
- 4 tbsp full-fat milk
- 2 tbsp plain flour
- 1 tsp vanilla extract
- 2 tsp cornflour
- 3 tbsp golden caster sugar

INSTRUCTIONS
1. Roll a long piece of foil into a sausage shape and roll into a coil. Put in the bottom of the slow cooker. Turn the slow cooker on to high and pour in hot water to come 4cm up the side.

2. Wrap the outside of a cake tin in two layers of clingfilm and then a layer of foil. Make sure there are no gaps for the water to seep through. Grease the tin, then line the bottom with greaseproof paper.

3. Blitz the biscuits and hazelnuts in a food processor to make fine crumbs. Tip the crumbs into the tin and press into the base using a spoon. Chill for 10 minutes.

4. In a small pan, heat the sugar and milk. Mix constantly until the sugar dissolves, then set aside to cool.

5. Beat the eggs, flour and vanilla into the cream cheese. Stir through the soured cream and sugar mix until combined. Tip the mixture into the tin and carefully put it in the slow cooker. Place a tea towel over the slow cooker, then put the lid on top.

6. Cook for 2 hours, then turn off the slow cooker. Leave the cheesecake in the slow cooker without taking the lid off for another 2 hours.

7. Cool the cheesecake at room temperature for another hour, then chill for 4 hours or overnight.

8. Put the cornflour, sugar, and half of the blackberries in a saucepan. Cook for 3 to 4 minutes over a high heat, crushing the blackberries a little until the mixture becomes syrupy. Toss in the rest of the berries and heat through.
9. Cool until you are ready to serve.

POACHED APRICOTS WITH ROSEWATER

SERVES 2 | PER SERVING - CALORIES: 161, FAT: 0G, CARBOHYDRATES: 41G, PROTEIN: 2G

INGREDIENTS

- 50g caster sugar
- 400g ripe apricots, halved and stoned
- Couple drops of rosewater
- Greek yoghurt to serve

INSTRUCTIONS

1. Put the apricots, sugar, and 100ml of water in the slow cooker. Cook on low for 2 hours until soft.
2. Splash in the rosewater and leave to cool.
3. Serve in glasses with Greek yoghurt.

TREACLE SPONGE

SERVES 4 | PER SERVING - CALORIES: 763, FAT: 43G, CARBOHYDRATES: 90G, PROTEIN: 10G

INGREDIENTS

- 175g unsalted butter, plus extra for greasing
- 3 tbsp golden syrup, plus extra to drizzle
- 1 tbsp fresh white breadcrumbs
- 175g caster sugar
- Zest of 1 lemon
- 3 eggs
- 175g self-raising flour
- 2 tbsp milk

INSTRUCTIONS

1. Use a small knob of butter to heavily grease a 1-litre pudding basin. In a small bowl, mix the golden syrup with the breadcrumbs, then tip into the pudding basin.
2. Beat butter with sugar and zest until light and fluffy, then add eggs gradually. Fold in the flour, then finally add the milk.
3. Tip the mixture into a pudding dish. Cover the dish with a double layer of foil and greaseproof paper, making a pleat in the middle to let the puddling rise. Tie the foil securely with string.
4. Place the pudding in the slow cooker. Pour in enough boiling water to come halfway up the sides, then cook for 4 hours on high.
5. Serve with clotted cream and a drizzle of extra golden syrup.

APPLE FLAPJACK CRUMBLE

SERVES 6 | PER SERVING - CALORIES: 447, FAT: 16G, CARBOHYDRATES: 9G, PROTEIN: 6G

INGREDIENTS

- 1kg apples, such as Coxes
- 3 to 4 tbsp apricot jam
- Juice of 1 large orange
- 140g porridge oats
- 100g plain flour
- 1 tsp ground cinnamon
- 100g butter
- 100g light muscovado sugar
- 1 tbsp golden syrup

INSTRUCTIONS

1. Peel, core, and slice the apples. Mix with the jam and orange in the bottom of the slow cooker.
2. Cook for 2 to 4 hours on low.

3. When they are nearly done, mix the porridge oats, flour, cinnamon, butter, and sugar together to create a crumble-light texture. Drizzle over the syrup and mix to form small clumps. Cook under a hot grill for a couple minutes until browned.
4. Transfer the fruit to a dish, sprinkle over the crumble, and serve with custard, cream, or ice cream.

TRIPLE CHOCOLATE BROWNIES

SERVES 14 | PER SERVING - CALORIES: 324, FAT: 18.6G, CARBOHYDRATES: 37.8G, PROTEIN: 5.8G

INGREDIENTS

- Non-stick cooking spray
- 170g plain flour
- 35g cocoa powder
- ¾ tsp baking powder
- ½ tsp salt
- 55g butter
- 225g dark chocolate
- 125g sugar
- 3 eggs
- 1 tsp vanilla extract
- 125g pecans
- 125g mixed chocolate chips

INSTRUCTIONS

1. Spray the inside of the slow cooker with non-stick spray, and line the bottom and sides with greaseproof paper. Lightly spray the paper with non-stick spray.
2. Stir the salt, cocoa powder, and baking powder into the flour in a bowl.
3. Melt the chocolate in the microwave, heating 30 seconds at a time and stirring in between until melted and smooth.
4. Mix the sugar into the chocolate, followed by the eggs and vanilla.
5. Fold the flour in to the chocolate gradually, then fold in the chocolate chips and pecans.
6. Pour the mix into the slow cooker, smoothing the top with a spatula.
7. Cook for 3 ½ hours on low, then cook for 30 minutes longer uncovered. Allow to cool on a wire rack before slicing and serving.

SALTED CARAMEL COOKIE BARS

SERVES 8 | PER SERVING - CALORIES: 432, FAT: 24G, CARBOHYDRATES: 49G, PROTEIN: 4G

INGREDIENTS

- 220g butter
- 125g sugar
- ¼ tsp salt
- 1 tsp vanilla
- 1 egg
- 270g plain flour
- 300g caramel chips or chunks
- ½ tbsp sea salt

INSTRUCTIONS

1. Beat together the butter, vanilla, and sugar, then add the egg and salt. Mix until combined.
2. Add the flour gradually and mix until you form a dough. Sprinkle some flour on the dough, then shape into a ball by hand.
3. Cut the dough in half, and put the first half in the slow cooker, pressing it down. Use a little extra flour if needed to stop it sticking to your hands.
4. Sprinkle the caramel over the crust, then crumble the remaining dough on top of the caramel.
5. Finish by sprinkling over the sea salt, then cook on low for 2 to 3 hours.

COOKIES AND CREAM FUDGE

SERVES 36 | PER SERVING - CALORIES: 113, FAT: 5G, CARBOHYDRATES: 14G, PROTEIN: 1G

INGREDIENTS

- 400g white chocolate
- 397g tin of condensed milk
- 130g of your favourite chocolate chip cookies

INSTRUCTIONS

1. Put the chocolate and condensed milk in the slow cooker. Cook on low for 40 minutes, stirring any ten minutes.
2. Crumble half of the cookies and stir through the fudge mix.
3. Tip the mixture into a pan lined with baking paper and smooth the top. Break the remaining cookies into pieces and press into the surface of the fudge.
4. Store in the fridge overnight until set, then slice into 36 squares.

1 INGREDIENT CARAMEL SAUCE

SERVES 10 | PER SERVING - CALORIES: 113, FAT: 5G, CARBOHYDRATES: 14G, PROTEIN: 1G

INGREDIENTS

- Tin(s) of condensed milk

INSTRUCTIONS

1. Put the sealed tin(s) in the slow cooker, and cover with water.
2. Cook on either medium or high for 8 hours, remove, and leave to cool completely before opening the cans.

DRINKS

SPICED WHITE HOT CHOCOLATE

SERVES 12 | PER SERVING - CALORIES: 393, FAT: 20G, CARBOHYDRATES: 50G, PROTEIN: 7G

INGREDIENTS
- 225g white chocolate
- 480ml single cream
- 960ml milk
- 1 can sweetened condensed milk
- 4 sticks of cinnamon
- 2 tsp vanilla extract
- ½ tsp ground cardamom
- ½ tsp ground nutmeg

INSTRUCTIONS
1. Put everything in the slow cooker. Cook for 2 ½ to 3 ½ hours on low, stirring occasionally.
2. Remove cinnamon sticks before serving.

CLASSIC HOT CHOCOLATE

SERVES 10 | PER SERVING - CALORIES: 337, FAT: 30G, CARBOHYDRATES: 19G, PROTEIN: 6G

INGREDIENTS
- 1 litre milk
- 300ml double cream
- 200g dark chocolate, chopped
- 100g milk chocolate, chopped
- Marshmallows, whipped cream, and grated chocolate to serve

INSTRUCTIONS
1. Pour the milk and double cream into the slow cooker. Tip in the chocolate, then cook on low for 2 hours. Stir halfway through the cook time.
2. Remove the lid and stir again, then continue to cook for a further 15-20 mins. Ladle into mugs and top with the marshmallows, dollops of cream and grated chocolate.

MULLED WINE

SERVES 10 | PER SERVING - CALORIES: 191, FAT: 0G, CARBOHYDRATES: 13G, PROTEIN: 0G

INGREDIENTS
- 100ml Cointreau
- 2x 750ml bottles of red wine
- 120g caster sugar
- 3 star anise
- 4 cloves
- 2 cinnamon sticks
- Zest of 1 lemon
- Peeled zest and juice of 2 large oranges
- Slices of orange to serve

INSTRUCTIONS
Put everything (except the orange slices) in the slow cooker. Cook on low for 1 to 1 ½ hours until hot. Ladle into glasses and serve with slices of orange.

SARA R. ADAMS

MULLED CIDER

SERVES 12 | PER SERVING - CALORIES: 68, FAT: 0G, CARBOHYDRATES: 15.8G, PROTEIN: 0.1G

INGREDIENTS

- 1 litre cider
- 3 lemon and ginger tea bags
- 1 orange
- 5 whole star anise
- 3 cinnamon sticks
- Brandy (optional)

INSTRUCTIONS

1. Pour the cider into the slow cooker and set on low. Cut the orange in half, and add it, along with the cinnamon, star anise, and tea bags to the slow cooker.
2. Cook for three hours, stirring occasionally.
3. Strain the cider to remove any bits and stir in brandy or rum to taste.

IRISH HOT CHOCOLATE

SERVES 6 | PER SERVING - CALORIES: 654, FAT: 39G, CARBOHYDRATES: 60G, PROTEIN: 10G

INGREDIENTS

- 1 litre whole milk
- 200ml Baileys liqueur
- 300ml double cream
- 397g condensed milk
- 30g cocoa powder
- 150g dark chocolate chips
- Whipped cream, chocolate sauce, and marshmallows to serve

INSTRUCTIONS

1. Put all the ingredients in the slow cooker and stir together. Cook on low for a minimum of an hour until the chocolate has all melted and everything is combined.
2. Serve topped with whipped cream, marshmallows, and a drizzle of chocolate sauce.

CARAMEL APPLE CIDER

SERVES 10 | PER SERVING - CALORIES: 280, FAT: 0.5G, CARBOHYDRATES: 43G, PROTEIN: 0.5G

INGREDIENTS

- 2L apple cider
- 60g soft brown sugar
- 240ml caramel syrup
- 475ml vodka
- 2 tbsp cinnamon
- 2 tsp ground cloves
- Sliced apples to serve

INSTRUCTIONS

Put all of the ingredients in the slow cooker and stir. Cook on low for 3 hours. Serve immediately with slices of apple and a drizzle of caramel sauce.

VIENNESE COFFEE

SERVES 4 | PER SERVING - CALORIES: 173, FAT: 7G, CARBOHYDRATES: 18G, PROTEIN: 1G

INGREDIENTS

- 720ml strong coffee
- 3 tbsp chocolate syrup
- 1 tsp sugar
- 80ml double cream
- 60ml either coffee or Irish liqueur

INSTRUCTIONS

1. Mix the sugar, syrup, and coffee in the slow cooker. Cook for 2 ½ hours on low.
2. Stir in the liqueur and cream, and cook for another 30 minutes.
3. Serve in mugs with whipped cream and grated chocolate.

SPICED CHERRY CIDER

SERVES 16 | PER SERVING - CALORIES: 159, FAT: 0G, CARBOHYDRATES: 39G, PROTEIN: 1G

INGREDIENTS

- 195g cherry jelly chunks
- 4.6L apple cider
- 2 cinnamon sticks

INSTRUCTIONS

Put the cider in the slow cooker with the cinnamon, and cook on high for 3 hours. Mix in the jelly, then cook for another hour. Discard the cinnamon sticks before serving.

Note
___

For a non-alcoholic version, swap the cider for apple juice.

NON-ALCOHOLIC SPICED PEAR CIDER

SERVES 20 | PER SERVING - CALORIES: 100, FAT: 0G, CARBOHYDRATES: 25G, PROTEIN: 0G

INGREDIENTS

- 2.8L unsweetened apple juice
- 1L pear juice
- 8 cinnamon sticks
- 1 tbsp whole allspice
- 1 tbsp whole cloves

INSTRUCTIONS

1. Combine the juices in the slow cooker. Wrap the cinnamon sticks, allspice, and cloves in a cheesecloth and tie into a bag. Place in the slow cooker.
2. Cook on low for 3 to 4 hours, then discard the spice bag. Serve warm.

BOOZY PEPPERMINT HOT CHOCOLATE

SERVES 12 | PER SERVING - CALORIES: 404, FAT: 19G, CARBOHYDRATES: 51.4G, PROTEIN: 10G

INGREDIENTS

- 2 litres whole milk
- 1 can sweetened condensed milk
- 510g dark chocolate chips
- 60ml crème de menthe (or vodka)
- 1 tbsp vanilla extract
- ¼ tsp salt
- Sweetened whipped cream and crushed candy canes to serve

INSTRUCTIONS

1. Mix all of the ingredients (excluding the candy canes and cream) in the slow cooker.
2. Cook on high for 2 hours until combined, whisking halfway through to help the chocolate melt.
3. Turn the slow cooker down to low to keep the hot chocolate warm throughout serving.
4. Pour into mugs, and top with whipped cream and crushed candy canes.

RED WINE HOT CHOCOLATE

SERVES 10 | PER SERVING - CALORIES: 389, FAT: 16.3G, CARBOHYDRATES: 48G, PROTEIN: 7.9G

INGREDIENTS

- 425g dark chocolate chips
- 750ml bottle of red wine
- Pinch salt
- 1.4 litres of whole milk
- 25g cocoa powder
- 100g granulated sugar
- Marshmallows and grated chocolate to serve

INSTRUCTIONS

1. Combine chocolate chips, cocoa powder, sugar, salt, milk, and wine in slow cooker. Cook on high for one hour, whisking every 20 minutes.
2. Ladle cocoa into mugs, and top with marshmallows and grated chocolate to serve.

SPICED CRANBERRY CIDER

SERVES 12 | PER SERVING - CALORIES: 389, FAT: 16.3G, CARBOHYDRATES: 48G, PROTEIN: 7.9G

INGREDIENTS

- 2 litres cranberry juice
- 1 litre apple cider
- 100g fresh cranberries
- 2 tbsp brown sugar
- 4 cinnamon sticks
- 1 tbsp whole cloves

INSTRUCTIONS

1. Mix cranberry juice, apple cider, cranberries, brown sugar, cinnamon sticks, and cloves in the slow cooker.
2. Cook for 2 to 3 hours on high.
3. Keep warm, stirring occasionally until you are ready to serve.
4. Ladle into mugs to serve.
5. If you like, add a shot of rum to each mug.

CARAMEL MOCHA

SERVES 6 | PER SERVING - CALORIES: 218, FAT: 17G, CARBOHYDRATES: 16.5G, PROTEIN: 3.9G

INGREDIENTS

- 240ml double cream
- 1 tbsp icing sugar
- 1 tsp vanilla extract
- 50g cocoa powder
- 240ml milk
- 960ml hot strong coffee
- 60ml caramel syrup

INSTRUCTIONS

1. In a small bowl, beat half the double cream until it begins to thicken. Add icing sugar and ½ teaspoon vanilla and beat until stiff peaks form.
2. Mix the cocoa, remaining double cream, milk, coffee, caramel syrup, and vanilla in a slow cooker. Cook on low for 2 to 3 hours.

EASY CHRISTMAS FRUIT PUNCH

SERVES 10 | PER SERVING - CALORIES: 79, FAT: 0.2G, CARBOHYDRATES: 18.3G, PROTEIN: 0.7G

INGREDIENTS

- 500ml hot tea
- 500ml apple juice
- 500ml orange juice
- 500ml pineapple juice

INSTRUCTIONS

Put all ingredients in a slow cooker. Cook on low for 3 to 4 hours, stirring every now and again.

SPICED BERRY PUNCH

SERVES 10 | PER SERVING - CALORIES: 148, FAT: 0G, CARBOHYDRATES: 36G, PROTEIN: 0G

INGREDIENTS

- 400g frozen mixed berries
- 60g caster sugar
- 2 cinnamon sticks
- 6 whole star anise
- 2 litres of raspberry juice
- Mixed fresh berries to serve (optional)

INSTRUCTIONS

1. Put the frozen fruit, sugar, cinnamon, star anise and raspberry juice in the slow cooker. Cook for 2 to 3 hours on low.
2. Strain the punch, discarding the frozen fruit and spices.
3. Serve garnished with fresh berries (optional).

SPICED LEMON PUNCH

SERVES 12 | PER SERVING - CALORIES: 98, FAT: 0.2G, CARBOHYDRATES: 25G, PROTEIN: 0.3G

INGREDIENTS

- 2 litres water
- 250g sugar
- 360ml orange juice
- 120ml lemon juice
- 60ml pineapple juice
- 1 cinnamon stick
- ½ tsp whole cloves

INSTRUCTIONS

1. Mix the water, sugar, and juices together in a slow cooker.
2. Wrap the cinnamon stick and cloves in a cheesecloth, and tie to form a bag. Place in the slow cooker.
3. Cook on low until heated through, for around 2 to 3 hours. Discard the spice bag before serving.

MINT MOCHA

SERVES 8 | PER SERVING - CALORIES: 72, FAT: 2G, CARBOHYDRATES: 12G, PROTEIN: 1.7G

INGREDIENTS

- 1.4 litres hot brewed coffee
- 4 tbsp instant hot chocolate powder
- 60g mint chocolate
- 4 tsp sugar
- ½ tsp ground cinnamon
- Mini marshmallows to serve

INSTRUCTIONS

1. Mix the coffee, hot chocolate powder, mint chocolate, and sugar in the slow cooker. Cook on low for 2 to 3 hours until hot.
2. Serve in mugs with a sprinkling of marshmallows and cinnamon.

PINEAPPLE AND ORANGE SPICED TEA

SERVES 12 | PER SERVING - CALORIES: 173, FAT: 0G, CARBOHYDRATES: 43G, PROTEIN: 1G

INGREDIENTS

- 2 litres boiling water
- 16 tea bags
- 2 cinnamon sticks
- ½ inch fresh ginger, peeled and sliced
- 4 cloves
- 110g sugar
- 300ml orange juice
- 300ml pineapple juice
- 240ml cranberry juice
- 120ml lemon juice

INSTRUCTIONS

1. Put the boiling water and tea bags in the slow cooker. Leave to steep for 5 minutes.
2. Meanwhile, wrap the cinnamon sticks, ginger, and cloves on a cheesecloth, and tie to form a bag, then dispose of the tea bags.
3. Stir in the remaining ingredients and add the spice bag. Cook, on low, for 2 to 3 hours until heated through. Discard the spice bag and stir before serving.

CHAI TEA

SERVES 12 | PER SERVING - CALORIES: 109, FAT: 3G, CARBOHYDRATES: 19G, PROTEIN: 3G

INGREDIENTS

- 15 slices fresh ginger (about 80g)
- 3 cinnamon sticks
- 25 whole cloves
- 15 cardamom pods, lightly crushed
- 3 whole peppercorns
- 3.3 litres of water
- 8 black tea bags
- 400g can sweetened condensed milk

INSTRUCTIONS

1. Wrap the ginger, cinnamon, cloves, cardamom and peppercorns in a cheesecloth and tie to form a bag. Put the spice bag and the water in the slow cooker. Cook on low for 8 hours, then discard the spice bag.
2. Add the tea bags, then let them steep for 3 to 5 minutes depending on your tastes.
3. Discard the tea bags, then stir through the milk and heat through.

SPICED COFFEE

SERVES 8 | PER SERVING - CALORIES: 64, FAT: 0G, CARBOHYDRATES: 15G, PROTEIN: 0G

INGREDIENTS

- 2 litres brewed coffee
- 80g sugar
- 60ml chocolate syrup
- 2 whole star anise
- 4 cinnamon sticks
- 1 ½ tsp whole cloves

INSTRUCTIONS

1. Mix the coffee, sugar, and chocolate syrup in the slow cooker.
2. Wrap the star anise, cinnamon and cloves in a cheesecloth and tie to form a bag, then put in the slow cooker. Cook on low for 2 to 3 hours.
3. Discard the spice bag before serving.

TROPICAL SWEET TEA

SERVES 10 | PER SERVING - CALORIES: 82, FAT: 0G, CARBOHYDRATES: 21G, PROTEIN: 0G

INGREDIENTS

- 1.4 litres boiling water
- 6 tea bags
- 360ml orange juice
- 360ml pineapple juice
- 60g sugar
- 1 medium orange, halved and sliced
- 2 tbsp honey

INSTRUCTIONS

1. Combine the boiling water and tea bags in the slow cooker. Leave the tea to stand for 5 minutes. Discard the tea bags.
2. Mix in the remaining ingredients, and cook for 2 to 4 hours on low.

GINGERBREAD LATTE

SERVES 6 | PER SERVING - CALORIES: 251, FAT: 11.1G, CARBOHYDRATES: 27.3G, PROTEIN: 11.1G

INGREDIENTS

- 2 litres whole milk
- 60ml maple syrup
- 2 tbsp brown sugar
- 2 tsp ground ginger
- 1 tsp vanilla extract
- 2 cinnamon sticks
- Pinch of cloves
- ½ tsp fresh ground nutmeg
- 840ml fresh strong coffee

INSTRUCTIONS

Put all ingredients in a slow cooker. Cook for 3 to 4 hours on low. Stir occasionally and make sure it does not start to boil.

EGGNOG LATTE

SERVES 6 | PER SERVING - CALORIES: 82, FAT: 0G, CARBOHYDRATES: 21G, PROTEIN: 0G

INGREDIENTS

- 1.5 litres eggnog
- 1.3 litres hot brewed coffee
- ½ tsp ground nutmeg
- ½ tsp cinnamon
- ½ tsp vanilla extract

INSTRUCTIONS

Put everything in the slow cooker and mix. Cook for 1 to 1 ½ hours on high.

DISCLAIMER

This book contains opinions and ideas of the author and is meant to teach the reader informative and helpful knowledge while due care should be taken by the user in the application of the information provided. The instructions and strategies are possibly not right for every reader and there is no guarantee that they work for everyone. Using this book and implementing the information/recipes therein contained is explicitly your own responsibility and risk. This work with all its contents, does not guarantee correctness, completion, quality or correctness of the provided information. Misinformation or misprints cannot be completely eliminated.

Printed in Great Britain
by Amazon